MW01114881

ZAGATSURVEY®

1997

WASHINGTON, D.C.
BALTIMORE
RESTAURANTS

Editor
Olga Boikess

Contributing Editor for Baltimore
Marty Katz

Published and distributed by
ZAGAT SURVEY, LLC
4 Columbus Circle
New York, New York 10019
212 977 6000

Acknowledgments

Besides thanking the nearly 3,200 Washington/Baltimore restaurant-goers who shared their dining experience with us, we are especially grateful to David Belchik, Jay Block, Tom Bryant, Al and Ellen Butts, Karen Cathey, Fred Deutsch, Lorraine Fitzsimmons, Gail Forman, Justin, Abe, Joey and Micheline Frank, Phyllis Frucht, Bill Greene, Jim Jacobi, Rochelle Jaffe, Barbara Johnson, Bill Kopit, Nira Long, Mary Martin, Carrie Matthews, Karen H. Seidenberg, Robert Singleton, George D. Stewart, and Bob and Bonnie Temple for their support. Our special thanks go to Jami Yuspa for her editorial assistance.

Contents

INDEXES (Cont.)

Introduction

Here are the results of our *1997 Washington, D.C/Baltimore Restaurant Survey* covering nearly 1,000 restaurants in the Washington, Baltimore and Annapolis area.

By regularly surveying large numbers of local restaurant-goers, we think we have achieved a uniquely current and reliable guide. We hope you agree. This year, nearly 3,200 people participated. Since the participants dined out an average of 3.5 times per week, this *Survey* is based on roughly 578,000 meals per year.

We want to thank each of our participants. They are a widely diverse group in all respects but one – they are food lovers all. This book is really "theirs."

To help guide our readers to the area's best meals and best buys, we have prepared a number of lists. On the assumption that most people want a quick fix on the places at which they are considering eating, we have tried to be concise and to provide handy indexes.

We are particularly grateful to Olga Boikess, a Washington lawyer and avid restaurant-goer, who has organized and edited this *Survey* since it was first published in the fall of 1986. Our special thanks also go to contributing editor Marty Katz, veteran news photographer and inveterate eater, for his insights on the Baltimore food scene.

We invite you to be a reviewer in our next *Survey*. To do so, simply send a stamped, self-addressed, business-size envelope to ZAGAT SURVEY, 4 Columbus Circle, New York, NY 10019, so that we will be able to contact you. Each participant will receive a free copy of the next *Washington, D.C./ Baltimore Restaurant Survey* when it is published.

Your comments, suggestions and even criticisms of this *Survey* are also solicited. There is always room for improvement with your help!

New York, New York   Nina and Tim Zagat
October 28, 1996

Foreword

On the 10th anniversary of the *Zagat Survey of Washington, D.C./Baltimore Restaurants*, we celebrate many healthy changes to the local dining scene. An abundance of new and revised places are serving wholesome, affordable food in settings that work for anything from a casual bite to a festive meal. Whether at a saloon or a showcase for one of the area's many talented chefs, most menus feature fresh produce and imaginative fish, fowl and vegetarian choices. And, spurred by the fact that Washingtonians dine out an average of 3.6 times a week (Baltimoreans an average of 3.4 times a week), restaurateurs have developed clever ways to keep meal costs down. In fact, the average tab is just $24.49 in D.C., $20.49 in Baltimore.

We also rejoice in the timeless appeal of some of the area's best values, most notably, the beloved L'Auberge Chez Francois, the epitome of Country French comfort food and open-handed hospitality. At the same time, clubby red meat houses are more popular than ever (with both sexes), as proven by the rapid institutionalization of relative newcomers like the Capital Grille and Sam & Harry's, which joined the Prime Rib, Morton's, Ruth's Chris and The Palm as fixtures of the power-dining scene.

Many of the top restaurants in this *Survey* opened in the past decade – Kinkead's, Ruppers, Obelisk, Gerard's Place, the Morrison-Clark Inn, Asia Nora and this *Survey*'s sleeper, the exquisite Makoto. All combine imaginative cooking and a user-friendly (though not necessarily informal) environment. Several also reflect the public's growing appetite for small-scale restaurants with personalized cuisine – perhaps as an antidote to the proliferating chains.

Washington, D.C.'s vibrant ethnic food scene makes it one of the nation's most interesting restaurant towns. Recently, Asian eateries have taken the lead in combining exciting design and upscale atmosphere with easy-on-the-wallet dining. So it's not surprising that Mark Miller (Red Sage) is refining his Asian diner concept, Raku, here before syndicating it nationally – or that Tara Thai, Busara and Oodles Noodles have lines out the door. Roberto Donna's (Galileo,

I Matti) imaginative Italian updates at the budget-friendly
Il Radicchio and Arucola pioneered this trend.

The same stimulating changes can be seen in Baltimore. Of
course, Tio Pepe, Prime Rib and Tersiguel's, along with a
host of classic crab houses and homey neighborhood bars,
remain popular choices. But, at the same time, a varied array
of ethnics are joining talented younger chefs like Nancy
Longo (Pierpoint), Linwood Dame (Linwood's, Due), Cindy
Wolf (Savannah) and Michael Gettier (M. Gettier) in providing interesting, accessible meals.

Thus, as we head for the uncharted millennium – and more
immediately, possible election-year shifts – we can exult in
the diversity of committed talents that keep Washington, D.C.
and Baltimore restaurants fresh and in front of the dining pack.

Washington, D.C.   Olga Boikess
October 28, 1996

Key to Ratings/Symbols

This sample entry identifies the various types of information contained in your Zagat Survey.

(1) Restaurant Name, Address & Phone Number

(2) Hours & Credit Cards

(3) ZAGAT Ratings

F	D	S	C
23	5	9	$19

Tim & Nina's ◗ Ⓢ ⊄

4 Columbus Circle (8th Ave.), 212-977-6000

◪ Open 7 days a week, 24 hours a day (some say that's "168 hours too much"), this wildly successful dive started the "deli-tapas craze" (i.e., tidbits of pastrami, corned beef, etc. on cracker-size pieces of stale rye bread); unfortunately, the place looks like a "none-too-clean garage" and Tim and Nina have "never heard of credit cards or reservations."

(4) Surveyors' Commentary

The names of restaurants with the highest overall ratings and greatest popularity are printed in **CAPITAL LETTERS**. Address and phone numbers are printed in *italics*.

(2) Hours & Credit Cards

After each restaurant name you will find the following courtesy information:

◗ .... *serving after 11 PM*

Ⓢ .... *open on Sunday*

⊄ .... *no credit cards accepted*

(3) ZAGAT Ratings

Food, **Decor** and **Service** are each rated on a scale of **0** to **30**:

F	D	S	C

F	....	*Food*
D	....	*Decor*
S	....	*Service*
C	....	*Cost*

23	5	9	$19

0 - 9	....	*poor to fair*
10 - 19	....	*good to very good*
20 - 25	....	*very good to excellent*
26 - 30	....	*extraordinary to perfection*

▽ 23	5	9	$19

▽ .... *Low number of votes/less reliable*

The **Cost (C)** column reflects the estimated price of a dinner with one drink and tip. Lunch usually costs 25% less.

A restaurant listed without ratings is either an important **newcomer** or a popular **write-in**. The estimated cost, with one drink and tip, is indicated by the following symbols.

–	–	–	VE

I	....	*below $15*
M	....	*$16 to $30*
E	....	*$31 to $50*
VE	....	*$51 or more*

(4) Surveyors' Commentary

Surveyors' comments are summarized, with literal comments shown in quotation marks. The following symbols indicate whether responses were mixed or uniform.

| ◪ | .... | *mixed* |
| ◼ | .... | *uniform* |

Washington's Favorites

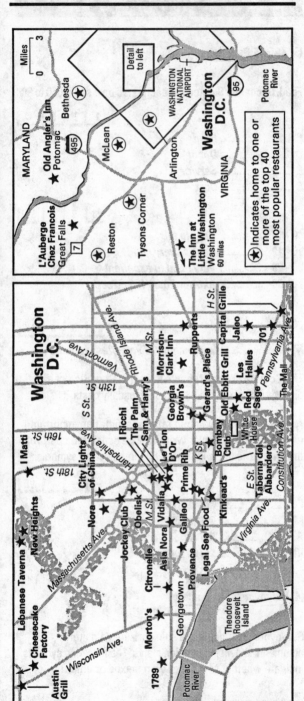

Top map (detail):

Miles 0 — 3

MARYLAND

Old Angler's Inn
Potomac

Bethesda

L'Auberge Chez Francois
Great Falls

7

Reston

McLean

Tysons Corner

495

Detail to left

WASHINGTON NATIONAL AIRPORT

Arlington

VIRGINIA

Washington D.C.

95

Potomac River

The Inn at Little Washington
Washington
60 miles

⊛ Indicates home to one or more of the top 40 most popular restaurants

Bottom map (detail):

Washington D.C.

Vermont Ave.

Rhode Island Ave.

H St.

M St.

Morrison-Clark Inn

Ruppert's

Capital Grille

Jaleo

701

Pennsylvania Ave.

13th St.

S St.

Georgia Brown's

Gerard's Place

Les Halles

Old Ebbitt Grill

The Mall

I Ricchi
The Palm
Sam & Harry's

Le Lion D'Or

Prime Rib

K St.

Bombay Club

White House

Red Sage

16th St.

I Matti

City Lights of China

18th St.

Nora

Jockey Club

Obelisk

Asia Nora

Vidalia

Galileo

Taberna del Alabardero

E St.

Constitution Ave.

New Heights

Massachusetts Ave.

Citronelle

Provence

Kinkead's

Legal Sea Food

Virginia Ave.

Lebanese Taverna

Cheesecake Factory

Austin Grill

Wisconsin Ave.

Morton's

1789

Georgetown

Theodore Roosevelt Island

Potomac River

New Hampshire Ave.

Washington's Most Popular Restaurants

Each of our reviewers has been asked to name his or her five favorite restaurants. The 40 spots most frequently named, in order of their popularity, are:

1. L'Auberge Chez Francois
2. Kinkead's
3. Inn at Little Washington
4. Galileo
5. Vidalia
6. Citronelle
7. Nora
8. Carlyle Grand Cafe
9. Prime Rib
10. I Ricchi
11. Red Sage
12. Gerard's Place
13. Provence
14. Bombay Club
15. Jaleo
16. Obelisk
17. Le Lion D'Or
18. Cheesecake Factory
19. 1789
20. Rio Grande Cafe
21. Morrison-Clark Inn
22. Old Angler's Inn
23. Lebanese Taverna
24. Taberna del Alabardero
25. Capital Grille
26. Palm
27. Rupperts
28. Morton's of Chicago
29. Old Ebbitt Grill
30. 701
31. Sam & Harry's
32. Georgia Brown's
33. New Heights
34. Austin Grill
35. I Matti
36. City Lights of China
37. Les Halles
38. Jockey Club
39. Legal Sea Food
40. Asia Nora

It's obvious that most of the restaurants on the above list are among the most expensive, but Washingtonians love a bargain. Were popularity calibrated to price, we suspect that a number of other restaurants would join the above ranks. Thus, we have listed over 150 "Best Buys" on pages 17 and 18.

Top Ratings*

Top 40 Food Ranking

29 Inn at Little Washington	Tachibana
28 Makoto	I Ricchi
L'Auberge Chez Francois	Peking Gourmet Inn
27 Kinkead's	Taberna del Alabardero
Obelisk	Haandi
Seasons	Vidalia
Le Lion D'Or	Provence
26 Gerard's Place	Duangrat's
Prime Rib	Pizzeria Paradiso
Galileo	Four & Twenty Blackbirds
Citronelle	Pesce
L'Auberge Provencale	New Heights
Rupp003	City Lights of China
Nora	Pilin Thai
Taste of Saigon	24 Melrose
Patisserie Cafe Didier	Sushi-Ko
Morton's of Chicago	Bombay Club
25 Morrison-Clark Inn	Jockey Club
1789	La Bergerie
Rabieng	Le Refuge

Top Spots by Cuisine

Top American (New)
27 Kinkead's
   Seasons
26 Ruppers
   Nora
25 Morrison-Clark Inn

Top Bar-B-Q
22 Rockland's
20 Red Hot & Blue
19 Starke's Head Hog BBQ
   Houston's
18 Old Glory BBQ

Top Breakfast†
26 Patisserie Cafe Didier
23 La Colline
   La Brasserie
19 Parkway Deli
   Old Ebbitt Grill

Top Brunch
27 Kinkead's
   Seasons
26 Citronelle
25 Morrison-Clark Inn
   New Heights

Top Business Lunch
27 Kinkead's
   Seasons
   Le Lion D'Or
26 Gerard's Place
   Prime Rib

Top Chinese
25 Peking Gourmet Inn
   City Lights of China
23 Mr. K's
22 Fortune
   Good Fortune

---

* Excluding restaurants with low voting.
† Other than hotels.

Top Continental
24 Jockey Club
Ritz-Carlton Grill
23 Ritz-Carlton Restaurant
22 Tivoli
— Baron's

Top Creole/Cajun/
New Orleans
24 R.T.'s
22 Warehouse Bar & Grill
21 Cajun Bangkok
Louisiana Express Co.
20 219

Top Family Dining
24 Lebanese Taverna
21 Rio Grande Cafe
20 Red Hot & Blue
Outback Steakhouse
19 Hard Times Cafe

Top French Cafe/Bistro
24 Le Refuge
Village Bistro
23 Le Gaulois
Bistrot Lepic
Lavandou

Top French Classic
28 L'Auberge Chez Francois
27 Le Lion D'Or
24 La Bergerie
23 La Miche
La Colline

Top French (New)
26 Gerard's Place
Citronelle
25 Provence
24 Maison Blanche
Cafe Bethesda

Top Hamburgers
23 Carlyle Grand Cafe
22 Occidental Grill
21 Mike's American Grill
Artie's
19 Old Ebbitt Grill

Top of the Hill
23 La Colline
La Brasserie
21 Two Quail
20 La Lomita
17 Bistro Le Monde

Top Hotel Dining
27 Seasons/Four Seasons
26 Citronelle/Latham
25 Morrison-Clark Inn
24 Melrose/Park Hyatt
Jockey Club/Ritz-Carlton

Top Indian
25 Haandi
24 Bombay Club
Bombay Bistro
22 Bombay Palace
Aditi

Top Italian
27 Obelisk
26 Galileo
25 I Ricchi
23 Goldoni
Il Pizzico

Top Japanese
28 Makoto
25 Tachibana
24 Sushi-Ko
23 Tako Grill
22 Hisago

Top Mex/Tex-Mex
21 Rio Grande Cafe
Mi Rancho
20 Lauriol Plaza
La Lomita
Enriqueta's

Top Middle Eastern
24 Lebanese Taverna
23 Moby Dick
Kazan
22 Pasha Cafe
Bacchus

13

Top Newcomers/Rated
- *24* Cashion's Eat Place
- *23* Goldoni
  - Jin-ga
  - Bistrot Lepic
- *22* T.H.A.I.

Top Newcomers/Unrated
- Bangkok St. Grill
- Cafe Atlantico
- Lespinasse
- Raku
- Thyme Square

Top Pizza
- *25* Pizzeria Paradiso
- *22* Coppi's
- *21* Faccia Luna Pizzeria
  - Eye St. Cafe
  - Red Tomato Cafe

Top Saturday Lunch
- *27* Kinkead's
- *26* Citronelle
  - Taste of Saigon
  - Patisserie Cafe Didier
- *25* Rabieng

Top Seafood
- *25* Pesce
- *23* Blue Point Grill
- *21* Sea Catch
  - Legal Sea Food
  - Crisfield

Top Southeast Asian
- *23* Asia Nora
  - Germaine's
- *21* Oodles Noodles
  - Straits of Malaya
- — Raku

Top Southern
- *25* Morrison-Clark Inn
  - Vidalia
- *22* Georgia Brown's
- *20* B. Smith's
- *18* Union St. Public Hse.

Top Southwestern
- *22* Red Sage
  - Gabriel
- *20* Santa Fe East
  - Cottonwood Cafe
- *18* Stella's

Top Steakhouses
- *26* Prime Rib
  - Morton's of Chicago
- *24* Sam & Harry's
  - Ruth's Chris
- *23* Capital Grille

Top Thai
- *25* Rabieng
  - Duangrat's
  - Pilin Thai
- *24* Tara Thai
- *23* Crystal Thai

Top Vegetarian Friendly
- *21* Greenwood's
- *19* Zed's
  - Vegetable Garden
- — Planet X
- — Thyme Square

Top Vietnamese
- *26* Taste of Saigon
- *22* Cafe Dalat
  - Queen Bee
  - Cafe Saigon
  - Saigon Gourmet

Top Worth a Trip
- *29* Inn at Little Washington/
  - Washington, VA
- *26* L'Auberge Provencale/
  - White Post, VA
- *25* 4 & 20 Blackbirds/
  - Flint Hill, VA
  - Stone Manor/
  - Middletown, MD
- *23* Bleu Rock Inn/
  - Washington, VA

Top 40 Decor Ranking

29 Inn at Little Washington
27 Willard Room
    L'Auberge Chez Francois
26 Taberna del Alabardero
    L'Auberge Provencale
    1789
    Morrison-Clark Inn
    Seasons
    Bombay Club
    Red Sage
25 Ritz-Carlton Grill
    Makoto
    Coeur de Lion
    Jockey Club
    Capital Grille
    Prime Rib
    Ritz-Carlton Restaurant
    Asia Nora
    Jin-ga
24 Old Angler's Inn

Provence
Bleu Rock Inn
Jefferson
B. Smith's
Two Quail
Le Lion D'Or
Melrose
Sequoia
701
T.H.A.I.
Gadsby's Tavern
Nora
23 Hibiscus Cafe
Goldoni
Galileo
Shelly's Woodroast
New Heights
I Ricchi
Busara
Occidental Grill

Top Outdoor

Bleu Rock Inn
Coco Loco
Gerard's Place
Inn at Glen Echo
La Brasserie
L'Auberge Chez Francois

Old Angler's Inn
Perry's
Radio Free Italy
Sequoia
701
Straights of Malaya

Top Rooms

Asia Nora
Bombay Club
B. Smith's
Coeur de Lion
Inn at Little Washington
Jockey Club
Lespinasse
Makoto
Morrison-Clark Inn

Old Ebbitt Grill
Provence
Red Sage
Ritz-Carlton Grill
Ritz-Carlton Restaurant
Seasons
1789
Taberna del Alabardero
Willard Room

Top Views

Bleu Rock Inn
Cedar Knoll Inn
Chart House
Gangplank
L'Auberge Chez Francois

Le Rivage
Perry's
Potowmack Landing
Roof Terrace Ken. Ctr.
Sequoia

Top 40 Service Ranking

29 Inn at Little Washington
27 Makoto
L'Auberge Chez Francois
26 Seasons
L'Auberge Provencale
Le Lion D'Or
25 Prime Rib
Obelisk
Taberna del Alabardero
Bombay Club
Rupperts
Ritz-Carlton Grill
24 Jockey Club
1789
Four & Twenty Blackbirds
Willard Room
Morrison-Clark Inn
Maison Blanche
Nora
Ritz-Carlton Restaurant

Melrose
Kinkead's
Gerard's Place
Coeur de Lion
Sam & Harry's
23 Galileo
701
Citronelle
Bleu Rock Inn
Jefferson
Kazan
Capital Grille
Mr. K's
Morton's of Chicago
Vidalia
New Heights
I Ricchi
Oval Room
Rabieng
La Bergerie

Best Buys*

Top 100 Bangs For The Buck

This list reflects the best dining values in our *Survey*. It is produced by dividing the cost of a meal into the combined ratings for food, decor and service.

1. Burro	51. Bertucci's
2. El Pollo Rico	52. Starke's Head Hog BBQ
3. Bob & Edith's Diner	53. La Lomita
4. Pho 75	54. Pizza de Resistance
5. Crisp & Juicy	55. Vox Populi
6. Hard Times Cafe	56. City Lights of China
7. C.F. Folks	57. Cafe Taj
8. Pho 95	58. Bua
9. Le Bon Cafe	59. Polly's Cafe
10. Moby Dick	60. Haandi
11. Patisserie Cafe Didier	61. State of the Union
12. Cafe Saigon	62. Pasha Cafe
13. Cafe Parisien Express	63. Mike's American Grill
14. Pilin Thai	64. Good Fortune
15. Florida Ave. Grill	65. Skewers/Cafe Luna
16. Generous George's	66. Pho Cali
17. Delhi Dhaba	67. California Pizza Kitchen
18. Full Key	68. Tara Thai
19. Ambrosia	69. Red Tomato Cafe
20. Cowboy Cafe	70. Hard Rock Cafe
21. La Madeleine	71. El Tamarindo
22. Cafe Dalat	72. Artie's
23. Ledo Pizza	73. Queen Bee
24. Faccia Luna Pizzeria	74. Thai Kingdom
25. Haad Thai	75. Louisiana Express Co.
26. Rockland's	76. Eye St. Cafe
27. Crystal Thai	77. House of Chinese Gourmet
28. Silver Diner	78. Hsiang Foong
29. Oodles Noodles	79. China Chef
30. Hunan Number One	80. Calvert Grille
31. Taste of Saigon	81. Saigon Gourmet
32. Nam Viet	82. Austin Grill
33. Pizzeria Paradiso	83. Shelly's Woodroast
34. Dean & DeLuca Cafe	84. Bugaboo Creek Steak Hse.
35. Benjarong	85. Duangrat's
36. Parkway Deli	86. Foong Lin
37. Garrett Park Cafe	87. Old Glory BBQ
38. Coppi's	88. Full Kee
39. Bombay Bistro	89. Kabul Caravan
40. T.H.A.I.	90. Rio Grande Cafe
41. King Street Blues	91. Panjshir
42. Luna Grill	92. Mick's
43. Little Viet Garden	93. Nam's
44. Dusit	94. Meskerem
45. Rabieng	95. Cactus Cantina
46. Taipei/Tokyo Cafe	96. Aditi
47. Food Factory	97. Fortune
48. Mi Rancho	98. Sala Thai
49. Easby's	99. Hunan Lion
50. Burma	100. Houston's

* Excluding coffeehouses.

Additional Good Values
(A bit more expensive, but worth every penny)

Aangan
Aegean Taverna
Arucola
Bangkok St. Grill
Bistro
Bistro Bistro
Bistro Francais
Bombay Club
Burrito Brothers
Busara
Cafe Deluxe
Cafe Mileto
Cajun Bangkok
California Tortilla
Carlyle Grand Cafe
Cheesecake Factory
Chicken Place
Clyde's
Eat First
Ecco Cafe
Enriqueta's
Eurogrill
Fern Street Bistro
Hibiscus Cafe
Il Pizzico
Il Raddichio
Jaleo
La Fourchette
Lauriol Plaza
Lebanese Taverna

Lite 'n' Fair
Malik
Mama Wok & Teriyaki
Mare E Monti
Martin's Tavern
Metro 29
Miss Saigon
Music City Roadhse.
Paolo's
Pasta Plus
Perry's
Pesce
Pho
Planet X
Saigon Inn
Saigonnais
Southside 815
Spices
Stella's
Sunny Garden
Sushi Chalet
That's Amore
Tom Tom
Union Street Public Hse.
Uptown Cafe
Vegetable Garden
Vienna's Grille
Wurzburg-Haus
Yin Yang
Zed's

Alphabetical
Directory
of Restaurants

Washington, D.C.

	F	D	S	C

Aangan 🅂 17 16 18 $21
4920 St. Elmo Ave. (bet. Old Georgetown Rd. & Norfolk Ave.), Bethesda, MD, 301-657-1262
■ "Undeservedly overlooked", this Bethesda Indian's "fresh and subtle" dishes suit an "American palate", while its colonial courtyard setting feels "sunny" on the darkest winter day; "very pleasant" (if "slow") service makes it a "warm and welcoming" "discovery."

Aaranthi 🅂 ▽ 18 14 17 $19
Danor Plaza, 409 Maple Ave. E. (Beula St.), Vienna, VA, 703-938-0100
☑ This suburban sibling of the well-thought-of Georgetown Indian, Aditi, receives mixed notices; while some delight in finding the same "delicious food" and a staff "that enjoys giving" good service, others insist it "must be adopted."

Aditi 🅂 22 16 19 $20
3299 M St., NW (33rd St.), 202-625-6825
■ "A step above the usual Indian", this second-story dining room produces "nicely representative" fare at lower-caste prices; despite the "lack" of decor, most rate it "worth the parking nightmare" in Georgetown (high praise).

Aegean Taverna 🅂 17 15 17 $17
2950 Clarendon Blvd. (Garfield St.), Arlington, VA, 703-841-9494
☑ "Pleasant patio dining" and being treated "like family" enhance the appeal of the "consistent" food dished out at this Clarendon Hellene; though a few find the fare "boring", it's welcome in an area with "few Greek choices"; the mood is "understated" – that is, "until the belly dancer arrives."

Alamo 🅂 ▽ 13 17 13 $16
1063 31st St. (M St.), 202-342-2000
☑ A newish Georgetown "neighborhood drop-in" joint where the Tex-Mex vittles don't live up to the "painstakingly detailed Western decor"; it tastes like a case of "too much tequila for the chef" or simply a kitchen that "needs to work out the kinks."

Alamo ◖🅂 13 18 14 $17
100 King St. (Union St.), Alexandria, VA, 703-739-0555
☑ A party-prime corner location in Old Town, "amazing margaritas" and country-rock bands are the "primary draws" of this Tex-Mex; happily, few of its youngish partisans get past the "great chips and salsa" sober enough to taste the "predictable" entrees.

Ambrosia ◐⇗   19 | 6 | 17 | $11
Congressional South, 1765 Rockville Pike (bet. Twinbrook Rd. & Alpine Dr.), Rockville, MD, 301-881-3636
■ "Long lines" tell the story about this great Greek "dive" in Rockville – the food is "good, cheap" and "plentiful", and the "factory setting" has so little atmosphere that it's considered "colorful" (or "depressing"); go for the "best gyro platter in the area" or lamb "done any way."

America ◐S   13 | 18 | 15 | $19
Union Station, 50 Massachusetts Ave., NE (North Capitol), 202-682-9555
Tysons Corner Ctr., 8008-L Tysons Corner Ctr. (Rte. 7), McLean, VA, 703-847-6607
☒ The terrific "*Mr. Smith Goes to Washington* views" from this Union Station megadiner, and Capitol gazing from its sidewalk cafe, are tempered by a "way-too-ambitious" American menu and "waiters with a bad attitude"; less demanding patrons point out it's "fun for out-of-towners" and "there's something for everyone"; P.S. the "barnlike cave" in Tysons Corner has a similar "luck-of-the-draw" menu sans the people-watching and pols.

American Grill ◐S   19 | 17 | 17 | $29
(fka Cafe Pierre)
Loews L'Enfant Plaza Hotel, 480 L'Enfant Plaza, SW, 202-484-1000
☒ An "oasis" in the L'Enfant Plaza "concrete jungle", this hotel dining room's "imaginative" Contemporary American menu and restful surroundings are a welcome respite; while not perfect, it's worth considering for a quiet lunch or dinner – especially since they "make one great dark chocolate cake."

Andalucia S   20 | 18 | 20 | $30
Shoppes of Bethesda, 4931 Elm St. (Arlington Rd.), Bethesda, MD, 301-907-0052
12300 Wilkins Ave. (Parklawn Dr.), Rockville, MD, 301-770-1880
■ These "congenial" Spaniards rank among suburban Maryland's "classier restaurants" despite their "commercial zone" (Rockville) and "glorified storefront" (Bethesda) settings; host-owner Joaquim Serrano establishes a "refined" environment in which to enjoy "straightforward" classics and "expertly prepared fish" – when he's around, things seem especially well-oiled.

Appetizer Plus S   – | – | – | M
1117 N. 19th St. (Lynn St.), Rosslyn, VA, 703-525-3171
Known for its "inexpensive" but uninspired all-you-can-eat sushi, this Rosslyn Japanese is a "good value" if you're not expecting thrills or frills; go hungry and be prepared to wait.

Aquarelle 🅂
–|–|–| E
Watergate Hotel, 2650 Virginia Ave., NW (New Hampshire Ave.), 202-298-4455
Following the much-publicized departure of superchef Jean-Louis Palladin from its kitchen, this dining room refocuses on its paintable Potomac River vistas complemented by classically based New American food and appointments; its new toque, Robert Wiedmaier, earned high marks at Cafe on M for his flavor palette and presentations.

Argentine Grill 🅂
16 | 14 | 16 | $20
2433 18th St., NW (Columbia Rd.), 202-234-1818
◪ At one of the "best sidewalk spots in Adams Morgan", local gauchos sample the cuisine of Argentina; although some find the service "surly" and the hearty fare focusing on chewy (read "tough") steaks and grilled specialty meats "much ado about nothing", the "lively" weekend scene is more like the "real thing" – "to South America we go."

Arizona
–|–|–| I
1211 Connecticut Ave. (M St.), 202-785-1211
Write-ins alerted us to "one of the city's best-kept new secrets" – a Southwesterner with lots of style, "unusual tastes" and a below-Dupont-Circle address; its "chicken mole comes with dreamy mashed potatoes" and "you can't beat the ribs."

Aroma 🅂
–|–|–| M
1919 I St. (20th St.), 202-833-4700
Not quite "undiscovered" (but hardly well-known), this intimate K Street–area Indian is one of several "top-notch" subcontinentals to open in the past few years; its classical menu of tandooris, curries and breads offers "delicate, mouthwatering food" at "reasonable prices."

Artie's 🅂
21 | 18 | 20 | $19
3260 Old Lee Hwy. (south of Fairfax Circle), Fairfax, VA, 703-273-7600
■ "Consistent", "attractive", "friendly and open late" on weekends are among the "good reasons" this all-purpose American is "often mobbed"; it's probably the best business lunch option in the Fairfax "restaurant wasteland" (though you'll "struggle to hear the deal"), with "addictive rolls", a "great prime rib" and draft microbrews.

Arucola 🅂
16 | 15 | 15 | $24
5534 Connecticut Ave., NW (Morrison St.), 202-244-1555
◪ "Tasty", "affordable" "meals on wheels" sums up this "trendy" Chevy Chase Italian where rolling carts are laden with pastas and antipasti accompanied by grilled meats and fish; the "smorgasbord approach" encourages family-style dining, but with "kids everywhere", "no reservations and no room to wait", some "only visit for lunch."

ASIA NORA   23 | 25 | 22 | $37
2213 M St., NW (bet. 22nd & 23rd Sts.), 202-797-4860
■ Nora Pouillon makes "exquisite use of small space" to achieve a "Zen"-like serenity at this West End Asian "adventure"; her "cool, fresh" fare synthesizes Japanese, Thai, Indonesian and Indian influences – it's "health-conscious", on the edge, "expensive" and strikes a few as "contrived"; still, you "always run into White House staff" and knowledgeable foodies.

Atami 🅂   18 | 10 | 16 | $20
3155 Wilson Blvd. (Clarendon Metro Stop), Arlington, VA, 703-522-4787
■ The $24.95 "unlimited" sushi special at this "dreary", "no-frills" Clarendon Japanese uses "good-quality" fish and "doesn't try to fill you up on rice"; however, unless you're famished or it's time for "that monthly sushi gorging", tempura, one-dish meals or sushi à la carte are more cost-effective options.

Athenian Plaka 🅂   17 | 18 | 18 | $21
7833 Woodmont Ave. (Fairmont Ave.), Bethesda, MD, 301-986-1337
☑ Although "you can do better" than this "agreeably kitschy" Greek for fine dining in Bethesda, it's not a bad choice "for an outdoor lunch on a sunny day"; you'll get lots of "homey", "garlicky" food in a "cheerful atmosphere."

Au Pied du Cochon ◗🅂   12 | 13 | 13 | $17
1335 Wisconsin Ave., NW (Dumbarton St.), 202-333-5440
☑ The charms of this "funky", 24-hour French "hole-in-the-wall" in Georgetown are elusive unless you've been there "at 3:30 AM" – supposedly, the "cheap" omelets, eggs Benedict and fries "are better then" and "people-watching" peaks; reopened last summer after a bout with the IRS, it still "needs a good scrubbing."

Austin Grill 🅂   19 | 15 | 17 | $17
2424 Wisconsin Ave., NW (Calvert St.), 202-337-8080
8430 Old Keene Mill Rd. (Rolling Rd.), W. Springfield, VA, 703-644-3111
7278 Woodmont Ave. (Elm Ave.), Bethesda, MD, 301-656-1366
South Austin Grill
801 King St. (Washington St.), Alexandria, VA, 703-684-8969
■ These "high-energy" cantinas "give Tex-Mex food a fresh look" (think "duck tacos", crabmeat quesadillas), swirl "addictive" margaritas and have a "country-western feel" that makes Texans feel "right at home"; they're "crowded" and "too loud to converse", but the Gen X crowd doesn't go here to talk.

Bacchus   22 | 18 | 20 | $25

1827 Jefferson Pl., NW (bet. M & N Sts.), 202-785-0734
7945 Norfolk Ave. (Del Ray Ave.), Bethesda, MD,
301-657-1722 S

■ Patron "loyalty is well deserved" by these "personable" Lebanese siblings for their "consistently good" food and "low-key" (if "dated") surroundings; they're "ideal for meze" (appetizers) and "good for an inexpensive business lunch" (with "great eavesdropping") in Dupont Circle; "spend a lot or not much – and get a good meal either way."

Balalayka S   ∇ 16 | 18 | 19 | $21

3300 M St., NW (33rd St.), 202-338-4544

☒ Step down into a Russian happening at this M Street basement cafe, where you'll find "lots of Russians", "very heavy food", garish decor, "live music" and offbeat fun; be sure to bring a designated driver.

B & C S   – | – | – | M

(aka Bread & Circus Cafe)
2323 Wisconsin Ave. (Calvert St.), 202-333-1866
Grocery shopping in Upper Georgetown takes on a new dimension at this "promising" in-store cafe, which uses "fresh, wholesome" ingredients from the market in its pastas, salads and grills; an 'in' spot for "breakfast" or a "light lunch", it also serves casual dinners.

Bangkok St. Grill & Noodles   – | – | – | I

5872 Leesburg Pike (bet. Columbia Pike & Glen Carlyn Rd.), Falls Church, VA, 703-379-6707
Head to Falls Church for a quick, inexpensive tour of Thailand's street-food stalls; here, Duangrat's young sprig reproduces the vendors' noodle, rice bowl and grill specialties in a spare, blond wood and white setting; this place is getting good press.

Bangkok Vientiane S   ∇ 18 | 9 | 13 | $15

926 W. Broad St. (bet. West St. & Ospring St.), Falls Church, VA, 703-534-0095
☒ Laos' location between Vietnam and Thailand explains the multinational menu and clientele at this Falls Church Asian; "hot", spicy food is the focus – "all else is left to chance" (translation: "depressing" decor, "slow service"); while a handful hint it's "gone downhill", most maintain it's "cheap" and "good."

Bardo Rodeo   9 | 12 | 11 | $13

2000 Wilson Blvd. (1 block east of Courthouse Metro Stop), Arlington, VA, 703-527-9399
■ One goes to this "postapocalyptic" "playground" in an "old car dealership painted like an LSD trip" for all-night pool, "bold" house brews and "raucous fun"; "forget the food" (mostly "veggie victuals") – this place is a one-of-a-kind, "love-it-or-hate-it", "great slumming beer joint."

Baron's　　　　–| –| –| M
Sheraton Premiere at Tysons Corner, 8661 Leesburg Pike (Westwood Ctr. Dr.), Vienna, VA, 703-448-1234
A "wonderful selection at Sunday brunch" ($29.95 including champagne) draws locals to this "beautiful", baronial Tysons Corner dining room; at night, soft lights and music provide a "pleasant" backdrop for the Contemporary Continental fare.

BeDuCi　　　　21 | 18 | 20 | $30
2100 P St., NW (bet. 20th & 21st Sts.), 202-223-3824
◪ "If only you could eat charm", this Dupont Circle Mediterranean might beat them all – not that a meal here isn't often "delicious" and "delightful"; "given the high price", however, many customers expect better food and comfort; N.B. its spring 1996 move to a bigger space, featuring a notable sidewalk cafe, addressed the latter complaint.

Bei Tempi S　　　　15 | 15 | 17 | $24
4930 Cordell Ave. (Old Georgetown Rd.), Bethesda, MD, 301-718-0344
◪ Regulars sing the praises of the warmth, willingness "to please", "traditional" fare and special deals at this popular, family-run Bethesda Neapolitan, but less-impressed patrons consider the name (which means 'beautiful times') a misnomer.

Belmont Kitchen S　　　　18 | 17 | 17 | $23
2400 18th St., NW (Belmont Rd.), 202-667-1200
◪ Long known for "providing Waspy food" in "DC's most ethnic neighborhood", and for its "people-watching" outdoor brunch, this Adams Morgan "nook" also has a rep for "bad service", but the staff is so "nice" that many overlook it.

Benjarong S　　　　22 | 18 | 20 | $18
Wintergreen Plaza, 855-C Rockville Pike (Edmonston Rd.), Rockville, MD, 301-424-5533
■ There are "some very nice dishes" on the comprehensive menu at this "classy", "reasonably priced" Rockville Thai, along with nice touches, such as artwork on display, that you wouldn't expect to find in a "cheap, ethnic" storefront; admirers judge it the "best Thai in suburban Maryland."

Benkay　　　　15 | 10 | 15 | $18
727 15th St., NW (bet. H St. & New York Ave.), 202-737-1515
◪ Fighting "lines and tourists" for "mass-produced", "mediocre" sushi at this Downtown Japanese's all-you-can-eat buffet isn't ideal, but you "can't beat the price" and the "set meals" are even more of "a bargain"; the utilitarian setting at least has "great TV."

Bertolini's S   15 17 15 $21
801 Pennsylvania Ave., NW (9th St.), 202-638-2140
White Flint Mall, 11301 Rockville Pike (Nicholson Ln.),
Bethesda, MD, 301-984-0004
◪ These strategically located chain places with upscale decor and "by the numbers" Italian food "aren't restaurants you'd travel miles to go to", but for a "reasonably priced" pizza and salad they're "surprisingly good" – and the "very slow" servers are kind to kids.

Bertucci's S   17 16 16 $15
1218-20 Connecticut Ave., NW (Jefferson Pl.), 202-463-7733
2000 Pennsylvania Ave., NW (bet. 20th & 21st Sts.),
202-296-2600
8027 Leesburg Pike (off Rte. 495), Vienna, VA, 703-893-5200
7421 Sudley Rd. (Nicholson St.), Manassas, VA, 703-257-5550
13195 Parcher Ave. (bet. Elden St. & Worldgate Dr.),
Herndon, VA, 703-787-6500
6525 Frontier Dr. (Franconia Rd.), Springfield, VA, 703-313-6700
6208 Multiplex Dr. (bet. Rte. 28 & Old Braddock Rd.),
Centreville, VA, 703-803-9300
◪ "Popular with families" for what they are – "cheap", "convenient" places for "pretty decent" pizza plus pasta and salads; as with any chain, you'll find "clueless" help, poor housekeeping and "mediocre food" on any given day at any location.

Bice S   23 23 21 $39
601 Pennsylvania Ave., NW (Indiana Ave.), 202-638-2423
◪ This "boisterous" Downtown Northern Italian "power" place for "trendy lunches at Fendi prices" has been "much maligned" (i.e. often pronounced "bitchy") despite its "fabulous" risotto, "reliable people-watching" and handsome setting; but with Francesco Ricchi (ex I Ricchi) overseeing the kitchen (post-*Survey*) and Francesco Pistorio out front, hold tight for the "upswing."

Bilbo Baggins S   18 18 18 $22
208 Queen St. (Lee St.), Alexandria, VA, 703-683-0300
◪ Fans of this "funky" Alexandria townhouse delight in its "interesting" American and veggie dishes (even when they "don't quite pan out") and don't mind the contrast between the "warm setting" and sometimes "colder-than-your-ex-in-laws" service; while its homemade raisin bread and sticky buns are a "habbit", a "serious" wine list is the sleeper.

Bistro S   – – – M
ANA Hotel, 2401 M St., NW (24th St.), 202-457-5020
Timothy Dean (recently honored by the James Beard House) is putting this "moderately priced" bistro on DC's culinary map with his Contemporary American menu; pleasant dining is made more so by the handsome wood and tile interior, secluded courtyard and "very helpful staff; "spectacular" Sunday brunch in the Colonnade room is not to be missed.

Bistro Bistro 🖪　　　20 | 18 | 18 | $22
Village at Shirlington, 4021 S. 28th St., Arlington, VA,
703-379-0300
Reston Town Ctr., 1811 Library St. (bet. Dulles Toll Rd. &
Reston Pkwy.), Reston, VA, 703-834-6300
☑ Designer American bistros with a "solid menu" that try to
create a "neighborhood" feel in "faux-urban" locales;
fans think they're best for hanging out with friends and
"post-movie fare", but detractors decry "bland" food,
"yuppie" pricing and a staff trained for "throughput."

Bistro Francais ◑🖪　　　20 | 18 | 18 | $26
3128 M St., NW (bet. 31st St. & Wisconsin Ave.), 202-338-3830
☑ "Where else in DC" can you get a real dinner "at 1 AM"?;
the later it gets, the more "wonderfully French" this
Georgetown "standby" becomes as it fills up with chefs,
nightowls and travelers on "late-night flights"; its steak
tartare and pommes frites are as legendary as its prix fixe
deals; "if service were better, it wouldn't seem so authentic."

Bistro Le Monde　　　17 | 14 | 17 | $21
223 Pennsylvania Ave., SE (bet. 2nd & 3rd Sts.), 202-544-4153
■ Prompted by congressional gift-ban rules, which are
drying up the Capitol Hill lunch trade, and an increasingly
health-conscious clientele, this House-side Gallic bar and
upstairs bistro (fka Le Mistral) have a new format and menu
of lower-priced salads, pastas and light entrees; downstairs
plays to "staffers and Hill locals", upstairs it's "Hill-itis."

Bistrot Lepic 🖪　　　23 | 19 | 21 | $34
1736 Wisconsin Ave., NW (S St.), 202-333-0111
■ "Très French" in a "Georgetowny" way, this "charming"
storefront with "true bistro" fare is "just the right size"
("a tad cramped") to be a "wonderful find"; it's "always
crowded, but one is never rushed."

Bistro Twenty Fifteen 🖪　　　21 | 19 | 21 | $32
Embassy Row Hotel, 2015 Massachusetts Ave. (off
Dupont Circle), 202-939-4250
☑ "Hidden" off Dupont Circle, this "quiet, restful" hotel
venue with a "wonderfully inventive" chef, Jim Papovich,
and fine service seems to be "struggling to find its image"
(currently Contemporary American); special events give
Papovich a chance to shine, although his cheering squad
wishes he were "given free play" more often.

Bleu Rock Inn 🖪　　　23 | 24 | 23 | $44
Rte. 211 (5 mi. west of Hwy. 522 N.), Washington, VA,
540-987-3190
☑ With its "romantic" Blue Ridge Mountain prospect, this
French-accented inn is a "delightful" overnight destination;
but its food and hospitality suffer by comparison with the
Inn at Little Washington nearby; surrounded by vineyards
and orchards, it's still a "nice Sunday jaunt" and especially
"lovely" at brunch (which the legendary Inn doesn't serve).

Blue & Gold S   – | – | – | M
3100 Clarendon Blvd. (Highland St.), Arlington, VA, 703-908-4995
Northern Virginia brewpubs are going "upscale" as
evidenced by this "overly ambitious" Clarendon entry; early
samplers report that the "delicious, Cajun-influenced" food
is "pretty pricey"; nevertheless, one "could get comfortable
here" – with earplugs.

Blue Point Grill S   23 | 17 | 20 | $31
600 Franklin St. (Washington St.), Alexandria, VA, 703-739-0404
◪ "Browse the antiques on King Street", then drop by
Sutton Place Gourmet for some of the "best seafood in
Alexandria" at its "spartan" cafe; the "exceptionally fresh"
fish doesn't come cheap, and the kitchen and servers
stumble, but more often than not the "innovative menu"
and good wine prevail.

Bob & Edith's Diner ◑ S ⇄   15 | 12 | 16 | $9
2310 Columbia Pike (Wayne St.), Arlington, VA, 703-920-6103
◪ It's "fast, friendly, filling and 'fordable" – and at 4 AM it
"beats waiting until 'real' places open for breakfast"; this
"classic", "very un-Washington" "grease pit" in Arlington
may also be the only place where "middle-aged women,
bikers and trendy gays fit in with yuppies."

Bombay Bistro S   24 | 13 | 19 | $17
3570 Chain Bridge Rd. (Lee Hwy.), Fairfax, VA, 703-359-5810
Bell's Corner, 98 W. Montgomery Ave. (Washington St.),
Rockville, MD, 301-762-8798
■ Respected by the local Indian community for their
"delicious" classics and regional specialties, plus an
"amazingly fresh" buffet lunch, these "always packed"
suburbanites are high on virtually everyone's "cheap
eats" list; if you "love good food more than fine dining",
they're a "real treat."

BOMBAY CLUB S   24 | 26 | 25 | $34
815 Connecticut Ave. (bet. H & I Sts.), 202-659-3727
■ One of Downtown DC's top "power-dining" rooms, this
"supercivilized" Anglo-Indian, with its "days of the raj"
opulence, "sophisticated" kitchen and "elegant" manners,
is surprisingly "low-key . . . for the price"; credit its savvy
owner, Ashok Bajaj, who "knows what DC wants."

Bombay Dining S   ▽ 23 | 18 | 19 | $23
4931 Cordell Ave. (Old Georgetown Rd.), Bethesda, MD,
301-656-3373
■ "Cordial" and a "great value for interesting food" sums
up the attraction of this "excellent" Indian in Bethesda; try
the "best-buy" lunch buffet, then go next door to Travel
Books to plan your trip.

Bombay Palace S   22 | 19 | 20 | $28
2020 K St., NW (bet. 20th & 21st Sts.), 202-331-4200
☑ This K Street Indian with "pretty, pink" decor is "not as upscale as the nearby Bombay Club", but it's "worthy in its own right"; many, in fact, think it's a "better value" and serves the "best traditional Indian food outside an Indian home" (i.e. spicy and rich).

B. Smith's S   20 | 24 | 18 | $28
Union Station, 50 Massachusetts Ave., 202-289-6188
■ Barbara Smith's soulful restaurant in a "majestic" Union Station setting successfully "combines down-home feel with elegance" and "welcomes all"; the "high-end Southern fare" can be "delicious" or "mediocre", but "it's worth the risk to see the room" and the "ultracool evening clientele" – a great choice "for foreign guests."

Bua S   21 | 16 | 19 | $18
1635 P St. (bet. 16th & 17th Sts.), 202-265-0828
■ Although the "atmosphere could use some work", this "relaxed", "reasonably priced" Thai with a "breezy deck" and "fresh, spicy" food is deemed a Dupont Circle East "trade secret" ("like a fishing hole only I know"); one of the few naysayers quips, "tiny portions explain the servers' trim waistlines."

Bugaboo Creek Steak House S   15 | 20 | 17 | $18
6820 Commerce Dr. (Backlick Rd.), Springfield, VA, 703-451-3300
15710 Shady Grove Rd. (Rte. 270, exit 8), Gaithersburg, MD, 301-548-9200
☑ "Kids love" these "goofy" steakhouses for their "Disneyish" decor and "novelty" atmosphere complete with "talking animals", while their parents love the price; the steak and ribs are "ordinary" if plentiful, though occasionally they talk back.

Buon Giorno   20 | 19 | 20 | $32
8003 Norfolk Ave. (Del Ray Ave.), Bethesda, MD, 301-652-1400
☑ In Bethesda, where Italian eateries abound, this family-run "favorite" has "maintained its standard" by staying "consistent", "traditional", "predictable" and "welcoming"; at the same time, it "hasn't improved over the years."

Burma S   21 | 10 | 18 | $15
740 Sixth St., NW (bet. G & H Sts.), 202-638-1280
☑ "Sweet service" and "exotic" fare make this "cheap-eats" Asian seem "far more elegant" than its "simple" decor and "run-down" Downtown "neighborhood would lead you to expect"; note that Burmese food, sometimes described as "Chinese with a kick", is not for "weak palates"; P.S. expect to stay awhile – "quick lunches take two hours."

Burrito Brothers 🅂♿
205 Pennsylvania Ave., SE (2nd St.), 202-543-6835
2418 18th St. (Columbia Rd.), 202-265-4048 ◗
3273 M St., NW (Potomac St.), 202-965-3963 ◗
1524 Connecticut Ave., NW (Q St.), 202-332-2308
We don't know why we left these major sources of
"nutritious fast food" served in "basic" countertop spaces
off the _Survey_, they provide a "grease-free" "meal of fresh
ingredients" at a "terrific price" (under $5), are "open late"
and sustain Generation X.

Burro ♿   19 | 12 | 15 | $8
1621 Connecticut Ave. (bet. Q & R Sts.), 202-483-6861 🅂
1134 19th St. (bet. L & M Sts.), 202-853-5041
■ "Fast food meets great ingredients" at these colorful Tex-
Mex takeouts dishing out "cheapo", grando burritos (and
low-fat chili, beans and soups) from countertop digs;
although some say the "fresh", "healthy" fillings are "not
so flavorful", many maintain they're "muy bueno."

Busara 🅂   23 | 23 | 20 | $23
2340 Wisconsin Ave., NW (Calvert St.), 202-337-2340
8142 Watson St. (bet. Leesburg Pike & Rte. 123), McLean,
_VA, 703-356-2288_
■ "Dramatic" neon and black decor, a "hip bar" and a
"gorgeous garden" lend a "sophisticated" touch to the
"straightforward" yet "yummy" food served at this popular
Upper Georgetown Thai; a few find the scenery (walking
and otherwise) "flashy but distracting" – "sunglasses
optional inside" and at the new Virginia locale.

Cactus Cantina 🅂   18 | 16 | 17 | $18
3300 Wisconsin Ave., NW (Macomb St.), 202-686-7222
◪ This "casual", "everyday" Tex-Mex in Cleveland Park
offers "decent, cheap food", a "great tortilla-making
machine" that keeps kids "occupied" and a "festive"
sidewalk setting for a group; it "keeps expanding", yet it
still gets gripes about waits – also "noise", "careless"
cooking and being "rushed."

Cafe Asia 🅂   _ | _ | _ | M
1134 19th St. (bet. L & M Sts.) 202-659-2696
Recommended for a lunchtime "trip around the Far East"
or sushi happy hour ($1 a piece) below Dupont Circle; this
smart-looking Pan-Asian earns kudos for "nice waiters",
"reasonable prices" and "doing everything" pretty well.

Cafe Atlantico   _ | _ | _ | M
405 8th St., NW (bet. D & E Sts.), 202-393-0812
In summer 1996, this former Adams Morgan hot spot
revamped historic Penn Quarter digs into a lively, multilevel
happening; DC trendies couldn't wait to check out its worldly
Nuevo Latino cuisine and clientele, along with paintings
done by talented Caribbean and South American artists.

Cafe Berlin [S]

F	D	S	C
18	16	19	$23

322 Massachusetts Ave., NE (bet. 3rd & 4th Sts.), 202-543-7656

■ One of the "best outdoor dining areas" on the Hill makes this German popular with "Senate staffers"; another attraction is the "bargain soup-and-sandwich lunch" plus lightened-up versions of regional specialties like potato pancakes, bratwurst and spaetzle washed down, of course, with an "excellent German beer."

Cafe Bethesda [S]

F	D	S	C
24	20	21	$35

5027 Wilson Ln. (bet. Old Georgetown & Arlington Rds.), Bethesda, MD, 301-657-3383
121 Congressional Ln. (next to Congressional Plaza), Rockville, MD, 301-770-3185

■ "Vest pocket" intimacy and "light" cooking are the drawing cards of this Bethesda Contemporary American and its modish, "never-know-you-were-in-Rockville" sib; however, make sure that "leisurely dining" is in your game plan, as well as paying real money "for a weekday dinner."

Cafe Dalat [S]

F	D	S	C
22	10	19	$14

3143 Wilson Blvd. (Highland St.), Arlington, VA, 703-276-0935

■ Setting a high "standard" for "good-value" grub, this venerable Vietnamese with a "fall-of-Saigon atmosphere" may be the "friendliest", "cheapest" and tastiest in the Clarendon cheap-eats corridor; fans go so far as to say it's "head and shoulders above its much-talked-about neighbor Queen Bee" (ratings reveal they're neck and neck).

Cafe Deluxe [S] 🚫

F	D	S	C
18	19	19	$21

3228 Wisconsin Ave., NW (Macomb St.), 202-686-2233

■ How could this "buzzing" Cleveland Park newcomer miss with its "LA atmosphere", martini and mashed potatoes "comfort food" and sidewalk cafe?; it's a "much-needed", unfussy, "neighborhood bar for the '90s" (albeit "still experimental") – hence the "long waits."

Cafe Milano [S]

F	D	S	C
19	19	16	$31

3251 Prospect St., NW (bet. Wisconsin Ave. & 33rd St.), 202-333-6183

◪ It's fashionable to trash this "flashy" Georgetowner for its much-publicized, late-night Euro scene ("poseur's palace", "snobissimo"), but whereas celebs and micro-minis are well-seated downstairs, upstairs is "quiet and private" – "pretty agreeable" for a "light" Northern Italian meal; there's also an off-street patio that's "lovely for lunch."

Cafe Mileto [S]

	F	D	S	C
▽	17	18	19	$19

Cloppers Mill Village Ctr., 18056 Mateny Rd. (Great Seneca Hwy.), Germantown, MD, 301-515-9370

■ This youngster's brick pizza oven, decorative setting and inviting terrace indicate a serious try at bringing Southern Italy to Germantown; neighbors are hoping that the fairly successful efforts to date are "not beginner's luck."

Cafe Mozart [S] 16 13 16 $18

1331 H St., NW (bet. 13th & 14th Sts.), 202-347-5732

◪ "Indistinguishable from countless in Vienna", this "dusty" old Downtown German deli is one of the few local places where the "best of the 'wurst' [and other hard-to-find groceries] can be found"; it also serves "hearty" Bavarian meals and desserts in a bright, noisy rear dining room to mixed reviews: "disappointing" vs. " a nice alternative."

Cafe New Delhi [S] ▽ 24 16 21 $16

1041 N. Highland St. (Clarendon Metro Stop), Arlington, VA, 703-528-2511

■ Northern Virginians tell us that this "excellent little" Indian "deserves to be mobbed" for its "especially tasty" vegetable dishes, breads and curries, "modest prices", "friendly" ways and "beautiful calm" that enhances the "wonderful food"; perhaps its "storefront look" keeps the crowds away.

Café Oggi [S] 19 18 19 $25

6671 Old Dominion Dr. (Lowell & Whittier Aves.), McLean, VA, 703-442-7360

◪ The food is definitely not Milano "modern" ("how do you say très ordinaire in Italian?"), but suburbanites are pleased to have this Italian in McLean; "predictable" and a bit "pretentious", it's also "pretty" and a "change of pace."

Cafe on M [S] 26 22 23 $39

Western Hotel, 2350 24th St., NW (M St.), 202-429-0100

◪ Shortly after this suave West Ender was 'discovered', its chef departed, putting the above ratings in doubt; new management is continuing the Contemporary American focus, but we hear that the changes may have blunted its edge; one thing remains the same, however – the "dark", windowless decor.

Cafe Parisien Express ⊄ 18 13 14 $12

118 King St. (Washington St.), Alexandria, VA, 703-683-3331
4520 Lee Hwy. (bet. Woodstock & Woodrow Sts.), Arlington, VA, 703-525-3332

■ "In Paris", as in the Northern Virginia suburbs, there are times when you want a "quick", "cheap" meal; these "pleasant", self-serve cafes speak "fast food" with a French accent and "live up to the promise of their name"; now "get rid of the Styrofoam plates."

Cafe Promenade [S] 19 21 20 $28

Mayflower Hotel, 1127 Connecticut Ave., NW (bet. L & M Sts.), 202-347-2233

■ Long a major power breakfast, lunch and afternoon tea site, this "classy" hotel dining space with "great people-watching" has gotten even better since chef Tino Buggio directed his energies here; his first-class Mediterranean food has "vastly improved" Downtown dining options – and made the above ratings obsolete.

Cafe Riviera S   – | – | – | M

Georgetown Inn, 1310 Wisconsin Ave., NW (bet. Dumbarton & N Sts.), 202-944-9600

A veritable 'cafe provencal' replacing Georgetown's short-lived Millennium; its new patron, Gerard Pangaud (Gerard's Place), installed a chef from Nice and warmed up the svelte, minimalist decor; given his oversight, its friendly prices ($13–$19 entrees) and the presence of some experienced hands out front, this venture just might last the year – if not the decade.

Cafe Rose S   – | – | – | M

Stratford Motor Lodge, 300 W. Broad St. (Little Falls St.), Falls Church, VA, 703-532-1700

This Falls Church motel/restaurant, an Iranian community hub, is a "very good" place to explore Persia's 4,000-year-old cuisine; here, it's prepared for you as for a guest in the owner's "home" (translation: "slow" dining).

Cafe Saigon S   22 | 13 | 19 | $14

1135 N. Highland St. (bet. Wilson & Clarendon Blvds.), Arlington, VA, 703-276-7110

■ One visits this no-frills Vietnamese lunch counter for its "excellent" pho, Hanoi pork and "special items available nowhere else" in Clarendon; "small and efficient", it's a "fun place to eat."

Cafe Taj S   23 | 20 | 21 | $20

1379 Beverly Rd. (Old Dominion Dr.), McLean, VA, 703-827-0444

■ Reviewers in McLean "love" this relatively "unknown", "really good Indian" for its tempting food and "modest" prices; a lovely courtyard and "soothing" postmodern interior and manners bring you as close as you can get to the "Bombay Club . . . in the suburbs."

Cajun Bangkok S   21 | 13 | 18 | $19

907 King St. (Alford St.), Alexandria, VA, 703-836-0038

■ The seemingly "strange" coupling of Cajun and Thai cuisines at this Old Town storefront pleases "spicy food" freaks; highlights of its bipartite menu include crying tiger, pecan-crusted catfish and shrimp étouffe – all authentically prepared and "helpfully" served amid "nonexistent decor."

Calasia   21 | 17 | 19 | $35

7929 Norfolk Ave. (Cordell Ave.), Bethesda, MD, 301-654-6444

☑ Since its original chef left and key staff followed suit, this "in" place in Bethesda "doesn't meet the expectations" of many surveyors; now its "California food with an Asian flavor or vice versa" is too often "disappointing" and with "only 11 tables" some think service could improve.

California Pizza Kitchen [S] 18 | 14 | 17 | $16

1260 Connecticut Ave. (N St.), 202-331-4020
Chevy Chase Pavilion, 5345 Wisconsin Ave., NW (Military Rd.), 202-363-6650
700 King St. (S. Washington St.), Alexandria, VA, 703-706-0404
Village at Shirlington, 4053 S. 28th St. (Randolph St.), Arlington, VA, 703-845-7770
12300 Price Club Plaza, Ste. C (W. Ox Rd.), Fairfax, VA, 703-802-2250
1201 S. Hayes St., Ste. F (12th St.), Arlington, VA, 703-412-4900
Tysons Corner Ctr., 7939-L Tysons Corner (Rte. 7), McLean, VA, 703-761-1473
Montgomery Mall, 7101 Democracy Blvd. (Westlake Dr.), Bethesda, MD, 301-469-5090

■ Though "grown-ups" are "embarrassed to admit it, they love the food" at these "Disney-does-nouveau-pizza" kitchens, as evidenced by the highest traffic in the *Survey*; serving pizzas topped with "weird" stuff and staffed by overly friendly "90210 types", their "formula" may be "yup food", but it's a "good deal" if you can deal with the bright lights and "spotless white-tile decor."

California Tortilla [S] – | – | – | I

4862 Cordell Ave. (bet. Norfolk & Woodmont Aves.), Bethesda, MD, 301-654-8226

Bethesda's "healthy" Mexican replaces fat with "fresh" ingredients and "flavorful" seasonings; what's more, it delivers the "whole package" at "cheap prices" in a breezy eat-in/carry-out format.

Calvert Grille [S] 18 | 10 | 19 | $15

Calvert Apts., 3106 Mt. Vernon Ave. (bet. E & W Glebe Rd. & Commonwealth Ave.), Alexandria, VA, 703-836-8425

■ When Del Ray parents "can't find a sitter", they head for the toy-filled "kids' room" at this "neighborhood joint"; Don and Lynn Abram run it like a "big family", serving "quality breakfasts", "stick-to-your-ribs American fare" and well-selected brews at "reasonable prices."

Cambodian ▽ 15 | 11 | 16 | $16

1727 Wilson Blvd. (Quinn St.), Arlington, VA, 703-522-3832

◩ This colorful Cambodian "dive" in Arlington is possibly the "best source for a cuisine worth exploring"; most appreciate its low prices and "sweet service", but some find the Chinese-like dishes "unimpressive."

CAPITAL GRILLE [S] 23 | 25 | 23 | $41

601 Pennsylvania Ave., NW (6th St.), 202-737-6200

■ Decked out with "all the trappings" of a "clubby", "establishment" stronghold, DC's most Republican restaurant is packed with "fat cats talking on cell phones" and "first-time cigar smokers" ("all under age 25"); it has "great steaks, better drinks", smooth service ("regulars" preferred) and "expense-account" prices.

Capitol City Brewing Co. [S] 14 | 19 | 15 | $17
1100 New York Ave., NW (bet. H & 11th Sts.), 202-628-2222
2 Massachusetts Ave. (1st St.), 202-842-2337
◪ "Evenings are a yuppie group grope" at these raucous Downtown brewpubs where soft pretzels and burgers are the menu highlights and the help can't really cope with the crowds; still, the "microclimate" keeps lawyers, "young Republicans" and conventioneers "off the street."

CARLYLE GRAND CAFE [S] 23 | 21 | 21 | $24
4000 S. 28th St. (Quincy St.), Shirlington, VA, 703-931-0777
■ This "wildly popular" American bistro brings a "gourmet-for-the-common-man" approach to dining in Shirlington; chef Bill Jackson gives "fresh ingredients" an "innovative" twist but "doesn't forget that you have to eat the dish"; however, it's hard to forget that you're in a "suburban sprawl of a restaurant" with a "food court" feel; sit upstairs.

Cashion's Eat Place [S] 24 | 21 | 21 | $30
1819 Columbia Rd., NW (bet. Biltmore & Mintwood Sts.), 202-797-1819
■ Ann Cashion has created a "sophisticated" home away from home at her "urban" bistro where the bar and open-to-the-street dining space function as a neighborhood living room; her modern American "comfort food" is so appealing that customers, ranging from "Beltway bandits" to "tourists" to Euro expats, "want to try everything on the menu"; it could be the "best restaurant to hit Adams Morgan" in years.

Cedar Knoll Inn [S] 18 | 20 | 18 | $22
9030 Lucia Ln. (Vernon View Dr.), Alexandria, VA, 703-799-1501
■ Word has it that this Potomac viewplace, with its "Elks Lodge" decor, may "not be just for mothers-in-law anymore"; a 'real' chef and his Mediterranean-American fare have "vastly improved" dining prospects – though not to the level of the "lovely" river prospects.

C.F. Folks ⊄ 21 | 10 | 18 | $12
1225 19th St., NW (bet. M & N Sts.), 202-293-0162
■ Just-folks 'do lunch' at this Dupont Circle food stall (though you're likely to spot boldface names "saving a few bucks"); its "quirky" proprietor serves up "sandwiches and sass" along with "terrific" blackboard specials on a "limited" basis – closed after 3 PM and on weekends.

Chadwick's ☾ [S] 14 | 14 | 16 | $17
5247 Wisconsin Ave., NW (Jennifer St.), 202-362-8040
3205 K St., NW (Wisconsin Ave.), 202-333-2565
203 Strand St. (bet. Prince & Duke Sts.), Alexandria, VA, 703-836-4442
◪ Though some say these "comfortable" collegiate pubs "need a jump start", they're "always dependable", a "good value" and "handy" for a pre-movie burger and beer or "coming from the airport late at night."

Chardonnay S   ▽ 20 | 22 | 20 | $30

Doubletree Park Terrace Hotel, 1515 Rhode Island Ave.,
NW (Scott Circle), 202-232-7000

■ Garden ambiance, posh appointments, "good service"
and a "great wine list" recommend this "underrated", easy-
to-reach Contemporary American just off Scott Circle for
a "power lunch" or "romantic" dinner; supporters say it's
"one of the better reasonably priced hotel eateries."

Charlie Chiang's S   16 | 14 | 16 | $18

Village at Shirlington, 4060 S. 28th St. (Quincy St.),
Shirlington, VA, 703-671-4900
660 S. Pickett (Van Dorn St.), Alexandria, VA, 703-751-8888

▨ Despite their "health-conscious emphasis" and talented
kitchens, this "cheap", "convenient" Chinese duo gets very
mixed reviews: "always fresh", "reliable and consistent" vs.
"so many choices, so little flavor", "remarkably ordinary";
as with many seemingly "Americanized" Asians, it pays to
"ask for specials not on the menu."

Chart House S   19 | 21 | 19 | $28

1 Cameron St. (waterfront), Alexandria, VA, 703-684-5080

▨ "Beautiful locale", "boring food" sums up the majority
opinion on this waterfront viewplace whose steak, seafood
and salad-bar fare, "robotically cheerful" help and long
waits epitomize "chain" dining; still, for some, it embodies
"romance by the water" with "gorgeous" sights, "tasty"
eats and decadent mud pie.

CHEESECAKE FACTORY ◑S   19 | 18 | 17 | $20

Chevy Chase Pavilion, 5345 Wisconsin Ave., NW (bet.
Jennifer St. & Western Ave.), 202-364-0500
White Flint Mall, 11301 Rockville Pike (Nicholson Ln.),
Bethesda, MD, 301-770-0999

▨ "Hopeless waits", "gargantuan portions", "monstrous
desserts", an "unabridged" something-for-everyone menu —
there's "too much of everything" at these commercial
"crowd-pleasers", which is why so many "love" them; if
ever a restaurant chain epitomized the "homogenization
of New America", this is it.

Chesapeake Seafood   15 | 9 | 14 | $17
Crab House S

3607 Wilson Blvd. (bet. Nelson & Monroe Sts.), Arlington,
VA, 703-528-8888

▨ "Wacky" yet "worth surmounting the language barrier"
for the "cheap", "delicious" Vietnamese seafood dishes
served at this Clarendon hole; the "huge menu" of pho and
American-style fin fare can be daunting, ditto the "drab"
premises and service that's "ok on a good day", but the
Astroturf "patio is a trip."

Chicken Place [S] ▽ 19 10 16 $13
11201 Grandview Ave. (Reedie Dr.), Wheaton, MD, 301-946-1212
■ Crisp-skinned roasted chicken, "great fries" and unusual Peruvian sides – "for a very few pesos" you can turn "weeknight" refueling into a low-budget "adventure" at these Andean rotisseries; but unless you count the tempting smells and late-night music and dancing, the ambiance is nil.

China Canteen [S] ▽ 23 10 21 $15
808 Hungerford Dr. (off Ivy League Ln.), Rockville, MD, 301-424-1606
■ It's not as well-known as it should be, yet Rockville Sinophiles swear by this "crummy"-looking, "homestyle Chinese" with its "chalkboard menu and lumpy seats", "great food, bargain prices and a staff that tries to explain exotic dishes" – "what more would you want?"

China Chef [S] 18 12 17 $16
11323 Georgia Ave. (University Blvd.), Wheaton, MD, 301-949-8170
◪ Although this Wheaton Cantonese wins local "loyalty" for its weekend dim sum, lobster special and "doting" on kids, we also hear the food is "now very ordinary" (like the decor); nevertheless, it's cheap enough to be worth a try.

China Inn ◐ [S] 19 13 16 $19
631 H St., NW (bet. 6th & 7th Sts.), 202-842-0909
◪ It looks "worn", yet this "reliable old Chinatown standby" is still capable of producing exciting dishes like "spicy eggplant", "drunken crabs" and daily dim sum; but some surveyors increasingly find less reason to visit this "shabby neighborhood" – especially at night.

"Ciao baby" Cucina 18 20 18 $26
Washington Sq., 1736 L St., NW (bet. 18th St. & Connecticut Ave.), 202-331-1500
◪ Young K Street strivers favor this too-"trendy" Italian for its "high-end" atmosphere and free "happy-hour chow", but not for the high-end prices (unless "someone else pays") or "magazine food" ("looks better than it tastes"); there's a popular lunch buffet and a back room for "celebrations."

Cintra [S] ▽ 23 13 20 $22
5216 Wilson Blvd. (bet. Florida St. & George Mason Dr.), Arlington, VA, 703-525-1170
■ An Iberian addition to the area's international palate, this Portuguese offers "unusual" food in a Ballston storefront brightened with ethnic touches; *paelha* and pork with clams are some of the interesting choices – along with an interesting bar.

Cities S   20 | 23 | 18 | $28
2424 18th St., NW (Columbia Rd.), 202-328-7194

☑ This "campy" bar/restaurant "brings the world to Adams Morgan", periodically revamping the decor and menu to showcase a "different city"; while it's "still a great place for dinner and then Latin dancing later" (upstairs) and for a laid-back brunch, its founding chef, Mary Richter, is "missed" by many who feel the food is "uneven and uninspired" these days.

CITRONELLE S   26 | 23 | 23 | $47
Latham Hotel, 3000 M St., NW (30th St.), 202-625-2150

■ Michel Richard's "very Californian" take on French dining (à la LA's Citrus) is the "best expense-account splurge" in Georgetown; filled with "romantic nooks" and "famous faces", it's where the "upscale" crowd goes "when the meal is the main event" – and with a new chef, Larbi Darouch (ex Palladin), it could peak.

City Lights of China S   25 | 14 | 19 | $19
1731 Connecticut Ave., NW (bet. R & S Sts.), 202-265-6688

■ "The best Chinese food in DC served efficiently by surly waitresses" is the short of it; the rest of the story on this "cramped", "no-decor" ("but who cares?") Dupont Circle step-down is that in a "town devoid of good Chinese", its "light sauces" and "fresh ingredients" stand out; yes, that was "Mick Jagger"; "quick delivery", too.

Clyde's ◑S   17 | 21 | 18 | $21
Georgetown Park Mall, 3236 M St., NW (Wisconsin Ave.), 202-333-9180
Reston Town Ctr., 11905 Market St. (Reston Pkwy.), Reston, VA, 703-787-6601
8332 Leesburg Pike (Rtes. 7 & 123), Vienna, VA, 703-734-1901
70 Wisconsin Circle (bet. Wisconsin & Western Aves.), Chevy Chase, MD, 301-951-9600

☑ With their commitment to providing "wholesome food" at a "good price", these "handsome", hometown saloons are reinventing themselves while preserving their "great burgers" appeal; the "stunning" new Chevy Chase locale is a "smash" hit, though working out "kinks" – and Georgetown has been impressively overhauled; a few naysayers respond "too bad you can't eat the decor."

Coco Loco   20 | 22 | 18 | $28
810 7th St., NW (bet. H & I Sts.), 202-289-2626

■ A "high-energy", "off-the-wall" South American hot spot where pinstripes, pols and cosmopols find common ground; it has added words like caipirinhas (80-proof, lime-flavored knockout drops), Mexican tapas and churrascaria (an all-you-can-eat "carnivore extravaganza") to the Downtown dining vocabulary; late at night, when Brazilian dancers rev up the room, critics call it "overexposed."

COEUR DE LION S   24 25 24 $43
*Henley Park Hotel, 926 Massachusetts Ave., NW (10th St.),
202-638-5200*
■ When you "take someone you love" to this "jewel"
set in a Downtown hotel, its "beautiful setting", "romantic"
ambiance, "creative" Contemporary American fare and
after-dinner dancing will burnish your glow; it's also a
"pleasure" for business or brunch and "perfect for
special occasions."

Connaught Place S   ▽ 25 19 24 $21
*10425 North St. (Rte. 236 W. & University Dr.), Fairfax, VA,
703-352-5959*
■ This "refined" suburban subcontinental rewards those
who "find it" (in Fairfax City) with "first-class food and
service" reminiscent "of London's" famed Anglo-Indian
restaurants; the seafood, chicken tikka and "lamb anything"
are "excellent" – "light", "not oily" and "fresh."

Coppi's S   22 19 18 $18
1414 U St., NW (bet. 14th & 15th Sts.), 202-319-7773
◪ In the not-quite-gentrified New U area, this brick-oven
pizzeria is "packed" on weekends with a lively mix of
resid'Uers and tourists from the 'burbs; they find plenty of
attitude, along with "creative" salads and toppings and a
deadly Nutella (chocolate-hazelnut paste) calzone.

Cottonwood Cafe S   20 20 19 $27
*4844 Cordell Ave. (bet. Wisconsin Ave. & Old
Georgetown Rd.), Bethesda, MD, 301-656-4844*
◪ "Too spicy", "too pricey", "too unvarying" say some
surveyors – so why is this "Red Sage knockoff" usually
packed to the max?; because "Bethesda is desperate
for good Southwestern food" but willing to settle for a
reasonable proxy if it's "close", "friendly" and happens to
have a "great patio."

Cowboy Cafe S   14 12 15 $12
*Adams Square Shopping Ctr., 2421 Columbia Pike (bet. S.
Barton & Cleveland Sts.), Arlington, VA, 703-486-3467
4792 Lee Hwy. (N. Glebe Rd.), Arlington, VA,
703-243-8010
6151 Richmond Hwy. (Rte. 1), Alexandria, VA,
703-660-2320*
■ "Music rules" at this "terrific neighborhood" hitching
post in S. Arlington, which means that "Thursday night is
pork chops and The Grandsons" (a country-rockabilly band)
or a "good cheap burger" and microbrew; but what locals
like best is that "over the years the staff's enthusiasm has
not waned" – ditto at newer locations; P.S. "nonsmokers
need an iron lung."

Crisfield S　　　21 10 16 $25

Lee Plaza, 8606 Colesville Rd. (Georgia Ave.), Silver Spring,
MD, 301-588-1572
8012 Georgia Ave. (East-West Hwy. & Railroad St.), Silver
Spring, MD, 301-589-1306

☑ A fried-fish field trip to these Old Maryland culinary "landmarks" may be a "go once" experience given their "high" price tag, "dowdy" appearance and "surly" help; yet they are edible history, with "some of the best seafood on the East Coast" and lots of "character" in the original Silver Spring location.

Crisp & Juicy S　　　20 5 13 $9

Sunshine Sq. Shopping Ctr., 1331-G Rockville Pike
(Congressional Plaza), Rockville, MD, 301-251-8833
Leisure World Plaza, 3800 International Dr. (Georgia Ave.),
Silver Spring, MD, 301-598-3333
Lee Heights Shopping Ctr., 4520 Lee Hwy. (Lorcom Ln.),
Arlington, VA, 703-243-4222 ⊅

■ This trio of "roadside chicken stands" serving "great", cheap, "greasy" chicken, a "scrumptious" hot sauce and must-try Latin sides are "cheaper and better than eating at home"; although the "lack of any attempt at decor has a certain charm", most prefer takeout.

Crystal Thai S　　　23 17 21 $18

Arlington Forest Shopping Ctr., 4819 Arlington Blvd.
(Park Dr.), Arlington, VA, 703-522-1311

■ At this Arlington Thai, crystal chandeliers and white walls contrast pleasantly with "well-prepared" food that's "spicier than at most Thai restaurants"; its "light touch" with traditional recipes and "pauper's prices" please most, but its performance can be "erratic."

Da Domenico　　　20 17 20 $28

1992 Chain Bridge Rd. (Rte. 123), McLean, VA, 703-790-9000

☑ "The veal chop sings" and so does the opera-loving proprietor of this "old-fashioned" Tysons Corner Italian, as he and his "attentive" staff transform an ordinary meal in "dated" surroundings into a "pleasant evening"; however, it is said that "Chef Boyardee could make it at this location."

Dar es Salaam S　　　19 21 20 $25

3056 M St., NW (bet. 30th & 31st Sts.), 202-337-6680

■ Visit Morocco on M Street at this dramatically lit, authentically crafted replica; recline on pillowed seating and sample multicourse feasts or (mostly) "delicious" à la carte specialties while the belly dancers whirl; it's an "inviting" "getaway" from Georgetown traffic.

Dean & DeLuca Cafe 19 | 14 | 13 | $13
3276 M St., NW (33rd St.), 202-342-2500 S
1299 Pennsylvania Ave., NW (bet. 13th & E Sts.), 202-628-8155
1919 Pennsylvania Ave., NW (bet. 19th & I Sts.), 202-296-4327
☑ "Snack central" for Georgetown shoppers and people-watchers, this "stylish" sidewalk cafe serves tempting sandwiches, salads and light fare based on "what's best that day" in the adjacent gourmet shop; many find it "far too easy to spend too much" despite the "NY" attitude – ditto at D&D's Downtown bean bars.

Delhi Dhaba S 19 | 7 | 13 | $11
7236 Woodmont Ave. (bet. Bethesda Ave. & Elm St.), Bethesda, MD, 301-718-0008
2424 Wilson Blvd. (bet Barton St. & Clarendon Blvd.), Arlington, VA, 703-524-0008
■ Blaring Indian MTV sets the tone at these suburban down 'n' Delhis, where "hefty portions" of spicy curries and breads at "rock-bottom prices" substitute for amenities like atmosphere and service; no wonder surveyors say they're strictly for takeout or "on-the-run" meals.

Dixie Grill S 12 | 15 | 14 | $15
518 10th St., NW (bet. E & F Sts.), 202-628-4800
☑ A "great happy hour" and "shooting pool upstairs" draw Capitol Hill types to this Downtown Confederate pretender; reputedly, presidential "policies are hashed out here over a beer", but only a Republican would call the "greasy" fare real Southern food.

Donatello ◑ S 21 | 18 | 21 | $28
2514 L St., NW (Pennsylvania Ave.), 202-333-1485
☑ "On a summer night", the front porch of this "reliable", "relaxed" West End Italian is awfully "romantic"; it does "great everyday business lunches" and Kennedy Center ticketholders "would be lost" without its pre- and post-theater prix fixe menu, yet it has "never achieved liftoff" – possibly because it's "unexciting."

DUANGRAT'S S 25 | 21 | 21 | $23
5878 Leesburg Pike (Glen Forest Rd.), Falls Church, VA, 703-820-5775
■ One of the *Survey*'s top-rated Thais "never fails to please" with its "fragrant, deliciously flavored" dishes, pastel "elegance", waitresses in "custom dress" and "charming" weekend dance show; it's a "soothing" oasis in Bailey's Crossroads that can be "very impressive" for entertaining "at a fair price."

Duca Di Milano 18 | 20 | 18 | $34

2 Wisconsin Circle (Wisconsin & Western Aves.), Chevy Chase, MD, 301-656-3822

◪ Shameless glitz, "arrogant" too, yet this Northern Italian haunt of Chevy Chase/Bethesda's "beautiful people" has something "authentically European" about it; what's more, it's capable of producing "very good" – though "variable" of late – food; it's quiet at lunch, "flashy" at the bar.

Dusit [S] 21 | 16 | 19 | $17

2404 University Blvd. W. (Georgia Ave.), Wheaton, MD, 301-949-4140

◪ In Wheaton, with its wealth of inexpensive ethnic eateries, this "typical lavender" Thai gets good grades for comfort and for some "well-priced" dishes that "really shine", like BBQ beef salad and "satisfying curry"; perhaps naysayers haven't "learned what not to order."

Dynasty ◐ [S] ▽ 18 | 14 | 15 | $15

11123 Viers Mill Rd. (Wheaton Metro Station), Wheaton, MD, 301-942-3070

◪ Dinner at this unprepossessing Hong Kong outpost in Wheaton gives Westerners a chance to try exotic dishes and "authentically" prepared, "great fresh fish" as enjoyed by its Chinese clientele; however, gelatinous sea cucumbers and "goopy brown sauce" may not be your destiny.

Easby's Buffet [S] 11 | 9 | 11 | $10

8053 Leesburg Pike (Gallows Rd.), Tysons Corner, VA, 703-893-2072

1488 Rockville Pike (Montrose Rd.), Rockville, MD, 301-770-7710

Herndon Ctr., 428 Elden St. (Herndon Pkwy.), Herndon, VA, 703-435-5348

◪ Cheaper and easier than eating at home, these suburban family "feeding stations" let you "bulk up" on plain American food at their unlimited "smorgasbords"; but like your "school cafeteria", they elicit barbs such as "what decor? what service?", "I'd rather eat at an interstate rest area."

Eat First [S] 18 | 5 | 14 | $12

728 7th St., NW (bet. G & H Sts.), 202-347-0936

◪ "Surprisingly novel and tasty dishes" reward frequent visits to this Hong Kong "hole" in Chinatown; the "respectful staff guides you to make interesting choices" and is "kind enough to warn against goose feet . . . and other exotica", yet some would eat here last.

Ecco Cafe [S] 20 | 17 | 19 | $20

220 N. Lee St. (Cameron St.), Alexandria, VA, 703-684-0321

◪ Credit Diana Damewood's warm "welcome" along with double-sized pastas, pizzas and prize-winning salads for "making this place tick"; although it looks like it was decorated at a "yard sale", it's where they "power lunch Virginia-style" and "Old Town natives" dine "once a week."

El Caribe S   19 | 17 | 19 | $23
3288 M St., NW (bet. Potomac & 32nd Sts.),
202-338-3121
8130 Wisconsin Ave. (bet. Cordell Ave. & Battery Ln.),
Bethesda, MD, 301-656-0888
■ They may be "tired-looking", but these late-night
Latinos are "enjoyable" and "attentive" and produce
"interesting", "hearty" plates; "like the Redskins",
however, there are "a few great ones" (fried calamari,
paella and black beans), plus some "duds."

El Gavilan S   ▽ 18 | 10 | 18 | $16
8805 Flower Ave. (Pine Branch Rd.), Silver Spring, MD,
301-587-4197
■ Among the many Central Americans in this Silver
Spring enclave, this one is favored for being relatively
"nice-looking" and for "authentic" Salvadoran food
that goes beyond "good" fajitas and salsa; on weekends,
"loud" music adds another "authentic" note.

El Pollo Rico S⊟   23 | 7 | 16 | $10
2915-2917 N. Washington Blvd. (10th St.), Arlington, VA,
703-522-3220
7031 Brookfield Plaza Rd. (Amherst Ave.), Springfield, VA,
703-866-1286
2541 Ennalls Ave., Wheaton, MD, 301-942-4419
■ "Yummy", mouthwatering roasted chickens virtually fly
out the door of these high-volume charcoal grills largely
because "you don't find better value and your food comes
almost before you've finished ordering"; eat "shoulder to
shoulder" off "Styrofoam plates" in one of the area's "true
democratic restaurants" – or opt for "to go."

El Tamarindo S   17 | 10 | 16 | $14
7331 Georgia Ave., NW (Fessenden Rd.), 202-291-0525
4910 Wisconsin Ave., NW (42nd St.), 202-244-8888 ☽
1785 Florida Ave., NW (bet. 18th & U Sts.), 202-328-3660 ☽
■ Rated on a "calorie to dollar ratio", these low-rent
Salvadorans zoom off the charts; their "hearty, simple but
good" platters are the mainstay of students, moviegoers
and hungry families; after midnight, the food, "great
music" and goodwill get even better; squeamish diners
"bring the Rolaids."

Elysium S   – | – | – | E
Morrison House Hotel, 116 S. Alfred St. (bet. King &
Prince Sts.), Alexandria, VA, 703-838-8000
Although this secluded and "formal" dining room in a posh
Old Town hotel has suffered from a series of chef changes,
it still can make "special occasions" more so; its herb-
scented, Contemporary American focus sounds promising
and the staff is almost "too attentive" to your needs.

43

Enriqueta's 🅂   20 | 15 | 18 | $20
2811 M St., NW (bet. 28th & 29th Sts.), 202-338-7772
◪ One of the area's few "real" Mexicans, it's the place to
taste mole and Mayan dishes; but Georgetown parking,
too-"quick" service, "close" seating and chairs that could
double as "torture devices" do not encourage "lingering."

Eurogrill   – | – | – | M
*8401 Connecticut Ave. (Chevy Chase Lake Dr.), Bethesda,
MD, 301-907-0368*
From offering a "good choice of well-presented food" to
garage parking "on a rainy night", this "pleasant suburban
Continental" does basic things right; its "fixed-price menus
are an outstanding value"– and one reason why its
Bethesda neighbors treat the place like their living room.

Evans Farm Inn 🅂   13 | 19 | 16 | $25
1696 Chain Bridge Rd. (Rte. 123), McLean, VA, 703-356-8000
◪ "If only they'd sold to Jean-Louis" (ex Palladin), one of
the area's top toques – imagine what he could have done
with this lovely "bucolic setting", "tired" decor and kitchen
mired in the American '60s – not to mention its "cozy" pub, a
McLean favorite for "quiet cheats"; that would really wake
up the grandmothers who flock here on Mother's Day.

Eye St. Cafe   21 | 16 | 18 | $18
1915 I St., NW (bet. 19th & 20th Sts.), 202-457-0773
■ Although Mary Richter (ex Cities) has left this "casual"
Mediterranean, her legacy makes it a "find" for an
uncrowded dinner; the menu features Lebanese vegetarian
choices and pizza at lunch, when "too-close" seating and
"rushed" service draw fire; still, "in an area [K Street] short
on reasonably priced" dining, its customers are forgiving.

Faccia Luna Pizzeria 🅂⊘   21 | 15 | 17 | $15
2400 Wisconsin Ave., NW (Calvert St.), 202-337-3132
2909 Wilson Blvd. (Filmore St.), Arlington, VA, 703-276-3099
■ "It's the crust"– "oven burnt" – and "fresh", thoughtful
toppings that make these "lively neighborhood pizzerias";
but "even if you don't eat pizza", salads, hoagies, pastas,
microbrews, "good" sounds, "sports on the tube" and "love-
in-bloom photos on the wall" make them great "hangouts";
"slow service" seems to be the only "negative."

Falls Landing 🅂   20 | 21 | 20 | $31
*Village Ctr., 774 Walker Rd. (Georgetown Pike), Great
Falls, VA, 703-759-4650*
◪ "Central casting couldn't do Sunday dinner in the '50s
more accurately" than this "colonial" Virginian with its blue-
haired clientele, "living room"–like decor and cream-sauced
seafare; nevertheless, it offers the "freshest fish" and stately
treatment in a "serene setting."

Fatt Daddy's S   12 | 12 | 12 | $16
316 Massachusetts Ave., NE (bet. 3rd & 4th Sts.), 202-547-7014
◾ On Capitol Hill, "le bon temps roule" with "very mixed results" at this New Orleans facsimile; while it wins points as an "outdoor option" with "upbeat" help, virtually everything but the location "needs help."

Fedora Cafe S   18 | 19 | 18 | $22
8521 Leesburg Pike (bet. Rte. 123 & Dulles Access Rd.), Tysons Corner, VA, 703-556-0100
◾ A "comfortable", polished wood and brass backdrop for briefcase dining, after-work unwinding and "pre–Wolf Trap" snacks in Tysons Corner explains this Cal-Ital's "puzzling" (to those inside the Beltway) popularity; while there's nothing wrong with the eats, they're "not the main attraction."

Felix S   21 | 20 | 19 | $30
2406 18th St., NW (Belmont Rd.), 202-48-FELIX
◾ This "NY chic" New American has been having its "moment"; its "innovative", internationally accented food, "decadent" desserts and "fantasy" cityscape design "have found a good home" in Adams Morgan – but its "NY prices" and "pretensions" have not; check out the "hip" (for DC) bar and billiard scene.

Fern Street Bistro   ▽ 23 | 17 | 20 | $23
Burke Ctr., 6025-A Burke Ctr. Pkwy. (corner of Burke Commons), Burke, VA, 703-425-9463
◼ "Thirtysomethings" in Burke bless this strip-mall site for creating an "exciting atmosphere" with an Eclectic menu and a neat "gimmick" – choosing beer or wine from the adjacent retail store; it's "still a great secret" but small enough that "reservations are a must on weekends."

Filomena Ristorante S   20 | 19 | 19 | $29
1063 Wisconsin Ave., NW (bet. M & K Sts.), 202-338-8800
◾ The "finomenal" portions of "heavy" pasta dished out at this "gargantuan" Georgetown "tour bus" stop bring groans from some gastronomes; overlook the "hustle and bustle" and "snob attitude", however, and you may be "surprised by who" you see ("Pat Buchanan") and even "occasionally surprised by" what you eat.

Firehook Bakery & Coffeehouse S   24 | 16 | 17 | $9
1909 Q St., NW (19th St.), 202-588-9296
106 N. Lee St. (bet. King & Cameron Sts.), Alexandria, VA, 703-519-8020
◼ From "crusts to crumbs", the "stellar" artisan bread and fresh focaccia from these bakery/cafes, like their "scrumptious" pastries, are "arguably the best" in town; eaten in "warm" surroundings that double as local living rooms or in Old Town with fillers from the adjacent gourmetisserie, they give good bang for the buck; N.B. look for a new location on 17th Street.

Fleetwood's S 14 20 14 $23
44 Canal Ctr. Plaza (N. Fairfax Circle), Alexandria, VA,
703-548-6425
☑ "Great" live music and Potomac River views at Mick
Fleetwood's namesake blues club/eatery are "cheapened
by the inexperienced staff" and "uninspiring" American
food; perhaps a recent reorganization will tune up this
"theme restaurant without much of a theme."

Flint Hill Public House S ▽ 16 20 18 $30
Rte. 522 (Rte. 647), Flint Hill, VA, 540-675-1700
■ "Lovely new owners" are turning this turn-of-the century
property into a "wonderful place to visit" (despite some
"iffy" days); everyone from "bikers" to bankers are welcome
to sample the seasonal Contemporary American fare in a
pub or parlor setting that suits a wide range of appetites
and occasions; Blue Ridge Mountain vistas from the
outdoor deck are "worth the trip."

Florida Ave. Grill 19 12 16 $13
1100 Florida Ave., NW (11th St.), 202-265-1586
☑ DC's "best greasy breakfast", served at this soul kitchen
in a "borderline" 'hood, includes "waitresses calling you
'baby'", "grits and biscuits buttered to order", photos of
"famous patrons" and "plastic plants"; the food "could be
made with less fat", but then it wouldn't be "great down-
home cooking"; P.S. "it's cheap", too.

Food Factory S🈯 20 5 11 $11
4221 N. Fairfax Dr. (Glebe Rd.), Arlington, VA, 703-527-2279
1116 Herndon Pkwy. (Elden St.), Herndon, VA, 703-435-3333
8145-G Baltimore Ave. (University Blvd.), College Park,
MD, 301-345-8888
■ "It's another world" at "Kebabs R Us", a Pakistani
cafeteria in Ballston with less than "zero decor" but "huge
servings" of "great kebabs", breads and spicy curries at
rock-bottom prices; this (or its unrated brethren) is the
place to go when you want to "fill your stomach" and
"can't afford to eat at home."

Foong Lin S 20 15 20 $19
7710 Norfolk Ave. (Fairmont Ave.), Bethesda, MD,
301-656-3427
■ Bethesda's "Sunday night" Chinese has "redecorated
into the '90s" ("a welcome change") while preserving
its "retro" menu of standards; prized for its fresh fish,
willingness to "prepare foods as requested" ("Peking
chicken") and "gracious, unflappable" help, it's summed
up by surveyors as "high quality but uninspired."

Fortune [S] 22 | 12 | 17 | $18

Greenforest Shopping Ctr., 5900 Leesburg Pike (Bailey's Crossroads), Falls Church, VA, 703-998-8888
North Point Village Ctr., 1428 Reston Pkwy. (bet. Rte. 7 & Baron Cameron Rd.), Reston, VA, 703-318-8898

■ "Go on Sunday for the full effect" of the "festive", fast-paced scene at these Virginia dim sum palaces where rolling carts serve "fantastic" Chinese tidbits in a "gymnasium" filled with "Chinese families", "Vietnamese weddings" and non-English-speaking waiters; weekday dim sum, backed by a compendium of Chinese seafood dishes, is also "like Taipei."

49 Twelve Thai [S] ▽ 19 | 15 | 19 | $19

4912 Wisconsin Ave., NW (bet. Ellicott & Fessenden Sts.), 202-966-4696

■ Some say this "very good" Northwest neighborhood Thai where they "really try hard" deserves wider attention for its "beautiful presentation" of assertively seasoned food; although comfortable, "summer dining outside" sums up the decor.

FOUR & TWENTY BLACKBIRDS [S] 25 | 22 | 24 | $33

Route 522 (Rte. 647), Flint Hill, VA, 540-675-1111

■ A reminder of the small-town snugs in rural England, with its wooden tables and rustic charm, this eclectic Contemporary American in the Virginia foothills not only gets rave reviews from media critics, but it also passes the real people test – it's a one-and-a-half-hour drive from DC, yet there's a "line for Sunday brunch."

Four Rivers [S] 18 | 9 | 16 | $16

184 Rollins Ave. (E. Jefferson St.), Rockville, MD, 301-230-2900

■ To find out why this "dumpy" Rockville storefront is "where Chinese eat Chinese", ask for a "suggestion from the Chinese menu" or try one of the Szechuan specialties or "great veggie" choices; food and service is "better and more exciting when in groups" – and you get to sample lots of dishes.

Fran O'Brien's Steak House ◐ [S] ▽ 19 | 18 | 19 | $30

Capitol Hilton Hotel, 1001 16th St., NW (L St.), 202-783-2599

◩ Making a play for "Duke Zeibert's crowd", ex-Redskin Fran O'Brien has turned a wood-paneled, near-the-White House space (ex Trader Vic's) into a clubby, "old-fashioned" steakhouse/sports bar; its "great ambiance", "mammoth" portions and "good lunch prices" earn yardage but not a touchdown – the final score is "middle-of-the-road political hangout."

Full Kee ◐ [S] 🚫 — 19 | 5 | 14 | $13
509 H St., NW (bet. 5th & 6th Sts.), 202-371-2233
■ One of DC's "best" for Chinese is even better "at 2 AM", when top chefs drop by this Chinatown Cantonese for clams in black bean sauce and shrimp dumpling soup; at that hour, no one cares about "language problems", "abrupt service" or no booze or decor – the fact is the "food can't be beat" and "it's cheap."

Full Key ◐ [S] — 22 | 8 | 16 | $12
Wheaton Manor Shopping Ctr., 2227 University Blvd. W. (Georgia Ave.), Wheaton, MD, 301-933-8388
◪ "Unusual" meal-sized soups, noodle dishes and "Hong Kong specialties" that "you have to be adventurous to eat" establish this Wheaton Cantonese's authenticity; but the flip side is that it's "tough to communicate" and the 'atmosphere' is supplied by Chinese families focusing on the "good, inexpensive" food.

Gabriel [S] — 22 | 18 | 20 | $26
Radisson-Barcelo Washington Hotel, 2121 P St., NW (bet. 21st & 22nd Sts.), 202-956-6690
■ Check out the "intriguing" spread of "inventive" tapas at this Contemporary Latin's "good-value" buffet lunch ($9.50), "good-time" happy hour (Wednesday-Friday $7.50) or "lavish" brunch; equally "exciting" entrees can be ordered full sized or as little plates; though busy, this attractive, "not-your-average" hotel dining room is still something of a Dupont Circle secret.

Gadsby's Tavern [S] — 18 | 24 | 20 | $25
138 N. Royal St. (Cameron St.), Alexandria, VA, 703-548-1288
◪ Follow in George Washington's footsteps to this Old Town restoration and museum for a "history lesson come alive" with costumed staff, period appointments and colonial food and drink; while it's a "tourist must", with a great courtyard for parties, some say the "olde" gimmick must be "backed up by better food."

Galaxy [S] — – | – | – | M
Tower Square Ctr., 155 Hillwood Ave. (Annandale Rd.), Falls Church, VA, 703-534-5450
"Some of the best Vietnamese food" in the area can be found at this relatively unknown Falls Church Indochinese whose menu offers a galaxy of regional choices; its performance is both "high high and low low" ("very spotty"), but it won't cost much to try your luck; N.B. dine early on weekends or you'll find yourself a part of the adjacent nightclub scene.

GALILEO S
26 | 23 | 23 | $49

1110 21st St., NW (bet. L & M Sts.), 202-293-7191

■ The "best Italian moments in town" take place in Roberto Donna's "handsome", "celebrity"-lined dining room; his "sophisticated" menus reinterpret Northern Italian classics "showcasing" the "best of everything" in that day's market and are backed by an "amazing" wine list and "attentive" help; "when it's on" (and it almost always is), it's "excellent."

Gangplank S
14 | 17 | 14 | $24

600 Water St., SW (7th St. & Maine Ave.), 202-554-5000

☑ In a "lucky" marina setting for catching "tourists and Arena Stage" ticketholders, this floating fish house baits its hook with seafood, steak, good parking and "pleasant river views"; enthusiasts insist it's "far better than its reputation" (and ratings), while critics quip "throw it back if it comes out of the kitchen."

Garrett Park Cafe S
19 | 18 | 18 | $17

4600 Waverly Ave., Garrett Park, MD, 301-929-0486

■ A "folksy, small-town" eatery with a "big heart", where Garrett Park locals linger on the front porch or inside over thick, "homemade" sandwiches and "tasty" American entrees – and "hope its being listed here doesn't ruin it"; "charming" and "relaxing", it's a "slow-paced" "time warp."

Generous George's S
17 | 15 | 16 | $13

7031 Little River Tpke. (John Marr Dr.), Annandale, VA, 703-941-9600
Concord Shopping Ctr., 6131 Backlick Rd. (Commerce St.), Springfield, VA, 703-451-7111
3006 Duke St. (Roth St.), Alexandria, VA, 703-370-4303

☑ The "bizarre" (to put it kindly) "circus atmosphere" at these pizza parlors is strictly for "high school dates" and families with "screaming kids" intent on "scarfing" up "tons of food" for little dough; only 'George' has the crust to pile "pasta on pizza" and serve it in surroundings so "tacky" that it's like "eating in a fraternity basement the morning after the party."

Genji S
▽ 22 | 15 | 21 | $20

Lee-Graham Shopping Ctr., 2816 Graham Rd. (Lee Hwy.), Falls Church, VA, 703-573-0112

■ Northern Virginians have "been going to this traditional Japanese forever", which should tell you something about its "excellent food" and manners; it's located in an area of Falls Church with a scarcity of nice restaurants and is quite "good for large parties."

Georgetown Seafood Grill ◐ S   18 | 13 | 17 | $25
3063 M St., NW (bet. 30th & 31st Sts.), 202-333-7038
1200 19th St., NW (bet. M & N Sts.), 202-530-4430
☑ Georgetown "neighborhood charm and great bloodies"
are best enjoyed at this "casual" raw bar and seafooder
during Sunday brunch or on Saturday afternoons; during
"tourist season", it can be "awfully loud, crowded" and
"inconsistent"; the new (unrated) below Dupont Circle
location has the space and decor this one lacks.

Georgia Brown's S   22 | 23 | 21 | $31
950 15th St., NW (K St.), 202-393-4499
■ A "lively mix of patrons" and "hearty helpings" of "good
food" distinguish this high-profile restaurant near the White
House; it "takes chances", playing "imaginative" riffs on
Carolina Low Country cuisine and design elements while
making its diverse clientele feel "comfortable."

Geppetto S   17 | 14 | 16 | $18
Wildwood Shopping Ctr., 10257 Old Georgetown Rd.
(Democracy Blvd.), Bethesda, MD, 301-493-9230
☑ It's usually a toss-up between the thin-crust white pizza
with "tons of garlic" and the deep-dish pie with "mounds
of pepperoni" at this "crowded" and "slow" Bethesda family
place; its efforts at cooking pasta and Neapolitan entrees
are likened to "an Italian opera sung in English – poorly."

Geranio S   22 | 19 | 21 | $26
722 King St. (bet. Washington & Columbus Sts.),
Alexandria, VA, 703-548-0088
■ To old-time Alexandrians, this trattoria is one of those
"special places" where a meal is more than the sum of its
parts; at a quiet "winter dinner by the fire", with the pasta
and seafood enhanced by "special attention" from the
staff, it's easy to overlook the rather "shabby decor" and
enjoy food that's "comfortingly pleasing year after year."

GERARD'S PLACE S   26 | 21 | 24 | $50
915 15th St., NW (McPherson Sq.), 202-737-4445
■ It's one of the top-rated restaurants in the *Survey*, yet
Gerard Pangaud's fans insist his "intimate", "most Parisian"
Downtown bistro is "underappreciated", raving "best
French food outside Paris", "food graduated from finishing
school, it's so refined", "from pigs feet to mango tart –
wow!"; diners also "love" being treated "like friends."

Germaine's S   23 | 18 | 21 | $32
2400 Wisconsin Ave., NW (Calvert St.), 202-965-1185
☑ You "never know what or who you'll find" in this legendary
lady's Upper Georgetown dining room; her distinctive,
"light but filling" Pan-Asian cuisine has "stood the test of
time" and her "charm" puts everyone, from presidents to
poets, "at ease"; last spring's redecoration could
improve the already "great people-watching."

Ginza's ▽ 20 | 16 | 20 | $24
1009 21st St., NW (bet. K & L Sts.), 202-833-1244
◪ "At least you can get into" this "moderately priced" Midtown Japanese, and "if you know what to order" (ask what the Tokyo business suits are having) you'll do fine; it's said to have "good" cooked entrees and the "best sushi under $30"; neither the setting nor service is noteworthy.

Goldoni [S] 23 | 23 | 22 | $43
1113 23rd St., NW (bet. L & M Sts.), 202-293-1511
◪ Fabrizio Aielli, a Roberto Donna (Galileo) protégé, has "sculpted" a skylit West End space into a "serious" Italian and, although it's still "finding its feet", it's producing some "outstanding" seafood and pasta dishes; so far, he's had the smarts to pare a too-ambitious menu and to capitalize on Kennedy Center accessibility with an $18.50 prix fixe.

Good Fortune ◐ [S] 22 | 14 | 16 | $17
2646 University Blvd. (bet. Viers Mill Rd. & Georgia Ave.), Wheaton, MD, 301-929-8818
■ The "best dim sum" in the Wheaton area and some of the best "seafood noodle dishes" are among the highlights of this multiregional Chinese whose "simple interior" is "more tasteful" than most similar places; its "family-style" set-price dinners are a "steal" and a great way to sample the rest of its "extensive menu."

Granja de Oro [S] – | – | – | I
2920 Annandale Rd. (Rte. 50), Falls Church, VA, 703-534-5511
The victuals at this Peruvian "chickout" in Falls Church extend beyond "delicious", "cheap", rotisserie chicken to country-style BBQ meats, saltados (sautés), seafood and fried yucca with a green hot sauce that gives customers "new reason to live"; the visuals are watching soccer on the tube and live weekend entertainment.

Greenwood's 21 | 14 | 18 | $29
Esplanade Bldg., 1990 K St., NW (20th St.), 202-833-6572
◪ "Don't be put off by the mezzanine location" in an office building or the sterile decor – this "sophisticated" youngster's fresh approach to "meat-free dining" is worth "checking out"; sure, it's got some "growing pains" ("disorganized" service), but the Eclectic fare is so "interesting" that reviewers "want it to work."

Grillfish [S] – | – | – | M
1200 New Hampshire Ave., NW (M St., NW), 202-331-7310
◪ This West Ender's slogan – 'fresh fish, friendly prices, no tuxedo' – couldn't be more '90s in its casual appeal; the high ceiling, open-bar setting and simple fish and pasta menu seem made to order for neighborhood suits, cliff dwellers and diners on the way to Kennedy Center.

Grill from Ipanema 🖪
20 | 19 | 17 | $25

1858 Columbia Rd., NW (Belmont Rd.), 202-986-0757
🔳 Something like "Rio de Janeiro", especially after a caipirinha or two, this offbeat Adams Morganite appeals to a "chic" crowd that "dresses for the [black on black] decor"; go early for "Brazilian home cooking", late for "international people-watching"; the unimpressed say the "food isn't as clever as the name."

Guapo's 🖪
17 | 13 | 17 | $17

4515 Wisconsin Ave., NW (Albermarle St.), 202-686-3588
Rio Mall, 9811 Washingtonian Blvd., Gaithersburg, MD,
301-977-5655
🔳 "Solid margaritas", fajitas and "cheap", "cheese-laden, deep-fried Mexican food" keep these kid-friendly Tex-Mexicans "mobbed on weekends"; the Tenleytown shack looks so "realistic you don't drink the water" – a far cry from its "plastic" Gaithersburg kin.

Gulf Coast Kitchen 🖪
16 | 17 | 16 | $18

7750 Woodmont Ave. (bet. Cheltenham Dr. & Old
Georgetown Rd.), Bethesda, MD, 301-652-6278
🔳 This deliberately "tacky" "Biloxi" boathouse replica is where Bethesda singles "chill with a brew and a po' boy" or oysters from the raw bar and a meal of sides; it's "loud", "young" and "friendly", with sandwiches, salads and Creole plates (introduced post-*Survey*); happy hour on the roof deck is bedlam.

Haad Thai 🖪
23 | 19 | 19 | $18

1100 New York Ave., NW (11th St.), 202-682-1111
🔳 What a "great addition to Downtown/Convention Center dining" – a "pretty" Thai with "fresh-tasting food", "quick" service, "terrific prices" and tranquility; the "chic", sunset-at-the-beach decor shows what tasteful touches and good lighting can do for a storefront space; reserve for lunch.

HAANDI 🖪
25 | 18 | 22 | $21

Falls Plaza Shopping Ctr., 1222 W. Broad St. (Rte. 7), Falls
Church, VA, 703-533-3501
4904 Fairmont Ave. (Old Georgetown Rd.), Bethesda, MD,
301-718-0121
🔳 "Buried" in the suburbs, these "very small", "very professional" "great values" earn top Indian honors in the *Survey*; their "well-prepared", judiciously spiced food gets a "thumbs up" from natives and novices alike, while their "civilized" manners eclipse "threadbare decor" (Falls Church); as a result, "go early" or wait.

Hard Rock Cafe ◐S   14 | 21 | 16 | $17
999 E St., NW (10th St.), 202-737-ROCK

☑ You'd be surprised how many "self-respecting residents" consider this Downtown rock 'n' roll "tourist trap" a "fun place" for a burger and fries with "good music" and people-watching; one goes to the "bar upstairs" to avoid the kids; but even there, "sensory overload" is inevitable.

Hard Times Cafe S   19 | 16 | 18 | $13
Woodley Gardens Shopping Ctr., 1117 Nelson St. (Rte. 28), Rockville, MD, 301-294-9720
K-Mart Shopping Ctr., 394 Elden St. (bet. Herndon Pkwy. & Van Buren St.), Herndon, VA, 703-318-8941
1404 King St. (West St.), Alexandria, VA, 703-683-5340
3028 Wilson Blvd. (Highland St.), Arlington, VA, 703-528-2233

■ "On a snowy winter night", nothing beats a bowl of "the best chili in the cosmos", "terrific onion rings" and a beer at these beloved "greasy [literally] spoons"; with "rustic decor" and "1950s country-western music on the jukebox", they're "fun, relaxed" and "still the king of value."

Hautam Kebobs S   – | – | – | M
Ritchie Ctr., 785-D Rockville Pike (Wootton Pkwy.), Rockville, MD, 301-838-9222

Subtly seasoned and precisely grilled kebabs, classically served with freshly baked flat bread and rice, are the specialty of this surprisingly attractive Iranian storefront in Rockville's Ritchie Center; fish, chicken or meat kebabs are featured along with "authentic" appetizers and desserts.

Havana Cafe S   18 | 13 | 16 | $18
3100 Clarendon Blvd. (Washington Blvd.), Arlington, VA, 703-524-3611

☑ "Tasty, homestyle Cuban food" like ropa vieja and black beans and rice, served with "graciousness" in a "pleasant patio setting", generates "lots of activity on an otherwise quiet Clarendon block"; but expats wish it tasted more like old Havana – or even Miami Beach.

Herb's S   14 | 13 | 15 | $18
Governor's House Holiday Inn, 1615 Rhode Island Ave., NW (17th St.), 202-333-4372

☑ "Theatrical" memorabilia, a "literary atmosphere" and crowd, and half-price burgers on Sunday nights – relics of former owner Herb White's reign – save this "middle-America" Downtown hotel dining room; it's best for a "sunny outdoor lunch" or "late snack", when the "room service" quality of the American fare is less evident and helped by the "friendly" staff.

Hibiscus Cafe 22 | 23 | 18 | $25

3401 K St. (34th St.), 202-965-7170

■ Adding a "splash of color" to DC nighttime dining with its crayon bright, "neon and metal" design, "torrid" Caribbean cuisine and "lots of hip folks", this Islander's "hideaway location" (under the Whitehurst Freeway) lends a sense of discovery that, even with its "long waits" and "dubious service", makes it seem "different, adventurous, fun."

Hinode [S] 22 | 18 | 20 | $23

Bethesda Shopping Ctr., 4914 Hampden Ln. (Arlington Rd.), Bethesda, MD, 301-654-0908

■ This "family-oriented" Japanese has found a niche in Bethesda, where its "low-fat food", "quick service" and "calming Zen atmosphere" please the "neighborhood"; sushi, tempura and cooked dishes are also popular choices.

Hisago [S] 22 | 20 | 20 | $39

3050 K St., NW (Washington Harbour), 202-944-4181

◪ An across-the-board drop in ratings since our last *Survey* signals local resistance to "outrageous prices for teensy portions" and "brusque" service at this Washington Harbour Japanese; designed for "business-oriented" Japanese, it offers "excellent" sushi and choreographed kaiseki dinners (plus an à la carte menu) in a "lovely", classic setting.

Hogate's [S] 11 | 14 | 13 | $23

800 Water St., SW (bet. 9th St. & Maine Ave.), 202-484-6300

◪ "Retirements" and "rum buns" are the excuses locals give for visiting this Maine Avenue "seafood factory" "inundated" with tour buses; even the "strong" drinks, jazz and river views can't rescue the "mass-production" food and "mechanical" hospitality.

House of Chinese Gourmet [S] 20 | 12 | 18 | $16

1485 Rockville Pike (1 block north of Congressional Plaza), Rockville, MD, 301-984-9440

■ "Delicious", "beautifully served" Peking duck and a wealth of equally impressive vegetarian possibilities are a few reasons why Chinese food mavens take this Rockville mainstay seriously; priced for everyday family dining (with a $2.95 lunch), some think it's the area's "best Chinese."

Houston's [S] 19 | 17 | 18 | $19

1065 Wisconsin Ave., NW (M St.), 202-338-7760
7715 Woodmont Ave. (bet. Cheltenham Dr. & Old Georgetown Rd.), Bethesda, MD, 301-656-9755
12256 Rockville Pike (Montrose Rd.), Rockville, MD, 301-468-3535

◪ The model of what you could "expect from a chain" – a "little style", a "staff that hustles", "great" burgers, ribs and other "simple food prepared remarkably well" with "classy" touches like freshly squeezed juice; factor the "wait and parking hassles" into the "formula."

Hsiang Foong 🅂   18 | 10 | 17 | $15

2919 N. Washington Blvd. (bet. Filmore & Garfield Sts.), Arlington, VA, 703-522-1121

☑ With the exception of "certain dishes", i.e. "ants on the tree" (a pork and noodle dish), some find little reason to "go back" to this "humble" Clarendon Chinese, though fans praise its "creative" fare and say "good when it works."

Hunan Chinatown 🅂   20 | 15 | 18 | $19

624 H St., NW (bet. 6th & 7th Sts.), 202-783-5858

☑ Close to Downtown galleries, one of the few places in Chinatown "with tablecloths" does classy post-opening events; the reliable Hunan and Szechuan fare can be had "old-style" or "stir-fried in broth", but it would be a pity to eliminate the tea-smoked duck from your diet.

Hunan Lion 🅂   19 | 20 | 19 | $20

2070 Chain Bridge Rd. (Old Courthouse Rd.), Vienna, VA, 703-734-9828

Hunan Lion II

18140 The Galleria (near Tysons II), Tysons Corner, VA, 703-883-1938

☑ Their lordly manner may promise a bit more than these "dependable suburban Chinese" siblings deliver; but for "sit-down" dining near Tysons Corner, they beat the competition cold: "gladly sell my first born for the sweet and sour spare ribs."

Hunan Number One ●🅂   21 | 15 | 19 | $16

3033 Wilson Blvd. (Garfield St.), Arlington, VA, 703-528-1177

☑ It's "very popular", "authentic", inexpensive, kid-proofed ("plastic on the chairs") and open late (after 1 AM), yet you "can always get a table" at this Northern VA Chinese; the weekend dim sum ties up Wilson Boulevard traffic and the Hong Kong–style dishes on the menu are "very good", too.

Hunan Palace 🅂   ▽ 20 | 12 | 18 | $19

Shady Grove Ctr., 9011 Gaither Rd. (Shady Grove Rd.), Gaithersburg, MD, 301-977-8600

☑ This Northern Chinese in Gaithersburg specializes in the flavorful cooking of Taiwan and Shanghai; go for the "wonderful" dim sum, then explore the rest of the bilingual menu for some of that area's "best" food.

Ichiban   17 | 17 | 18 | $20

637 N. Frederick Ave. (near Lake Forest Mall), Gaithersburg, MD, 301-670-0560

☑ In Gaithersburg, where locals are "always on the lookout" for sushi and places to entertain a group, "beautiful landscaping" and lots of space draw attention to this Japanese-Korean; while many shrug off its faulty English and "only ok" food, an increasing number complain "food went downhill, prices up."

Il Borgo S
22 | 22 | 22 | $31
1381-A Beverly Rd. (bet. Old Dominion Dr. & Elm St.), McLean, VA, 703-893-1400
■ At his "happy" Italian in McLean, chef-owner Vittorio Testa (a "charmer" who "pays a visit to each table") has turned a plush shopping-strip space into a "great hangout"; he's "justifiably proud" of his "wonderful" "Italian cruise line food" but is "willing to cook anything you want."

Il Cigno S
▽ 19 | 17 | 19 | $29
Lake Anne Plaza, 1617 Washington Plaza, Reston, VA, 703-471-0121
▨ "Sitting outdoors" by Lake Anne at this Northern Italian is one of Reston's summer indulgences; its "consistent" food and service are good enough to make for a pleasant "outing", though inside dining may be another story ("better food nearby").

Il Pizzico
23 | 15 | 19 | $20
Suburban Park, 15209 Frederick Rd. (Gude Dr.), Rockville, MD, 301-309-0610
■ "Good deals" on "quality" Italian food are still to be found at this "unpretentious" Rockville trattoria – despite price hikes that pushed it off our Bang for the Buck list; it's unquestionably the best Italian in the area, with "terrific" homemade pasta and always "a surprise in store", but it's so "crowded" (causing service glitches) that "weeknights are the only time to go."

Il Radicchio S
18 | 16 | 16 | $19
1211 Wisconsin Ave. (M St.), 202-337-2627
1509 17th St., NW (bet. P & Q Sts.), 202-986-2627
1801 Clarendon Blvd. (Rhodes St.), Arlington, VA, 703-276-2627
■ At these "amusing" Italians, you can "go cheap and still get stuffed" – with "al dente" spaghetti galore plus "tasty" sauces to "share", rustic pizzas or "peasant" platters; Roberto Donna's (Arucola, Galileo, I Matti) "innovative" format for "affordable" dining is so successful that prime-time waits (especially at Dupont Circle) draw fire.

Il Ritrovo S
▽ 22 | 18 | 21 | $30
4838 Rugby Ave. (bet. Woodmont & Auburn Aves.), Bethesda, MD, 301-986-1447
■ Bethesda's "promising" Pan-Mediterranean earns kudos for its "broad menu" ("how do they do so many things so well?"), "attractive" appearance, "experienced personnel" and "easy parking"; its weak points – "unevenness" and a few "pedestrian" dishes – don't deter "repeat visits."

I Matti [S] 22 | 19 | 19 | $30

2436 18th St., NW (bet. Belmont & Columbia Rds.), 202-462-8844

■ DC's "best" surrogate for an "evening in Florence" brings "all the essential tastes of Italy" to Adams Morgan; at this "cosmopolitan", "accessibly priced" trattoria, you'll find rustic pastas and regional dishes, "excellent fish", "knowledgeable waiters" and an "upbeat" ambiance; despite "occasional lapses", it seems "just right."

India Kitchen [S] – | – | – | I

Shady Grove Ctr., 9031 Gaither Rd. (Shady Grove Rd.), Gaithersburg, MD, 301-212-9174

Not yet well known outside of Gaithersburg, this "pleasant" Indian's broad menu reflects that nation's cultural diversity, ranging from the tandooris and biryanis of the meat-loving North to the fiery vegetarian dishes of Southern India's Hindus; the pretty room engenders a "relaxing, get-away-from-it-all atmosphere."

Inn at Glen Echo 18 | 20 | 18 | $29

6119 Tulane Ave. (MacArthur Blvd. & Cabin John Pkwy.), Glen Echo, MD, 301-229-2280

◪ The "charm potential" of this former roadhouse's "lovely setting" overlooking Glen Echo Park isn't fully realized; despite efforts to upgrade, it remains an "ok neighborhood place" with "spotty" American "nostalgia" food and service; the outdoor deck and Sunday night jazz are bright points.

INN AT LITTLE WASHINGTON [S] 29 | 29 | 29 | $81

Inn at Little Washington, Middle & Main Sts., Washington, VA, 540-675-3800

■ Improving on "perfection" isn't easy, yet Patrick O'Connell and Reinhardt Lynch manage it; how else could their Virginia countryside inn (No. 1 for food, service and decor in this *Survey*) meet everyone's stratospheric "expectations"; with flawless Contemporary American food and service as "precise and flowing as modern dance", a meal here is best described by paraphrasing Oscar Wilde – 'my tastes are simple, I only want the best.'

I RICCHI 25 | 23 | 23 | $42

1220 19th St., NW (bet. M & N Sts.), 202-835-0459

◪ "Heartwarming on a dreary day", this popular Northern Italian's "down-to-earth" pastas, risottos and "succulent" grills are a "biz lunch bonanza" and "delightful" for a high-end "celebration"; yes, the "waiters have personality" (which can be tough to take), but "when it's good, its very, very good", though it's best if you're "known."

JALEO ◑ [S] 22 | 21 | 19 | $25

480 Seventh St., NW (E St.), 202-628-7949

■ A high-energy Downtown setting earns this Spanish tapas bar its name (Jaleo means 'revelry' as well as 'racket'); it's indispensable for biz lunches or a "bite" before or after "Shakespeare"; putting together a meal of the zesty "finger foods" or more substantial plates also can be a "complete evening's" entertainment – but allow for waits.

Jean-Michel [S] 22 | 19 | 21 | $37

Wildwood Shopping Ctr., 10223 Old Georgetown Rd. (Democracy Blvd.), Bethesda, MD, 301-564-4910

◩ The epitome of an "old French restaurant" thrives in a suburban strip mall, where its "classic" cooking and "personal" cosseting never go out of style; apart from K Street prices, its coterie of fans finds little to fault: "lifesaver for lunches", "safe place to take the in-laws for a lovely meal"; others, however, liken it to "flat champagne."

Jefferson Restaurant [S] 23 | 24 | 23 | $42

Jefferson Hotel, 1200 16th St., NW (M St.), 202-833-6206

◩ This "intimate", "European"-feeling hotel dining room near the White House is often chosen for "quiet lunches"; long considered one of "DC's premier kitchens", with "incomparable" service, it's undergone "too many changes" at the stove recently, but the post-*Survey* arrival of a new Contemporary American chef bodes well.

JIN-GA [S] 23 | 25 | 22 | $28

1250 24th St., NW (bet. M & N Sts.), 202-785-5319

■ "'Seoul food' at its best" (plus some Japanese standouts), served in a "gorgeous" space, adds an exciting option to West End dining; most appreciate getting the "Korean royal" treatment at this Asian import but warn that "authentic" doesn't always mean "pleasing to the US palate" and that you should be "prepared to cook for yourself."

JOCKEY CLUB [S] 24 | 25 | 24 | $46

Ritz-Carlton Hotel, 2100 Massachusetts Ave., NW (21st St.), 202-659-8000

■ This Kennedy-era, "upper-crust" Continental looks more like a hunt club than ever; its "wonderful seafood" and service are legendary and, notwithstanding some cracks ("quiet to the point of coma"), it remains *the* place to "experience Washington"; P.S. "don't miss the bar."

J. Paul's ◑ [S] 15 | 16 | 16 | $20

3218 M St., NW (bet. Potomac St. & Wisconsin Ave.), 202-333-3450

◩ Its open-to-the-street raw bar with good brews on tap generates good "people-watching" and "pickups", yet this Georgetown watering hole is sometimes considered a "backup pick"; it does an "ok" job with burgers, bar food and brunch and "really buzzes" if you're single.

Kabob Bazaar S ▽ 19 | 12 | 17 | $13 |
3133 Wilson Blvd. (bet. N. Highland St. & Washington Blvd.),
Clarendon, VA, 703-522-8999
■ The enticing smells of grilling kebabs at this Clarendon-
area Persian might be "tempting even to vegetarians", but
chances are its list of authentic, unusual vegetarian sides
and salads would interest them more; although the setting is
simple, the staff is "gracious" and the generously portioned
food is "outstanding for the price."

Kabul Caravan S 24 | 20 | 20 | $22 |
Colonial Shopping Ctr., 1725 Wilson Blvd., Arlington, VA,
703-522-8394
■ Don't let the strip mall location deter you – this Arlington
Afghan "pioneer" offers "excellent", reasonably priced
food in intriguing surroundings; locals insist it's a "cozy
getaway" and a comfortable place "to linger"; NYers swear
there's "nothing as good in the Big City."

Kawasaki – | – | – | E |
1140 19th St., NW (bet. M & L Sts.), 202-466-3798
Like the motorcycle, this business district Japanese's
sushi is precision-made and priced for fast-trackers (i.e.
the check can accelerate at "breathtaking" speed); it's
also functionally designed and delivers a high-"quality"
product, though the international clientele appears to have
less trouble with the service department than locals do.

Kazan 23 | 19 | 23 | $27 |
McLean Shopping Ctr., 6813 Redmond Dr., McLean, VA,
703-734-1960
■ This Northern Virginia storefront is known locally for
"wonderful" Turkish cuisine, including "excellent" doner
kebab and lamb, and "outstanding" service, which make
up for the "tired surroundings" and lack of "privacy."

King Street Blues S 18 | 20 | 18 | $17 |
112 N. St. Asaph St. (King St.), Alexandria, VA, 703-836-8800
■ "Dominion beer makes the menu" at this "raucous" Old
Town fun fair where the colorful "papier-mâché" decor and
live entertainment please kids of all ages; highlights of the
"good, greasy", cheap, all-American comfort food include
the "best cheese fries in creation", "dessert"-sweet BBQ
and "meat loaf 'n' mashed potatoes done right."

KINKEAD'S S 27 | 22 | 24 | $40 |
Red Lion Row, 2000 Pennsylvania Ave., NW (I St., bet. 20th
& 21st Sts.), 202-296-7700
■ Bob Kinkead's urban bistro, with its "elegantly casual"
two-tier setting, is the most popular in-town eatery in this
Survey; "no one does fish better" or more "imaginatively"
reinterprets regional American dishes and few can resist
his "incredible" desserts; most reviewers would go back
in a heartbeat despite a few "ups and downs."

Kramerbooks & Afterwords Cafe ☾ S
| 15 | 16 | 14 | $17 |

1517-21 Connecticut Ave., NW (bet. Q St., NW & Dupont Circle), 202-387-1462

◪ Browsing books while "waiting for a table is half the fun" at this '60s-era bookstore/cafe off Dupont Circle – a haven for "bookish" singles, late-night sucrophiles, jazz fiends and artistic types; since the American kitchen is little more than a "closet and a microwave", and service is hardly top-shelf, keep it simple.

Krupin's S
| 17 | 10 | 15 | $16 |

4620 Wisconsin Ave., NW (Chesapeake St.), 202-686-1989

◪ "Tacky" and overly "bright", this is a "real NY-style deli where rudeness" is part of the shtick; however, DC deli mavens would prefer their corned beef and pastrami, along with the "best pickled herring", boiled chicken and matzo-ball soup, served without a side of condescension.

La Bergerie
| 24 | 23 | 23 | $40 |

218 N. Lee St. (bet. Queen & Cameron Sts.), Alexandria, VA, 703-683-1007

■ "Every diner is treated like a valued old customer" at this Classic French in Old Town whose "Basque-accented" menu and plush quarters hark back to a more "gracious" era; but this is not a place to go when rushed – everything is done "right", but a bit "slow."

La Bonne Auberge
| 20 | 21 | 21 | $37 |

Great Falls Shopping Ctr., 9835 Georgetown Pike (Walker Rd.), Great Falls, VA, 703-759-3877

◪ In contrast to the rusticity of nearby L'Auberge Chez Francois, this "dressy" French in Great Falls provides a formal setting for more "classic" dining; the "romantic" ambiance works well for special occasions, and although the food strikes some as "unexciting", the "raspberry soufflé makes it worth a trip."

La Brasserie S
| 23 | 20 | 20 | $33 |

239 Massachusetts Ave., NE (bet. 2nd & 3rd Sts.), 202-546-9154

◪ There is no more "charming" setting for outdoor dining on Capitol Hill than this "once great" French brasserie; the food is still "good" and "hearty", but with the exception of some signature dishes and a notable crème brûleé, it "won't interfere" with your pitch and service can be "awkward and slow"; N.B. Sunday brunch is a buy.

La Chaumiere
| 22 | 22 | 21 | $35 |

2813 M St., NW (bet. 28th & 29th Sts.), 202-338-1784

■ Julia Child's visit to this "cozy" Country French 'cottage' in her old Georgetown neighborhood focused attention on its comforting, "old-fashioned" fare and "warm", welcoming atmosphere; "in winter", cozy up to the fire and dig into the cassoulet (Thursday nights).

La Colline 23 | 19 | 22 | $35
400 N. Capitol St., NW (bet. D & E Sts.), 202-737-0400
■ Before the congressional gift ban, this deceptively "dull"-looking French bistro was known for the "best working lunch" on the Hill; but now that fewer pols come to "see pals", surveyors hope that its "consistently" "great", market-driven menu, "excellent" staff and dinner prix fixe ($19.95) will be enough of a draw; "fine fare, fair price" is the word.

La Cote d'Or Cafe [S] 23 | 21 | 22 | $37
6876 Lee Hwy. (bet. Washington Blvd. & Westmoreland St.), Arlington, VA, 703-538-3033
◪ Falls Church blesses this neighborhood bistro for bringing "Gallic charm and cuisine" to a culinarily deprived area; it may be "pricey for a low-rent district", and the "food can be hit or miss", but "when it's good it's a wonderful asset."

Lafayette [S] ▽ 26 | 29 | 27 | $46
Hay-Adams Hotel, 800 16th St., NW (H St.), 202-638-2570
■ A meal in this "most elegant dining room" is a "true Washington experience" and "as close as most of us will get to dinner at the White House" (across the square); the aura of "power", awesome service and rubbernecking nearly eclipse its "tasty" Contemporary American fare.

La Ferme [S] 21 | 23 | 21 | $38
7101 Brookville Rd. (East-West Hwy. & Western Ave.), Chevy Chase, MD, 301-986-5255
◪ Parking plus a somewhat "formal" environment and "enjoyable" if "unimaginative" French food endear this Chevy Chase destination to the "old guard"; although this "pretty" place is often called "romantic", it's a bit too "ladylike" for amour; "no great flair, no great flaws."

La Fourchette [S] 22 | 20 | 20 | $27
2429 18th St., NW (bet. Kalorama St. & Columbia Rd.), 202-332-3077
◪ Charming, "family-run" French bistros casually dishing up escargot, moules and pommes frites "throughout the day" are "basic" in Paris, but not in Adams Morgan, which is why this one is considered a "petit trésor", especially from the vantage point of its "bohemian" sidewalk cafe.

La Lomita [S] 20 | 13 | 20 | $17
1330 Pennsylvania Ave., SE (G St.), 202-546-3109
■ "Hill rats" burrow into these "cheerful" Tex-Mexicans for "great margaritas" and "cheap", spicy food; with their "tasty offerings beyond the standards", "no attitude" and low-down, eat-in-a-"garage" appeal, they're a "good place to crash after work."

La Madeleine French Bakery S   17 18 15 $14
3000 M St., NW (30th St., NW), 202-298-6978
500 King St. (Pitt St.), Alexandria, VA, 703-739-2853
5861 Crossroads Ctr., Bailey's Crossroads (Leesburg &
Columbia Pikes), Falls Church, VA, 703-379-5551
1833 Fountain Dr. (bet. Baron Cameron & Reston Pkwy.),
Reston, VA, 703-707-0704
7607 Old Georgetown Rd. (Commerce St.), Bethesda, MD,
301-215-9142
Mid-Pike Plaza, 11858 Rockville Pike (Montrose Rd.),
Rockville, MD, 301-984-2270
☑ "Vive la quiche" is the motto of these self-serve, French-style cafe/bakeries, although their "phenomenal tomato basil soup" and "fabulous rotisserie chicken" are the big draws; though critics pan "slow fast food" and their made-in-America Country French atmosphere, they rise to some occasions as an "unhurried place to have a light bite."

La Miche S   23 21 22 $36
7905 Norfolk Ave. (bet. Wisconsin Ave. & Old Georgetown
Rd.), Bethesda, MD, 301-986-0707
☑ Lace curtains in the window tell Bethesda passersby that this "accomplished" French bistro does things in a "traditional" way; it's a "solid" performer with a few highs ("high consistency, high prices", "hit a good night and it's a 10") and a few lows ("cramped", "fusty").

La Mirabelle S   17 17 19 $30
6645 Old Dominion Dr. (McLean Sq.), McLean, VA,
703-893-8484
☑ McLean locals go to this "very personable" yet "little known" suburban French to "get away" from the kitchen and get together with friends; aside from "heavy sauces" and "dingy" decor, regulars find it "extremely pleasant."

Landini Brothers S   22 18 20 $28
115 King St. (Union St.), Alexandria, VA, 703-836-8404
☑ At "Old Town's power lunch spot", run by people who "appreciate your business", you can find "everything from a loan to a lawyer at the bar" and old-fashioned ("too much garlic") Italian seafood and pasta in back; it may look like a "dark, scary" tourist trap, but it's not.

La Panetteria S   18 15 19 $21
4921 Cordell Ave. (bet. Old Georgetown Rd. & Norfolk
Ave.), Bethesda, MD, 301-951-6433
☑ "Welcoming and friendly", this old-timer's comfortable cooking, garden setting and a "reasonable early bird" keep it competitive in Bethesda's "saturated Italian market"; it's "handy for family Sunday night dinner" or entertaining friends, when it doesn't really matter if the food is "not as good as you expect."

La Tomate [S] 17 18 18 $26
1701 Connecticut Ave., NW (Dupont Circle), 202-667-5505
◩ Prime people-watching from the patio and window seats make this popular Italian a great Dupont Circle hangout, but not necessarily a great place to dine; reviews run the gamut from "good day-in, day-out choice" to "inattentive", "pricey", "location is the only good thing about this place."

L'AUBERGE CHEZ FRANCOIS [S] 28 27 27 $47
332 Springvale Rd. (2 mi. north of Georgetown Pike), Great Falls, VA, 703-759-3800
■ Utterly comfortable because it's "not haute anything", our surveyors' favorite place is set in a rustic "French farmhouse" that embraces diners in a "warm, friendly hug", feeds them hearty Country French fare and makes them feel their money is well spent; a meal here is always a "charming and unforgettable experience" and, "on a moonlit night", the garden is "dreamy."

L'AUBERGE PROVENCALE [S] 26 26 26 $57
L'Auberge Provencale, Rte. 340 (Rte. 50), White Post, VA, 540-837-1375
■ In the Virginia countryside near White Post, Alain Borel and his charming wife re-create the ambiance of a country restaurant near his native Avignon, where patrons laze on the front porch and experience "happiness on a plate"; if asked whether it's a "little too French for Americans" (i.e. heavy food, "stuffy" help), most would answer 'mais non.'

Lauriol Plaza [S] 20 17 18 $22
1801 18th St., NW (S St.), 202-387-0035
◩ Sitting outside, drinking margaritas and eating "too many chips" amidst the "diverse" Adams Morgan/Dupont Circle "hubbub" is such "fun" that few mind the "ridiculous" crowds or waits at this urban Latin (or want to be inside); popular for fajitas, paella and roast pork, the "reasonably priced", recently revised menu tilts toward Mexican, with several Spanish "faves."

Lavandou [S] 23 17 20 $31
3321 Connecticut Ave., NW (bet. Macomb & Newark Sts.), 202-966-3002
■ The "warmth of Provence" pervades this quintessential neighborhood bistro in Cleveland Park, where everything from its flavorful, "affordable" cooking, friendly charm and "hopelessly cramped" quarters are straight from a book; while hardly perfect, nearly everyone wishes "everyone else would please stop going."

LEBANESE TAVERNA 🗌   24 | 18 | 20 | $22
2641 Connecticut Ave. (bet. Calvert St. & Woodley Rd.),
202-265-8681
5900 Washington Blvd. (McKinley Rd.), Arlington, VA,
703-241-8681

LEBANESE TAVERNA MARKET
4400 Old Dominion Dr. (bet. Lee Hwy. & Lorcom Ln.),
Arlington, VA, 703-276-8681
■ Consistently rated a "big yum" for their "impressive variety of meze" and "many vegetarian" choices served by waiters who "care if you clean your plate", these "congenial" Lebanese siblings are "great values for outstanding food"; enjoy the "family show" (VA) or join "in the city fun"; no reserving means waits.

Le Bon Cafe   19 | 14 | 13 | $12
210 2nd St., SE (bet. Pennsylvania Ave. & C St., SE),
202-547-7200 🗌 ⊟
1310 Braddock Pl. (West St.), Alexandria, VA, 703-519-1777
◪ Hilltoppers head to the "cutest cafe" on the "uncivilized House side" to "reward" themselves with "quality" salads, sandwiches and soup; since it's "crowded, cramped" and staffed with "good intentions", you can be sure that if the "food wasn't good they wouldn't go"; the Braddock metro location (lunch only) is less rewarding.

Le Caprice 🗌   23 | 19 | 21 | $37
2348 Wisconsin Ave., NW (Calvert St.), 202-337-3394
■ Brass lamps glow in the parlor dining rooms of this top-flight, "charming" Upper Georgetown Alsatian, whose good value is reflected in an "outstanding prix fixe" ($29.50), "wonderful" Monday night couscous ($13.50–$21) and "indoor picnic" lunch ($8.50); best of all, with chef-owner Edmond Foltzenlogel back from France after a year's commute, look for new, exciting and "original" dishes.

Ledo Pizza 🗌   17 | 10 | 15 | $12
2420 University Blvd. E. (Westpark Dr.), Adelphi, MD,
301-422-8622
13444 New Hampshire Ave. (Randolph Rd.), Silver Spring,
MD, 301-384-5400 ⊟
16-18 E. Ordinance Rd. (Ritchie Hwy.), Glen Burnie, MD,
410-590-2222
7213 Muncaster Mill Rd. (bet. Redland & Shady Grove
Rds.), Rockville, MD, 301-869-7900
Boulevard Shops, 14609 Baltimore Ave. (Rte. 1), Laurel,
MD, 301-498-5336 ⊟
1319-H Rockville Pike (Twinbrook Pkwy.), Rockville, MD,
301-309-8484 ⊟
5425 River Rd. (Kenwood Station), Bethesda, MD,
301-656-5336 ⊟
1035 S. Edgewood (Columbia Pike), Arlington, VA,
703-521-1760

Ledo Pizza (Cont.)
*7510 Leesburg Pike (Idlewood Rd.), Falls Church, VA,
703-847-5336*
*Battlefield Shopping Ctr., 1037 Edwards Ferry Rd. (15
Bypass), Leesburg, VA, 703-777-9500* ⊘
☑ "Memories of College Park" whet appetites for the
"unique" ("greasy", pie-crusted, "sweet sauced")
rectangular pizza at the original location in Adelphi; the
franchised operations use the same recipe, "tolerate
children very well", have no better decor and are just
as "cheap"; yet many think Ledo "lost its soul in the
expansion" – it's a "nostalgia thing."

Legal Sea Food 🆂   21 | 18 | 18 | $31 |
2020 K St., NW (bet. 20th & 21st Sts.), 202-496-1111
*Tyson Galleria, 2001 International Dr. (Rte. 123), McLean,
VA, 703-827-8900*
☑ Calling these up-market fish houses the "best export
from Boston since the Babe was traded to the Yankees"
overstates the case; but plenty of local fin fanciers cheer
their wide selection of "fresh" seafare – if not always the
way they cook it, their settings ("expense account" in DC,
"mall world" at Tysons Corner), "premium" pricing and no
reserving (Tysons); rookie staffers "need full training."

Le Gaulois 23 | 20 | 21 | $30 |
*1106 King St. (bet. Fayette & Henry Sts.), Alexandria, VA,
703-739-9494*
☑ Like a "true friend", you can count on this "cozy" Old
Town bistro to put you at ease and provide you with
"satisfying", well-priced, "unspectacular" French
"comfort food"; most lapses are treated with a Gallic
shrug ("too crowded, too rushed"), but it's never been
forgiven for having "left DC."

LE LION D'OR 27 | 24 | 26 | $57 |
1150 Connecticut Ave., NW (bet. 18th & M Sts.), 202-296-7972
☑ Jean-Pierre Goyenvalle, the "accomplished artist"
directing this Downtown French classic, is first among his
peers and a "superb" dinner in his formal dining room will
make a "major impact" on your peers; it's considered
Washington's "best" French ("more clearly so" with the
post-*Survey* closing of Jean-Louis at The Watergate), yet
some find it too "stiff" and in need of a "second wind."

Le Paradis 25 | 14 | 21 | $31 |
*Festival Shopping Ctr., 347 Muddy Branch Rd. (bet. Great
Seneca Hwy. & Clopper Rd.), Gaithersburg, MD, 301-208-9493*
■ Reports of "city food hiding out" at a "tiny", very plain
storefront in Gaithersburg have made this Franco-Asian a
very "crowded" find; its French provincial with a "Pacific
Rim twist" dishes are "creative" and often successful, but
people are starting to notice that they carry a city price tag.

Le Refuge 24 | 20 | 21 | $32
127 N. Washington St. (bet. King & Cameron Sts.), Alexandria, VA, 703-548-4661
◪ If this tarted-up Old Town French bistro "were larger" or less brazen "it would lose its appeal"; as it is, it's the near-home "bet for most romantic" dining and "very friendly, too"; most (not all) find it "worth the crowding because the food's so good."

Le Rivage [S] – | – | – | M
1000 Water St., SW (bet. Maine Ave. & 9th St.), 202-488-8111
"Everyone slips up sometimes", as we did when we left this French waterfront viewplace off the *Survey*; treasured for its "affordably priced" seafood and early-bird specials, it gets ticketholders to the Arena Stage on time and hosts romantic "sunset" dinners with equal aplomb.

Les Halles ☾ [S] 21 | 18 | 18 | $32
1201 Pennsylvania Ave., NW (12th St.), 202-347-6848
◪ From Paris by way of NY, this "Left Bank" steakhouse with a "breezy Gallic informality" verges on "authentically rude"; it's the place to come for frites, moules and onglet steak and to join the tourists, theatergoers and Pennsylvania Avenue pinstripes on the sidewalk terrace – who are escaping the cigar smoke inside.

Lespinasse – | – | – | E
Sheraton Carlton Hotel, 923 16th St., NW (K St.), 202-879-6900
Dripping with elegance that provides magnificent window dressing for a deal, and only two blocks from the White House, this stately, newly refurbished hotel dining room was slated to reopen in early October 1996 as an offshoot of NYC's celebrated French-Asian Lespinasse, with a chef trained at the NYC original; given such glittering prospects, this former yo-yo palace could soar.

Le Vieux Logis [S] 22 | 20 | 22 | $38
7925 Old Georgetown Rd. (Auburn Ave.), Bethesda, MD, 301-652-6816
◪ This agreeably cluttered "French cottage" in Bethesda, and its "good cooking" and cosseting, "never disappoint" its discriminating "older crowd"; but its "French food without all the fuss" approach leaves some younger diners cold ("boring and traditional", "small, cramped").

Listrani's [S] 17 | 14 | 16 | $20
5100 MacArthur Blvd., NW (Dana Pl.), 202-363-0619
◪ A "good place to grab a bite, with no high hopes" of more than "average" Italian dining is how surveyors sum up this MacArthur Boulevard "pizza and salad standby"; despite perennial complaints about its "tacky" appearance, waits and "spotty" service, it's "cheerful", comfortable, "satisfies the pickiest of children" – and there's not much else around.

Lite 'n' Fair   ▽ 18 | 6 | 13 | $16
*1018 King St. (bet. Patrick & Henry Sts.), Alexandria, VA,
703-549-3717*

Lite 'n' Fair/Belle View Seafood S
*Belle View Shopping Ctr., 1510 Belle View Blvd. (Fort
Hunt Rd.), Alexandria, VA, 703-660-6085*

☑ Offering "high-class" Italian, French or Asian-influenced
food at a "low price", including a "super portobello
sandwich" and "tarragon chicken salad" you'd love to
"replicate", this pocket-sized King Street deli manages to be
"very creative in a very small space"; its Belle View sister, a
real restaurant specializing in seafood, also "has its charms."

Little Viet Garden S   21 | 16 | 17 | $17
3012 Wilson Blvd. (Garfield Rd.), Arlington, VA, 703-522-9686
☑ More cosmopolitan than its neighbors on "Virginia's Ho
Chi Minh Trail" and "very busy", this "funky" Vietnamese
does a good ("not the best") job with its specialties and has
a "cute garden" which, alas, borders "deafening traffic"
and the parking lot; those who love it most "go for lunch."

Los Chorros S   19 | 12 | 17 | $14
*2420 Blue Ridge Ave. (Georgia Ave.), Wheaton, MD,
301-933-1066*
*8401 Snouffer's School Rd. (Center Way), Gaithersburg,
MD, 301-840-5894*

■ Please "don't tell anyone how good" these "family-run"
Salvadorans are, beg reviewers who worry that the
remodeling at Wheaton will attract too much trade; as it is,
their "good food" and "great value" keep them packed to
the max – go for the "papusas" and "shrimp anything."

Louisiana Express Co. S   21 | 9 | 15 | $15
*4921 Bethesda Ave. (Arlington Rd.), Bethesda, MD,
301-652-6945*
☑ "They know the meaning of Tabasco" at this Bethesda
Cajun-Creole "dump" with counter service (loosely
speaking) and zip decor; spicy stuff like jambalaya,
catfish beignets, "po' boy sandwiches and alligator stew"
are "cheap", "greasy" and "good" enough to keep the
joint "overcrowded"; "not bad", say natives, if you've
"never been to New Orleans."

Luigino S   22 | 20 | 19 | $30
1100 New York Ave., NW (bet. H & 12th Sts.), 202-371-0595
☑ This "slick and smartly done" Northern Italian striver is
one of the top biz lunch places near the Convention Center,
which could explain the complaints about "unreliable"
service and dishes that aren't "up to" their prices; still,
"in a city filled with Italian" restaurants, it's "worth going"
to and "underappreciated for dinner."

Luna Grill & Diner S
| 18 | 16 | 17 | $16 |

1301 Connecticut Ave., NW (N St.), 202-835-2280

■ Amid the "bars, chains and carryouts, just south of Dupont Circle", this spiffy-looking "urban diner" provides a reality check and some pretty good homestyle food (like "addictive" sweet potato fries); it's "cheap", "chaotic" and crowded, but the "chili is reason enough" to go.

Maharaja S
| – | – | – | M |

Cipriano Square Shopping Ctr., 8825 Greenbelt Rd. (Cipriano Rd.), Greenbelt, MD, 301-552-1600

The "shortage" of good restaurants in Prince Georges County is one reason why Greenbelt is "lucky to have" this Indian; others are its tandoor-baked breads and meats, savory stews and "good-deal" lunch buffet ($6.95 Tuesday–Friday); all the above make reports that it's "becoming a little seedy" unsettling.

Maison Blanche
| 24 | 23 | 24 | $46 |

1725 F St., NW (bet. 17th & 18th Sts.), 202-842-0070

◨ It's "staid" and "getting gray" (like its clientele) and has an aura of "faded glamour", but the food at this "formal" French "is still quite good", the unflappable service even better and it's near "lots of offices" and the World Bank (the White House, too); happy hour is surprisingly active and the $28.95 prix fixe is an "excellent" pre-concert deal.

MAKOTO S
| 28 | 25 | 27 | $42 |

4822 MacArthur Blvd., NW (Reservoir Rd.), 202-298-6866

■ An "incredible dining experience", an "immersion in Japanese culture" – whether you "sit ringside" at the 10-seat sushi bar of this largely "unknown", exquisite Nipponese "hidden" on MacArthur Boulevard or at one of the four tables for an "innovative" kaiseki dinner, you're in for some of the "finest Japanese dining outside of Japan."

Malik S
▽ | 23 | 19 | 21 | $17 |

(fka Mali Thai)
1805 18th St., NW (bet. S & T Sts.), 202-986-5124

■ "Suitable for casual" or "romantic" dining, this attractive Thai is giving nearby Bua "competition" in Dupont Circle East; if reports that the "waiters couldn't be nicer – so polite and unobtrusive", and the food (including a long vegetarian menu) is "wonderful" hold true, it won't be "quiet" long.

Mama Wok & Teriyaki S
▽ | 21 | 5 | 13 | $11 |

Rockville City Ctr., 595 Hungerford Dr. (N. Washington St.), Rockville, MD, 301-309-6642

■ Those who don't "expect much" from "Asian cafeteria food" may be pleasantly surprised by this "best bargain" Sino-Japanese off Rockville Pike; it's adept at a mix of Chinese and Japanese dishes, made with the critters swimming in the fish tanks (which constitute the decor) and sold for a pittance.

Mare E Monti S ▽ 23 | 17 | 19 | $22 |
Freestate Mall, 15554-B Annapolis Rd. (off Hwy. 197),
Bowie, MD, 301-262-9179
◪ Finding "homemade pasta" in a "suburban mall" is
"impressive", particularly in Bowie, where cucina Italiana
alternatives are pizza joints and chains; those who have
discovered this "consistently good, interesting" place wish
the service lived up to the "homey atmosphere" and food.

Market St. Bar & Grill S 22 | 21 | 22 | $28 |
Hyatt Hotel, 1800 President St. (Market St.), Reston, VA,
703-709-6262
▉ One of the highlights of the exurban mix of restaurants,
shops and entertainment in Reston Town Center, this
Contemporary American hotel dining room provides "first-
class food and service in a lively setting"; praise for the
"creative" menu, brunch and weekend jazz is tempered
mostly by concerns about last spring's chef change.

Martin's Tavern S 17 | 18 | 18 | $21 |
1264 Wisconsin Ave., NW (N St.), 202-333-7370
▉ This historic Georgetown tavern, "an island of stability in
a world of change", is as "easy and comfortable" now as in
the days of "FDR and the '40s"; go for an "old-fashioned"
breakfast or "evening snack" of solid American fare and
"feel like Washington is your old hometown."

Matuba S 22 | 13 | 19 | $21 |
2915 Columbia Pike (Walter Reed St.), Arlington, VA,
703-521-2811
4918 Cordell Ave. (Old Georgetown Rd.), Bethesda, MD,
301-652-7449
▉ "Fresh", "friendly", "fast", "no-frills" family sushi stops
that work well for everyday eating when presentation and
surroundings don't matter as much as "reasonable prices"
and "smiles"; "even if you don't eat sushi, there's lots that's
good" – "ask for specials not on the specials board."

Mediterranean Blue S – | – | – | M |
1910 18th St., NW (bet. T St. & Florida Ave.), 202-483-2583
"Colorful" – that goes for the eponymous exterior, ambiance
and company at this youthful Middle Eastern "fun spot"
below Adams Morgan; write-ins say it has "potential" – after
all, "where else can you listen to the *Laverne & Shirley*
theme while eating shish kebabs", grilled veggies and rice?

Mediterranee S – | – | – | E |
3520 Lee Hwy. (Monroe St.), Arlington, VA, 703-527-7276
In summer 1996, this warm Mediterranean bistro in Arlington
replaced the similarly named Mediterraneo; although it
also focuses on the sunny cuisine of Southern Europe,
which complements the white-walled, rustic space, the
management and kitchen are new.

Melati   – – – M
3506 Connecticut Ave., NW (bet. Ordway & Porter Sts.),
202-537-1432
Uptown moviegoers recommend this small Cleveland Park
Indonesian-Malayasian for its "intriguing" menu, sidewalk
seating and good value, but not for its decor; the staff will be
delighted to tell you about dishes you won't find elsewhere.

Melrose   24 24 24 $42
Park Hyatt Hotel, 24th & M Sts., NW, 202-955-3899
■ Its "urban garden" elegance and hush make this
"polished" West End hotel dining room perfect for a biz
lunch; diners find "flashes of brilliance" in the Contemporary
American kitchen and a sensory cornucopia – a cascading
fountain on the sunken patio, museum-quality art, "jumpin'"
Saturday night jazz and the "best" wine bar, tea and brunch.

Memphis Bar-B-Q Co. S   – – – I
Ballston Commons, 4238 Wilson Blvd. (Glebe Rd.),
Arlington, VA, 703-875-9883
13067-H Lee Jackson Hwy., Fairfax, VA, 703-449-0500
Like Red Hot & Blue, these new BBQ joints pay homage to
Memphis with wet or dry ribs, pulled pork, chicken, onion
straws, sides – and BBQ pizza just in case Elvis drops by;
too bad their designer-distressed, mall-based settings are
a far cry from down-home pits.

Meskerem ● S   21 18 18 $20
2434 18th St., NW (Columbia Rd.), 202-462-4100
☑ Adams Morgan Ethiopian serving "really ethnic food"
in attractive surroundings; one sits upstairs on hassocks
at basketweave tables attended by "beautiful waitresses"
and scoops up fiery stews with "sour", sponge-like bread;
romantics and vegetarians enjoy it, but novices be warned:
it's an "adventure."

Metro Center Grille S   18 17 18 $23
Marriott at Metro Ctr., 775 12th St., NW (bet. H & J Sts.),
202-737-2200
☑ This "comfortable" Marriott restaurant is making major
efforts to upgrade its image – namely, hiring an "ambitious
chef" whose "fresh" Contemporary American menu is
"worth the price"; but some still think of it as serving
"pedestrian business fare" – spillover from its "colorless"
appearance and Convention Center location perhaps?

Metro 29 ● S   – – – I
4711 Lee Hwy. (Glebe Rd.), Arlington, VA, 703-528-2464
Bright and shiny and looking like a diner should, this
Arlington entry is a "real" one with "class"; write-ins tell us it
has the basics aced with "platter"-sized portions, terrific
desserts and "lines out the door" for its "great breakfast."

Mick's 🅢   16 | 16 | 16 | $16
2401 Pennsylvania Ave., NW (24th St.), 202-331-9613
Fair Oaks Mall (Junction Rtes. 50 & 66), Fairfax, VA,
703-934-9716
Springfield Mall (Franconia Rd.), Springfield, VA, 703-971-6106
▣ Retro Americana and a "mishmash" menu for mix 'n'
match dining doesn't take these mock saloons much beyond
"TGIF" level now that the "excitement has dimmed";
"convenience counts for something", of course, but so
does "variable" performance.

Mike's American Grill 🅢   21 | 20 | 20 | $20
6210 Backlick Rd. (Old Keene Mill Rd.), Springfield, VA,
703-644-7100
▣ "Seating is a major headache" and reviewers, charitably,
"won't comment on the parking situation", yet they jam
this "standard American" warehouse in Springfield "for
what it is" – a place with "fern bar food", "dependable"
prime rib and a "suburban" environment that "tries to be
hip" – and because there isn't much else out there.

Mi Rancho 🅢   21 | 16 | 21 | $18
8701 Ramsey Ave. (Fiddler Ln.), Silver Spring, MD,
301-588-4872
■ Happily, this effort to simulate the Rio Grande Cafe in
Silver Spring (tortilla machine, cement floors, stacked
cartons and all) isn't entirely successful – while its
Tex-Mex menu seems familiar, the atmosphere is less
"frenetic", more genuine; on-site "owners take great
pride in the food – and it shows"; P.S. it's one of the few
places thereabouts with "patio dining."

Miss Saigon 🅢   21 | 15 | 18 | $20
1847 Columbia Rd., NW (18th St.), 202-667-1900
3057 M St. (Thomas Jefferson St.), 202-333-5545
▣ Best liked for its quail and noodle soup, "garden
atmosphere" and "very kind staff", this Adams Morgan
Vietnamese does a brisk takeout trade; eat-in diners
divide: "best cheap Vietnamese in DC" vs. "just ok" –
ergo it may be "inconsistent"; its smashing new sister in
Georgetown should be a hit.

Miyagi   – | – | – | M
6719 Curran St. (Old Dominion Dr.), McLean, VA,
703-893-0116
That this pocket-sized Japanese is not well known beyond
its McLean environs is one of its drawing cards; after all,
when one serves "the best sushi in the area, hands down"
and has only eight tables and a sushi bar, the fewer who·
vie for a seat, the better.

Mo Bay Cafe ◐ S   16 | 13 | 14 | $18
(fka Montego Cafe)
2437 18th St., NW (bet. Belmont & Columbia Rds.), 202-745-1002
◪ Aside from some of the best sidewalk seats in Adams Morgan, a "pulsating" reggae beat and a couple of deadly drinks, fewer are finding this "soft-core Jamaican" joint fun; it used to have "good Caribbean cuisine" (a few say it still does), but lately it's been "lackluster all-around."

Moby Dick ⊘   23 | 6 | 13 | $11
7027 Wisconsin Ave. (Leland St), Bethesda, MD,
301-654-1838 S
Buchanan Mall, 2103 S. Jefferson Davis Hwy. (23rd St.),
Crystal City, VA, 703-413-5100
6864 Old Dominion Dr. (Rte. 123), McLean, VA,
303-448-8448 S
■ Perhaps this area's "best" and most "authentic" Persian kebabs (making them is an art requiring precise timing and skillful grilling) can be found at this ramshackle Bethesda carryout-plus whose "healthy", "delicious", "filling" and "cheap" versions put it (and its kin) high on our Bang for the Buck list; they also earn kudos from "kids."

Monocle   15 | 17 | 17 | $29
107 D St., NE (1st St.), 202-546-4488
◪ This "clubby" Senate-side fixture will probably survive lobbying reform just fine – the 'members' (of congress) have been bringing their families and staff here for years for "old-fashioned" (aka "boring") American food in a "comfortable" setting; besides, no place is as "close to Senate offices" and handy to the Supreme Court; indeed, on any given day you could probably get the votes for a majority decision in the dining room.

Montgomery's Grille S   16 | 17 | 16 | $20
7200 Wisconsin Ave. (Bethesda Ave.), Bethesda, MD,
301-654-3595
◪ While wishing that Bethesda's "we-have-everything" American had food as "happening as the bar" and that it didn't treat customers "like herded cows", locals find it useful for a "no-nonsense bite", "nice Sunday brunch", outdoor dining, "game watching" and shopping for "Mr. or Ms. Right" – it's also where "the girls" "do" lunch.

MORRISON-CLARK INN S   25 | 26 | 24 | $39
Morrison-Clark Inn, 1015 L St., NW (bet. 11th St. &
Massachusetts Ave.), 202-898-1200
■ Susan Lindeborg is "back and cooking up a storm" at this treasured Downtown Victorian, "assuring" its place among DC's "best" restaurants; her American "home cooking with a modern flair" is "innovative" yet "understated" and enhanced by a "lovely" setting and "staff that makes you feel special"; out-of-town "visitors are enthralled" – though not by the neighborhood.

MORTON'S OF CHICAGO [S] 26 | 21 | 23 | $47
3251 Prospect St., NW (Wisconsin Ave.), 202-342-6258
8075 Leesburg Pike (Aline Rd.), Tysons Corner, VA, 703-883-0800
■ "In your face – brisk, brusque and noisy", these "top-dollar" cow palaces are a "steak-eater's dream"; their "men's club" atmosphere virtually demands a "porterhouse, martini and a good cigar" (although they serve "great lobster" too); so what if it's "sinful"? – "roll your sleeves up, damn the cholesterol and dig in."

Mr. K's [S] 23 | 23 | 23 | $39
2121 K St., NW (bet. 21st & 22nd Sts.), 202-331-8868
◪ "Fine Chinese dining", as done in Hong Kong, provides an "elegant" backdrop for business dining at this K Street stalwart where the "royal treatment" nearly overwhelms the "outstanding" food; if you're on an expense account, it's quite a "show"; for everyone else, it may be "past its price."

Mrs. Simpson's [S] 21 | 21 | 21 | $33
2915 Connecticut Ave., NW (Cathedral Ave.), 202-332-8300
◪ The romantic theme of the Windsor-Simpson legend casts its spell over this "intimate", slightly "precious" restaurant, its "light", "eclectic, American menu" and "classy" brunch; with few exceptions, it charms Woodley Park and tourists on the way to the zoo; P.S. the "royal memorabilia" is worth a trip to the rest rooms.

Mr. Yung's ◐ [S] 19 | 11 | 18 | $18
740 Sixth St., NW (bet. G & H Sts.), 202-628-1098
■ A choice selection of dim sum is the "good lunch deal" at this Chinatown Cantonese storefront; the "very capable" kitchen does a good job with the "very extensive menu", but for best results (and to bypass "language barriers") "let Mr. Yung order for you."

Muer's Seafood 17 | 18 | 19 | $30
1101 Connecticut Ave., NW (L St.), 202-785-4505
◪ "Strictly for business lunches" near Farragut Square, this nautical-themed seafooder stays busy but mostly inspires yawns: "Eastern Shore basic, without the beach", "service and quality spotty"; on weeknights, piano jazz is the bait.

Music City Roadhouse [S] 15 | 19 | 17 | $18
1050 30th St., NW (bet. M & K Sts.), 202-337-4444
■ "The bigger [and hungrier] the group, the better" at this rollicking Southern roadhouse replica in Georgetown where they pile on the down-home eats (we're talking "serious grease") family-style ($10.95–$12.95) and then things really start rolling in the bar; the Sunday gospel brunch ($12.95) is a "blast"; N.B. parking is a major plus.

Mykonos   19 | 18 | 19 | $23
1835 K St., NW (19th St.), 202-331-0370
☑ With its "fresh, tasty" fare, staff that "couldn't be nicer" and a K Street setting that evokes its namesake island, this "traditional" Greek is as close to the Aegean "as one can get"; maybe you could find as good or "better" Greek "at lower prices" elsewhere, but it's still a "nice, quiet", reasonable place for dinner or "taking a client to lunch."

Nam's S   21 | 16 | 19 | $19
11220 Georgia Ave. (University Blvd.), Wheaton, MD, 301-933-2525
Nam's of Bethesda
4928 Cordell Ave. (bet. Woodmont Ave. & Old Georgetown Rd.), Bethesda, MD, 301-652-2635
■ These "high-end" Vietnamese siblings manage to please both the knowledgeable and novices with "refined", French-influenced food, "considerate" help and "relaxing" surroundings (Bethesda is prettier, Wheaton has "better" food); both are "family friendly" and at busy times have a "tendency to rush" ("wham bam, thank you Nam's").

Nam Viet S   21 | 14 | 19 | $16
1127 N. Hudson St. (Wilson Blvd.), Arlington, VA, 703-522-7110
■ Though it's often a second – or third – choice for Clarendon Vietnamese dining, supporters call this "sleeper" a "diamond in the lemongrass" for its "excellent grilled dishes", "low-stress" atmosphere, "interesting patrons" and "romantic" summer nights on the patio.

Nathan's S   17 | 17 | 17 | $28
3150 M St., NW (Wisconsin Ave.), 202-338-2000
☑ Lately, this "Center of Georgetown" corner tavern is more of a "popular drinking" and "singles scene" than the "clubby" neighborhood in-spot it once was; the barroom is where preppies munch and mingle, the "cozy" back room is where they take their "parents" for pasta and seafood cooked by chef Giusseppina Alessandrini's daughters.

New Heights S   25 | 23 | 23 | $38
2317 Calvert St., NW (Connecticut Ave.), 202-234-4110
☑ Matthew Lake, recently honored by *Food & Wine*, is the most recent culinary talent to reach new heights in this New Age American's risk-taking kitchen; set in an "airy", art-filled space overlooking Rock Creek Park, it's "very well-run" (if a bit "joyless") and the food – "fascinating combinations" of seasonal ingredients – can make an ordinary meal an "occasion", but it sometimes veers over the edge.

Nizam's [S] 21 18 20 $27
Village Green Shopping Ctr., 523 Maple Ave. W. (Rte. 123), Vienna, VA, 703-938-8948
◪ The "doner kebab is not to be missed" at this Ottoman outpost in Vienna, but the presence of the local Turkish community means there are other "interesting" dishes to try; it's "friendly", "cramped" and less ornately decorated than nearby compatriot Kazan.

NORA 26 24 24 $46
2132 Florida Ave., NW (bet. Connecticut & Massachusetts Aves.), 202-462-5143
■ Nora Pouillon's pioneering "philosophy" – transforming farm-grown products into a "distinctive", delicious Contemporary American cuisine – has been "realized" so successfully that her "romantic" converted stable is one of the city's most stylish "must go's"; consequently, with the "press", literati and pols competing for the limited seats, expect "waits."

Normandie Farms [S] 17 21 19 $31
10710 Falls Rd. (Democracy Blvd.), Potomac, MD, 301-983-8838
◪ Although this dignified country setting in Potomac has been "improved" since its longtime chef took charge, it hasn't been able to shake its image as a ladies' lunch/ "bountiful brunch"/wedding/popover place – perhaps because the Continental menu and clientele ("blue hair") are largely unchanged.

Notte Luna 19 18 18 $26
809 15th St., NW (bet. H & I Sts.), 202-408-9500
◪ While no longer "the rage", this neon-bright Cal-Ital continues to benefit from its "strategic" location (near offices, the best clubs and National Theatre), sidewalk cafe (decorated by "pretty people") and "trendy" pizza, pasta and calamari menu; noise and "cavalier" attitudes are minor deterrents.

Nova Europa 17 15 18 $24
Kemp Mill Shopping Ctr., 1311 Lamberton Dr. (Arcola Dr.), Silver Spring, MD, 301-649-6690
◪ This Silver Spring Continental, "trusted" by the "early-bird set" to provide a "satisfying" meal at an affordable price, is one of the few places hereabouts to try Portuguese specialties like *paelha*, caldo verde and "sardines and wine"; neither its shopping center premises, nor service, impress outsiders, but "when the kitchen is careful, the food can be quite good."

Nulbom [S] – | – | – | M
4870 Boiling Brook Pkwy. (Nicholson Ln.), Rockville, MD, 301-468-2930
"Consistently well-crafted food", including spicy, grill-your-own BBQ and standard Japanese, can be found at this spartan, Rockville shopping strip Korean that makes few concessions to Western ways; "if you don't mind being regimented", it's a cheap trip to Asia.

OBELISK 27 | 21 | 25 | $46
2029 P St., NW (bet. 20th & 21st Sts.), 202-872-1180
■ Every evening, Peter Pastan cooks dinner for 35 lucky people in his "soigné" boîte off Dupont Circle; his Northern Italian menus "always excite" and are complemented by "perfect bread" and wines and a "knowledgeable staff" that shares his "dedication"; "charming", "exceptional", "a respite" are some of the encomiums he earns as this *Survey*'s top Italian.

Occidental Grill [S] 22 | 23 | 21 | $35
Willard Complex (Pennsylvania Ave. & 14th St.), 202-783-1475
◪ The sense of history and "Washington power" conveyed at the present reincarnation of this "clubby" Downtown American enhances its updated fare and soothes any "disappointed expectations"; a "stalwart for pre-theater dining", it's been "hard to beat for a business lunch" for nearly a century.

O'Donnell's [S] 17 | 15 | 18 | $25
8301 Wisconsin Ave. (Battery Ln.), Bethesda, MD, 301-656-6200
◪ For senior citizens and tourists, this "Bethesda landmark" offers a snapshot of the "real" old Washington, its friendliness and the traditional ways seafood was prepared (dripping with butter or "fried"); the rest dismiss it as "mass feeding", yet sneak a rum bun to take home.

OLD ANGLER'S INN [S] 23 | 24 | 21 | $46
10801 MacArthur Blvd. (1 mi. past Clara Barton Pkwy.), Potomac, MD, 301-365-2425
◪ "One of DC's special places for lovers" offers some of the "best outdoor seating in the area" with "inventive" Contemporary American food "to match" – especially the tasting menus (pricey but worthwhile); drinks by the fire are also "romantic", less so the "garret" upstairs.

OLD EBBITT GRILL ◐ [S] 19 | 22 | 19 | $26
675 15th St., NW (bet. F & G Sts.), 202-347-4801
■ A "beautiful", bustling, polished wood and brass setting with a "political feel", "well run" and near everything, "steady" American fare and "lots of affordable choices" – it's "easy to see why this restaurant has stood the test of time", is patronized by suits, jeans and "throngs of tourists" and generates relatively few complaints – "it is Washington."

Old Glory BBQ ◐ [S] 18 18 18 $18

3139 M St., NW (bet. Wisconsin Ave. & 31st St.), 202-337-3406

◪ "Serious guy food" (BBQ and buckets of beers) – "cheap and lots of it" – "good babe watching" (from the open-window seats), loud music and "'Skins games" make for "rowdy" times at this "hyper" collegiate happening in Georgetown; it's so much "fun", who cares if it's "slow"?

Oodles Noodles 21 15 17 $16

1010 20th St., NW (K St.), 202-293-3138
4907 Cordell Ave. (Old Georgetown & Norfolk Rds.), Bethesda, MD, 301-986-8833

■ This compact, attractive noodle house off K Street is "top rated for value" by just about everyone for its "huge bowls of spicy soup" and "heaping portions" of "terrific" noodles that are "well prepared" in many Asian styles; being "patient" (during long waits) and "packed as tight as noodles in a box" is included in the "bargain price"; the new Bethesda locale is also packing them in.

Otello 19 15 18 $22

1329 Connecticut Ave., NW (½ block south of Dupont Metro Station), 202-429-0209

◪ A step down from Dupont Circle, this "red-checker-tablecloth" Italian is a pleasant antidote to trendy pastarias and chains; it's "dowdy" and "reliable", the food is "nothing spectacular", yet it's fine for "day-in, day-out" eating – and "being there makes you feel good."

Outback Steakhouse [S] 20 16 19 $21

Arlington Forest Shopping Ctr., 4821 N. First St. (off Rte. 50 at Park Dr.), Arlington, VA, 703-527-0063
Elden Plaza, 150 Elden St. #100 (Herndon Pkwy.), Herndon, VA, 703-318-0999
Twinbrooke Shopping Ctr., 9579-B Braddock Rd. (Twinbrooke Dr.), Fairfax, VA, 703-978-6283
Colonnade, 5702 Union Mill Rd. (Rte. 29), Clifton, VA, 703-818-0804
Potomac Festival, 14580 Potomac Mills Rd. (Bixby Rd.), Woodbridge, VA, 703-490-5336
Backlick Ctr., 6651 Backlick Rd. (Old Keene Mill Rd.), Springfield, VA, 703-912-7531
Giant Shopping Ctr., 315 Maple Ave. E. (Glyndon St.), Vienna, VA, 703-242-0460
Beacon Mall, 6804 Richmond Hwy. (Rte. 1), Alexandria, VA, 703-768-1063
10060 Lee Hwy., Fairfax, VA, 703-352-5000
7720 Woodmont Ave. (bet. Old Georgetown Rd. & Wisconsin Ave.), Bethesda, MD, 301-913-0176
Germantown Sq., 12609 Wisteria Dr. (Great Seneca Hwy.), Germantown, MD, 301-353-9499

Outback Steakhouse (Cont.)
Hilltop Plaza, 6868 Race Track Rd. (Rte. 450), Bowie, MD, 301-464-5800
◩ "Ersatz" Aussies – strictly for cheapsteaks – "fill the beef craving" with decent steaks, "oversize" appetizers, spicy sides, "frosty beer" and a "welcoming atmosphere" that many find "worth" the "hellacious lines" and "franchise sterility"; grape nuts say the "exceptional Aussie wine values beat the steaks."

Oval Room 23 | 23 | 23 | $37
800 Connecticut Ave., NW (H St.), 202-463-8700
■ The bright, young "star on the K Street corridor", with "imaginative" Contemporary American food, "outstanding" service and a "whimsical mural", has become something of a "celebrity" house, earning rave reviews like "wonderfully relaxed", "excellent bar", "chic for business lunches"; "go once and you'll keep returning."

Ozio ▽ 14 | 19 | 18 | $25
1835 K St., NW (19th St.), 202-822-6000
◩ Strictly for lounge lizards and smokers, this slick "cigar and martini" bar on K Street (with trendy nibbles) stocks all the latest quaffs and is reputedly an "after-dinner hot spot"; some go for the "atmosphere, drinks and cigars", the rest "for the secondhand smoke."

Palm, The [S] 23 | 19 | 21 | $42
1225 19th St., NW (bet. M & N Sts.), 202-293-9091
◩ At this testosterone-fueled "locker room" for "male dinosaurs", monster steaks and lobsters, "killer martinis", "New York waiters" and "cigar-smoking Republicans are the norm"; you "can always see someone from the Sunday morning TV squad" and it's more fun to "go with a face"; P.S. the food's "first-rate."

Panjshir [S] 24 | 13 | 18 | $19
224 W. Maple Ave. (Rte. 123), Vienna, VA, 703-281-4183
924 Broad St. (West St.), Falls Church, VA, 703-536-4566
■ "Modest surroundings belie the wonderful food" and "pleasant" atmosphere at these "Afghan champs" in Northern Virginia; here, you'll find "bold flavors" and "more sophisticated and complex dishes than at most Afghans", yet familiar ingredients (pumpkin, lamb, rice) make them "good places for people squeamish about trying strange food"; N.B. service can be slow.

Paolo's [S] 20 | 19 | 18 | $22
1303 Wisconsin Ave., NW (N St.), 202-333-7353 ◐
Reston Town Ctr., Market & Fountain Sts., Reston, VA, 703-318-8920

Paolo's (Cont.)
1801 Rockville Pike (Randolph Rd.), Rockville, MD, 301-984-2211
◪ "Pop Italians" with the right mix of an action-packed bar scene, outdoor/streetside dining and a pasta/pizza/salad menu to consistently pull crowds (read 'noise'); they hold the middle ground "between pizza and fancy Italian" and are usually enjoyable "despite all the yuppies"; the free tapenade and breadsticks get the rave food reviews.

Pappa-Razzi S | 17 | 21 | 17 | $23 |
1066 Wisconsin Ave., NW (M St.), 202-298-8000
◪ This Georgetown "movie-set" Italian makes "dramatic" use of a landmark firehouse and its "medium-priced" menu "covers the staples well" (pastas, pizzas and grills), making it easy to "eat light"; some warn of "formulaic" food and others find it "too franchisey."

Paradise S | 19 | 15 | 17 | $22 |
7141 Wisconsin Ave. (Montgomery Ave.), Bethesda, MD, 301-907-7500
■ A few knowledgeable foodies recommend this "pleasant" Bethesdan for some of the "best Iranian food around"; its picture-book menu introduces many "interesting" Persian and Afghan dishes and its lunch ($7.95) and dinner ($11.95) buffets are a "good buy of taste treats."

Parioli S | 19 | 18 | 18 | $28 |
4800 Elm St. (Wisconsin Ave.), Bethesda, MD, 301-951-8600
◪ Packed with suburbanites who "know 10 other people eating there", this Bethesda Italian "rec room" is also known for its "homemade" pastas, seafood and "great pricing scheme" (all pastas are one price); but lately locals register more complaints – a slide in ratings is a warning.

Parkway Deli S | 19 | 8 | 17 | $14 |
Rock Creek Shopping Ctr., 8317 Grubb Rd. (East-West Hwy., bet. 16th St. & Connecticut Ave.), Silver Spring, MD, 301-587-1427
■ It's "a guaranteed favorite for New York transplants"– this "plain, old" Silver Spring Jewish deli pays homage to the 'deli greats' with their photos on the wall, a "great pickle bar", "best matzo-ball soup" and all the other edible trappings of the real thing; the back dining room is the neighborhood "meeting place" for breakfast.

Pasha Cafe S | 22 | 17 | 21 | $19 |
Cherrydale Shopping Ctr., 2109 N. Pollard St. (Military Rd.), Arlington, VA, 703-528-2126
■ Explore "Egyptian variations on Middle Eastern" classics at this simple but "very appealing" room in Cherrydale, where "gracious" hospitality, "good food" and great value are rewarding it with many friends; a selection of "wonderful appetizers" (hummus, falafel) could be the centerpiece of a "delightful" meal.

Pasta Plus S   ▽ 21 | 14 | 19 | $20
Center Plaza, 209 Gorman Ave. (bet. Rtes. 1 & 198E), Laurel, MD, 301-498-5100
■ "Great surprise – Laurel has a good restaurant now"; any neighborhood would be proud of this attractive, family- run Italian with "homemade food", "fabulous wood-fired pizza" and "very good pasta" and prices; it "smells so good" almost anyone would be willing to "wait in line."

PATISSERIE CAFE DIDIER S   26 | 16 | 18 | $15
3206 Grace St., NW (bet. M & K Sts.), 202-342-9083
■ "World-class" pâtissier Didier Schoner's "sublime" confections, "fantastic soups, soufflés" and light entrees are showcased at this "charming" Georgetown bistro; it's a "warm", "very European" place to have breakfast or tea and "a lovely lunch stop – it feels like you're miles away"; N.B. Monsieur Didier also teaches at NYC's prestigious French Culinary Institute and may eventually leave this place.

PEKING GOURMET INN S   25 | 15 | 21 | $24
Culmore Shopping Ctr., 6029 Leesburg Pike (Glen Carlin St.), Falls Church, VA, 703-671-8088
▨ The specialty of the house, Peking duck, along with "delicious" garlic sprouts and other custom-grown produce are the reasons this Falls Church perennial wins Top Chinese honors; the "chaos" and lack of "creature comforts" (and hanging "too many Republicans on the wall") are not.

Perry's S   18 | 21 | 15 | $24
1811 Columbia Rd., NW (18th St.), 202-234-6218
■ On DC's "best", "hippest" roof deck, it's sushi "as entertainment" – and it's quite "a scene"; right now the food is fusion, the interior is "lime green, patent leather and red" and on Sundays there's a drag show brunch; but with an owner "addicted to change", who knows what's next?; it "can be exceptional or mundane" – but always over the top.

Persepolis S   17 | 12 | 16 | $20
7130 Wisconsin Ave. (bet. Bethesda & Miller Aves.), Bethesda, MD, 301-656-9339
▨ Most agree this Bethesda Iranian's popular buffet (lunch $6.95, dinner $11.95) offers a "good-value" sampler of Persian cuisine, but perceptions of quality range from "wonderful for large groups" to "not all that good"; plus it's "dark", "disorganized" and not always "helpful."

Pesce S   25 | 15 | 19 | $30
2016 P St., NW (bet. Dupont Circle & 20th St.), 202-466-FISH
■ "DC's best seafood restaurant", an "intimate" Dupont Circle "bistro with style", is "fresh, "imaginative", "congenial" and "thoroughly professional"; the "originality and excellence" of its food belie its "simple" storefront surroundings, not to mention its "reasonable prices"; all told "we need more restaurants like this."

Petitto's S
　　　　　　　　　　　　　　　　– ∣ – ∣ – ∣ M
2653 Connecticut Ave., NW (Calvert St.), 202-667-5350
On Woodley Park's restaurant row, this sprightly Connecticut
Avenue "neighborhood" Italian has "fresh pasta" and
enough pizzazz to pull tourists; there's weekend opera
(with "singers better than the food") and cappuccino and
desserts in Dolce Finale below; plan to spend "an evening."

Phillips Flagship S
　　　　　　　　　　　　15 ∣ 15 ∣ 15 ∣ $23
900 Water St., SW (9th St.), 202-488-8515

Phillips Seafood Grill S
*American Ctr./Signet Bank Bldg., 8330 Boone Blvd. (bet.
Rtes. 7 & 23), Tysons Corner, VA, 703-442-0400*
☑ "Uninspired" seafood spreads and "nearly invisible" help
don't impress locals at these Ocean City imports "made for
the tourist trade" visiting the DC and Baltimore waterfronts;
there's a great piano bar in Baltimore and an à la carte menu
and happy-hour raw bar in Tysons Corner.

Pho S
　　　　　　　　　　　　▽ 22 ∣ 11 ∣ 19 ∣ $14
615 Ash St. (H St., bet. 6th & 7th Sts.), 202-789-0211
■ You can find "everything you'd want in a pho" restaurant
at this Chinatown Vietnamese, i.e. "cheap", "wholesome",
meal-sized bowls of flavorful noodle soup and a selection of
unusual garnishes; if "so much soup" becomes a "bore",
its "interesting non-pho dishes" are mighty "tasty", too.

Pho Cali S
　　　　　　　　　　　　▽ 21 ∣ 12 ∣ 16 ∣ $16
*1621 S. Walter Reed Dr. (Rte. 395, Glebe Rd. exit), Arlington,
VA, 703-920-9500*
■ This Arlington Vietnamese "treasure" is prized for its
"great handling of seafood" as much as its "terrific" soups –
ask for clams in black bean sauce, crispy whole fish or
seafood fondue; inside is simple but cheery, in summer
there's a "nice outdoor terrace", and year-round, "lots of
expensive cars out front."

Pho 95 S
　　　　　　　　　　　　21 ∣ 10 ∣ 18 ∣ $12
*Ritchie Shopping Ctr., 595 Rockville Pike (near Rockville
Metro Station), Rockville, MD, 301-294-9391*
■ As the name implies, this tidy Rockville pho house opened
in '95, joining the growing number of Vietnamese places
where you can get a "low-cal filling meal" for a few bucks;
although there's a full menu, most go for the "fantastic",
"incendiary" soup – not the "inept" service.

Pho 75 S⇄
　　　　　　　　　　　　21 ∣ 8 ∣ 15 ∣ $10
*1510 University Blvd. E. (bet. N. Glebe Rd. & Pershing Dr.),
Langley Park, MD, 301-434-7844*
771 Hungerford Dr., Rockville, MD, 301-309-8873
3103 Graham Rd. (Rte. 50), Falls Church, VA, 703-204-1490

Pho 75 (Cont.)
1711 Wilson Blvd. (Quinn St.), Arlington, VA, 703-525-7355
■ The concept behind these "cheap", "communal", "good-for-the-soul" Vietnamese soup kitchens is "very simple" – eating "great noodle soup while sitting at long, camplike tables" and letting smiles smooth "tough communications"; they're the area's first pho restaurants and still "an exceptional value."

Pier 7 S   14 15 16 $25
Channel Inn, 650 Water St., SW (bet. 7th St. & Maine Ave.), 202-554-2500
☑ DC's long-running "office party" for pols and feds working near the SW waterfront (Arena Stage convenience brings in the rest of its local trade); though this seafooder is often dismissed as a "high-priced Ho Jo's" with "nice water views", too much tourist traffic and not enough in the way of food and service, we hear it's bobbing up.

Pilin Thai S   25 18 22 $17
116 W. Broad St. (Rte. 29), Falls Church, VA, 703-241-5850
■ A "contender for Virginia's top Thai" sums up patron praise for this "inviting" Falls Church storefront whose "delightful owners" pile on enough "excellent" food for "$10 to feed three starving students" or a family of four – it "seems to get better each time."

Pines of Florence S   15 9 15 $16
2053 Wilson Blvd. (Courthouse Rd.), Arlington, VA, 703-243-7463
Foxchase Shopping Ctr., 4603 Duke St. (Seminary Rd.), Alexandria, VA, 703-370-6383
7151 Lee Hwy. (bet. Graham Rd. & Annandale Rd.), Falls Church, VA, 703-533-0024
2100 Connecticut Ave. (California Ave., 2 blocks from Hilton Hotel), 202-332-8233
☑ Most go to this "true, non-yuppie Italian" in Arlington (with saplings elsewhere) "because it's cheap" and treats families well, "not because it's good"; while devoid of "atmosphere", the "home cooking" is nostalgic – "like being back in 1963."

Pines of Rome S   18 10 16 $18
4709 Hampden Ln. (Wisconsin Ave.), Bethesda, MD, 301-657-8775
☑ A "cheap eats" evergreen that looks "crummy", cooks red-sauce Italian, acts "rude" and is beloved by Bethesda families who don't want to spend money or cook at home; dissenters chop it down: "they get away with it because they're an institution", "overrated by the beatnik trust fund set."

Pirandello S   19 | 17 | 19 | $24
4922 Cordell Ave. (Old Georgetown Rd.), Bethesda, MD, 301-718-0800

☑ "When the Italian mood strikes" in Bethesda, you "can usually get in" here and (less consistently) "leave feeling good and full"; outdoor seating and "step-up-from-red-sauce" menu and decor give it an "adult" edge over "like-sounding restaurants" in the area; N.B. don't expect too much and you won't be disappointed.

Pizza de Resistance   18 | 18 | 16 | $17
Courthouse Plaza, 2300 Clarendon Blvd. (bet. Barton St. & Courthouse Rd.), Arlington, VA, 703-351-5680

☑ "Immense efforts" to distinguish itself from other pizza/pastarias with unique crusts, "bizarre" toppings, "artsy" presentations and "quality sarcasm" at the bar get a mixed verdict at Courthouse Plaza: "interesting dishes not always pulled off", "harried staff", "guilty of great food."

PIZZERIA PARADISO S   25 | 17 | 18 | $18
2029 P St., NW (bet. 20th & 21st Sts.), 202-223-1245

■ "Best pizza anywhere, bar none" – Obelisk offshoot's "heavenly" hearth-baked pizzas merit near unanimous acclaim; crisp-crusted, with just the right amount of primo toppings, they have "lots of character" – like the place; this "celestial sphere is a little crowded, so expect to wait."

Planet Hollywood ◑S   12 | 22 | 15 | $19
1101 Pennsylvania Ave., NW (11th St.), 202-783-7827

☑ Filled with props and glitter, movie memorabilia and Hollywood fantasy decor, this Downtown "amusement park" near the Mall is "rated NA-17 (no adult over 17 unaccompanied by "kids or foreign friends"); it's "way too commercial" and the $8 burgers and bar food are "not worth" the fuss, but film buffs have a "lot of fun."

Planet X ◑S   ▽ 16 | 19 | 14 | $13
7422 Baltimore Ave. (Regence Dr. & College Ave.), College Park, MD, 301-779-8451

☑ A green light for veggie alternative rock types in College Park; "'90s food meets '60s coffeehouse chic" over "cheap veggie" fare, "good desserts if you hit it right", herbal "smart drinks" (to sharpen your mental edge) and "beat poetry"; if that's not your universe, you'll find "bad-tempered granola types" and not much service.

Polly's Cafe ◑S   18 | 17 | 16 | $16
1342 U St., NW (bet. 13th & 14th Sts.), 202-265-8385

☑ New U "mainstay" where locals soak up the log cabin atmosphere over "winter suppers" and nurse hangovers at brunch; visitors enjoy the burgers, the bartenders and the vibes, but warn that the "strange combinations" on the specials go a bit too close to the "frontier."

Positano 🅂   18 | 18 | 19 | $27
4940 Fairmont Ave. (Old Georgetown Rd.), Bethesda, MD,
301-654-1717
◪ "Sitting outside under the grape arbor" at this "trusty"
Bethesda Southern Italian is always a pleasure and the fact
that the food "hardly ever changes" heightens its appeal;
the feeling that it's "not as good as it was" (though "still ok")
may reflect, in part, its "expansion" as well as changing
tastes ("can't compete with DC Italians" at the price).

Potowmack Landing 🅂   15 | 22 | 16 | $24
Washington Sailing Marina, George Washington Pkwy.
(1½ mi. south of National Airport), Alexandria, VA, 703-548-0001
◪ This rustic Park Service American near National Airport
has never had food and service to match its "wonderful
river setting" and fascinating runway views; hence,
customers complain about the waits and "government-
issue food" and go for the "ambiance."

PRIME RIB   26 | 25 | 25 | $45
2020 K St., NW (bet. 20th & 21st Sts.), 202-466-8811
■ Decked (and deco-ed) out like a *"Guys and Dolls"*
stage set lined with "celebrities", lawyers, lobbyists and
"lovelies", this "decadent-feeling" Downtown American
supper club is unequaled for "business or pleasure"; it's
one of the "best-run" restaurants in town and a bargain
at lunch, with DC's definitive prime rib and crab imperial;
"a step back in time, but oh what a time."

Primi Piatti   22 | 20 | 20 | $32
2013 I St., NW (bet. 20th & 21st Sts.), 202-223-3600 🅂
8045 Leesburg Pike (Gallows Rd.), Tysons Corner, VA,
703-893-0300
■ These "very sophisticated", "very Italian" trattorias
offer "excellent pasta", "fine fish and breads", "too little
room" and too much noise; they're best enjoyed by those
who "love the snotty waiters", sidewalk seating (DC) and
"private dining in the wine rooms."

PROVENCE   25 | 24 | 20 | $48
2401 Pennsylvania Ave., NW (L St.), 202-296-1166
▨ The "charm and beauty" of Provence is "on the plate" as
well as in the setting of Yannick Cam's West Ender; when
he's "on" (as he mostly is) his dishes "dazzle", but the
restaurant suffers from "superstar" success – it gets
"pressured" and "too loud" during busy times.

Queen Bee 🅂   22 | 12 | 18 | $17
3181 Wilson Blvd. (Washington Blvd.), Arlington, VA,
703-527-3444
◪ It's nearly "impossible to have a bad meal or spend much
more than $15" at this "homely" Clarendon Vietnamese; its
spring rolls and grilled meats shine, yet some can't "tune
out" the waits and "hurried" service.

RABIENG S
25 | 19 | 23 | $21

Glen Forest Shopping Ctr., 5892 Leesburg Pike (bet. Glen Forest Dr. & Payne St.), Falls Church, VA, 703-671-4222

■ Surprisingly edging out its showy cousin Duangrat as the *Survey*'s top Thai, this "understated", "often overlooked" sib focuses on food; here, one can explore the diversity of "regional Thai cooking" in a "quiet setting" where the "sparse decor and dismissive service don't matter" once the vivid, "spicy" tastes explode in your mouth.

Radio Free Italy S
15 | 12 | 14 | $17

The Torpedo Factory, 5 Cameron St. (Union St.), Alexandria, VA, 703-683-0361

☑ This entrepreneurial Old Towner bids for your frequency with Potomac views from outdoor tables, lotsa inexpensive Italian food, a $10 wine list and thoughtful touches like giving kids pizza dough to play with and letting them eat at a discount (or Wednesday after 5 PM for free); the consensus is "variable-quality food, consistently great views."

Raku ◑ S
– | – | – | I

1900 Q St., NW (19th St.), 202-265-7258

Jammed from day one, Mark Miller's Asian street food cafe concept is shaking down in Dupont Circle before being syndicated nationwide"; it's a New Wave "wow" with pre-fab food – a mix 'n' match of noodles, salads, skewers and dumplings prepared off-site – lots of "tight" solo seating and a "tiny tab"; early reports are "promising" provided you "stick with the staff's" advice.

Red Hot & Blue S
20 | 15 | 17 | $17

1120 19th St., NW (bet. L & M Sts.), 202-466-6731
1600 Wilson Blvd. (Pierce St.), Arlington, VA, 703-276-7427
Canterbury Ctr., 8637 Sudley Rd. (bet. Rtes. 234 & 28), Manassas, VA, 703-330-4847
3014 Wilson Blvd. (Highland St.), Arlington, VA, 703-243-1510 (carryout only)
208 Elden St. (near Herndon Pkwy.), Herndon, VA, 703-318-7427
16811 Crabbs Branch Way (Shady Grove Rd.), Gaithersburg, MD, 301-948-7333
677 Main St. (Rte. 216), Laurel, MD, 301-953-1943

■ "Elvis eats here" ... well, if he could, chances are he'd find that the "excellent" Memphis-style ribs, rings and sides ("those baked beans!") dished out at these too-popular, "picnic"-like BBQ joints meet a Tennessean's "high standard" at a "great price"; he'd even enjoy the sounds.

Red River Grill S
10 | 13 | 13 | $18

201 Massachusetts Ave., NE (bet. 2nd & 3rd Sts.), 202-546-7200

☑ An after-work scrum for "preppy congressional aides", its Southwestern aspirations are more evident in the stagey decor and "exotic"-sounding specials than what's slapped on the plate; most call it "mediocre" and best if you stick to the Tex-Mex basics and beer.

RED SAGE S
22 26 20 $36

605 14th St., NW (F St.), 202-638-4444

More than 1,100 surveyors attest to the long burn of Mark Miller's megamillion-dollar chili palace; whether upstairs for casual, more affordable snacking and a "great bar scene" or a "treat-yourself evening" in the Disneyesque dining room downstairs, his showmanship and imagination "bring excitement" to SW cuisine; that the portions are "measly", the help occasionally "arrogant" or that everything is "spicy" hasn't diminished the heavy traffic.

Red Sea ◗ S
20 14 18 $18

2463 18th St., NW (Kalorama Rd.), 202-483-5000

In nice weather, this Adams Morgan Ethiopian's outdoor seating gives it an edge over nearby compatriots; the food isn't for timid palates, but "you can't beat the price" and "eating with your hands can be fun" with the right group.

Red Tomato Cafe S
21 19 19 $19

4910 St. Elmo Ave. (bet. Old Georgetown & Norfolk Rds.), Bethesda, MD, 301-652-4499

With its "adorable" brick-oven pizzas, sampler platters, "trendy" wine bar and "down-to-earth" attitude, this "cute", "casual", "low-cost" Bethesda Cal-Ital sounds "promising"; let's see how it grows.

Renato S
19 18 19 $27

10120 River Rd. (Potomac Pl.), Potomac, MD, 301-365-1900

Potomac's "perfect" osteria – "overpriced but charming" – with great pizza, pasta and seafood (especially "when Nicky cooks"); it "can't grow fast enough" to suit a neighborhood willing to suffer "knee-to-knee" dining and being elbowed out by "important walk-ins."

RIO GRANDE CAFE S
21 18 18 $20

4301 N. Fairfax Dr. (Glebe Rd.), Arlington, VA, 703-528-3131
Reston Town Ctr., 1827 Library St. (Reston Pkwy.), Reston, VA, 703-904-0703
4919 Fairmont Ave. (Old Georgetown Rd.), Bethesda, MD, 301-656-2981

It's always party time at these Tex-Mex "theme parks"; the menu is "limited to the great stuff" (fajitas, quesadillas, cabrito), they consistently "do well" and you "can't get a better deal"; were it not for the "painful" queue and clatter, people would eat here "three times a week."

Ristorante Capri S
16 17 17 $27

4871 Cordell Ave. (Norfolk Ave.), Bethesda, MD, 301-654-8333

Though this Italian is welcomed for "casually refined" patio dining and an accommodating, Mediterranean-feeling room, it's rapped for inconsistency and inability to cope with the "Bethesda crush"; a new, ambitious chef and manager (post-*Survey*) is good news – the place needs to "work on service and timing."

RITZ-CARLTON, THE GRILL S   24 | 25 | 25 | $40
Ritz-Carlton at Pentagon City, 1250 South Hayes St. (bet. 15th St. & Army Navy Dr.), Arlington, VA, 703-415-5000

■ "Dining in the grand manner" at this luxury hotel's "gorgeous" Contemporary American dining room, with "lots of space for conversation" and "excellent food", is a great way to "conduct business" and even better for "special occasions"; the "languorous elegance" of afternoon tea is the perfect antidote to a Pentagon City shopping spree.

RITZ-CARLTON, THE RESTAURANT S   23 | 25 | 24 | $38
Ritz-Carlton at Tysons II, 1700 Tysons Blvd. (Galleria, International Blvd.), McLean, VA, 703-506-4300x7488

■ "An oasis in VA . . . or anywhere", this hunt-clubby hotel dining room epitomizes "quiet elegance" with the "finest service" and "beautifully presented" Continental food; the Friday night seafood spread and Sunday brunch buffet are "special occasion" treats — as is the "best English tea."

River Club S   19 | 22 | 19 | $40
3223 K St., NW (bet. Wisconsin Ave. & 32nd St.), 202-333-8118

◪ Dust off your dancing shoes, dress to the nines and head for deco glamour, champagne and caviar in Georgetown; known mainly for dancing, and for 'backside of 40' romancing, this "classy" supper club's Continental fare "can surprise" — and it's still the "best place to seduce your wife."

Rockland's S   22 | 12 | 16 | $15
2418 Wisconsin Ave., NW (Calvert St.), 202-333-2558
4000 Fairfax Dr. (Quincy St.), Arlington, VA, 703-528-9663

■ "Perfect" BBQ ribs, chicken, meats and veggies, "surprisingly tender grilled fish", "great sides", "free nuts" and the world's largest collection of hot sauces are all reasons to frequent this Glover Park carryout and eat-in counter; at its Arlington locale, you can even sit down.

Roof Terrace Kennedy Center S   17 | 22 | 18 | $38
Kennedy Ctr., 2700 F St. (New Hampshire Ave.), 202-416-8555

◪ Ticketholders "can't beat the convenience or the view" (or the curtain-timed service) at this Kennedy Center rooftop dining room; so word that "a new chef" is "improving" the Contemporary American food gets a round of applause; its "leisurely" Sunday brunch has always been a hit.

Royal Dragon S   ▽ 17 | 12 | 17 | $17
(fka Moshe Dragon)
Randolph Hills Shopping Ctr., 4840 Bollingbrook Pkwy. (Nicholson Ln.), Rockville, MD, 301-468-1922

◪ "When you need kosher Chinese", this uninviting Rockville eatery is probably your only choice; its certified kitchen woks out kosher versions of Chinese and American menu staples; until the staff cleans up its "sloppy" act, however, many carry out.

R.T.'s S

| 24 | 15 | 21 | $27 |

3804 Mt. Vernon Ave. (Glebe Rd.), Alexandria, VA,
703-684-6010

■ This neighborly pub in a "grubby" Alexandria 'hood serves some of the "best, unhealthy" New Orleans–style seafood around; it's "great for a casual evening" and, given the "high quality" fare, "a great buy."

R.T.'s Seafood Kitchen S

| 18 | 15 | 18 | $23 |

Courthouse Plaza, 2300 Clarendon Blvd. (bet. Barton St. & Courthouse Rd.), Arlington, VA, 703-841-0100

■ "Cholesterol never tasted so good" except, of course, at the original Alexandria R.T.'s; this Courthouse Plaza copy, with its "faux New Orleans" look, "pleasant" patio and "similar" Creole-Cajun menu, "falls short" of its parent foodwise, but it's "convenient."

RUPPERTS

| 26 | 21 | 25 | $40 |

1017 7th St., NW (bet. New York Ave. & L St.),
202-783-0699

■ "Just showing up" at this "cutting-edge" Contemporary American "confirms that you are a true DC insider"; it's doing some of the "best serious" cooking in town and everything from the "sparse, romantic room" to the "helpful" if overly "enthusiastic" staff is pretty much "just as it should be" (and priced accordingly) – that is, until one hits the not-yet-gentrified street.

Ruth's Chris Steak House S

| 24 | 21 | 22 | $39 |

1801 Connecticut Ave., NW (S St.), 202-797-0033
2231 Crystal Dr. (23rd St.), Crystal City, VA, 703-979-7275

◪ A safe bet for an "outstanding steak", this franchise's "sizzlicious", butter-drenched beef is top quality and "they know how to treat customers like no one else"; although they lack the "personality" of comparable steakhouses like Morton's or The Palm (notwithstanding Crystal City's "superb view"), they're "consistently good at what they do."

Sabang S

| 20 | 17 | 19 | $21 |

2504 Ennalls Ave. (Georgia Ave.), Wheaton, MD,
301-942-7859

◪ Novices find Indonesian food "interesting, like a cross between Indian and Chinese", a bit "oily" and more than a bit hot; if that sounds appealing, try this "attractive", "modest" "jewel hidden in a Wheaton strip mall"; but note that some find the "rice table [sampler] disappointing."

Saigon Gourmet S

| 22 | 16 | 21 | $19 |

2635 Connecticut Ave., NW (Calvert St.), 202-265-1360

◪ Surveyors debate whether this Woodley Park Vietnamese is DC's "best" (when you know what to order, i.e. shrimp rolls, fish) or merely very good (and boosted by "superior service"); either way, you get a "pleasant, inexpensive" meal

Saigon Inn 🇸   20 | 14 | 19 | $15 |
2614 Connecticut Ave. (Calvert St), 202-483-8400
2928 M St. (30th St), 202-337-5588
■ The 'four dishes for $4.50' lunch specials at these "eager" Vietnamese places in Georgetown and Woodley Park give tourists on budgets a break; they're "small" and "simple", with some good plates (spring rolls, caramel pork) and prices that are "worth the wait."

Saigonnais 🇸   20 | 16 | 18 | $22 |
2307 18th St., NW (Belmont Rd.), 202-232-5300
■ This "tranquil" Vietnamese on Adams Morgan's main drag is "treasured" for its "lovely atmosphere and exquisite cuisine" served "with balletic grace"; but be aware that the pace is andante and it's "more expensive than most."

Sala Thai 🇸   21 | 15 | 19 | $19 |
2016 P St., NW (20th St., near Dupont Circle), 202-872-1144
☑ Many find the pungent Thai standards as "tasteful" as the "lavender" decor at this "efficient lunch stop" in an "unassuming basement" off Dupont Circle; it seems like "they work hard to do things better than necessary" – though possibly less so lately.

Sam & Harry's   24 | 23 | 24 | $41 |
1200 19th St., NW (bet. M & N Sts.), 202-296-4333
■ "Honesty compels high marks" for this "polished" Dupont Circle steakhouse with top-notch beef, a "great prime rib and wine selection" and a "more diverse menu" than most; its power-dining patrons go for the "clubby ambiance", but a few enjoy themselves elsewhere more.

Sam Woo 🇸   20 | 16 | 18 | $20 |
1054 Rockville Pike (Edmonds St.), Rockville, MD, 301-424-0495
☑ "Luscious California rolls" draw Rockville workers to this commodious Korean-Japanese's lunch buffet ($7.40); as for the extensive Korean menu, "you don't always know what you're going to get" – but it's likely to be "quick", "spicy" and "good", if a bit "pricey."

Santa Fe East 🇸   20 | 21 | 19 | $26 |
110 S. Pitt St. (bet. King & Prince Sts.), Alexandria, VA, 703-548-6900
☑ With its secluded courtyard, intimate rooms and "great fireplace", this historic Alexandria building "is a setting you'd mistake for Santa Fe"; but last year's departure of chef Alison Swope has left reviewers less certain about the Southwestern fare: "food and service by Jekyll and Hyde."

Sarinah Satay House 🇸   18 | 19 | 17 | $22 |
1338 Wisconsin Ave., NW (bet. N & O Sts.), 202-337-2955
■ Rainforest-inspired greenery and a cozy fireplace lend romance to a leisurely Indonesian meal at this Georgetown hideaway; it's an unusual place with "interesting" cuisine where one goes for the ambiance more than for the food.

89

Savory S   17 | 20 | 14 | $11
7071 Carroll Ave. (Columbia Ave.), Takoma Park, MD, 301-270-2233
◪ A budding 'hood "haunt" with big, comfy couches to sink into while enjoying "big coffee drinks", homemade desserts, sandwiches and heated-up bistro fare; as a "limited" operation (counter service/precooked food) it's "good", but Takoma Park still "needs a real restaurant."

Sea Catch   21 | 21 | 20 | $34
Canal Sq., 1054 31st St., NW (M St.), 202-337-8855
◪ The "best tables on the canal", "marvelous" mussels at the raw bar, booths by the fire and "high-quality" seafood – this Georgetowner has "so much potential"; yet it feels "a bit industrial and impersonal", and "with the canal empty" (pending repairs), so is this "watering hole."

SEASONS S   27 | 26 | 26 | $49
Four Seasons Hotel, 2800 Pennsylvania Ave., NW (29th St.), 202-944-2000
■ The city's "best hotel restaurant", a "stylish retreat" in Georgetown, wows a "sophisticated clientele" with its "light" Contemporary American food and "extremely knowledgeable" staff; respondents rave: "as close to perfect as can be", "in heaven they serve the Sunday brunch seven days a week."

Sequoia ☽S   17 | 24 | 17 | $28
3000 K St., NW (Washington Harbour), 202-944-4200
◪ "Major drink scene" doesn't begin to describe the bedlam on the panoramic terrace of this Washington Harbour American on a warm summer night; and since one of DC's most "spectacular" settings has pressured help and a kitchen geared for "factory line production", it works best for "gazing", grazing and brunch.

Sesto Sento S   19 | 18 | 17 | $28
1214 18th St., NW (bet. M St. & Jefferson Pl.), 202-785-9525
◪ A "real Italian restaurant" near Dupont Circle with "real Italians" serving "sensibly priced", "authentic food" in a "European atmosphere" at lunch or dinner; "after 11 PM", it becomes a "flashy", "smoky", "Euro-hip", "nightlife" scene; the one constant is that it's "uneven."

701 S   24 | 24 | 23 | $36
701 Pennsylvania Ave., NW (7th St.), 202-393-0701
■ It all comes together at this "most civilized", "elegant" Downtown New American, where its "memorable" service and "imaginative" fare complement the "lovely", "spacious" room; hundreds of "grown-ups" have fallen in "love" with the "night views" from the terrace, the "power" buzz at lunch, the "cool green" champagne bar, "the way its run" and, especially, the fact that it's "not overpriced."

Seven Seas [S] | 20 | 12 | 17 | $19 |
Federal Plaza, 1776 E. Jefferson St. (bet. Montrose & Rollins Aves.), Rockville, MD, 301-770-5020
◪ It's "not worth going all the way" to this "dingy" Rockville Chinese to "order egg foo young"; but if you're looking for some of the area's "best, freshest seafood" prepared in "unusual, interesting" ways, ask this Taiwanese about the specials on its Chinese menu.

1789 [S] | 25 | 26 | 24 | $46 |
1226 36th St., NW (Prospect St.), 202-965-1789
■ Old Washington "charm amid the hustle and bustle of Georgetown" – this historic townhouse has always had "atmosphere and then some", and now that chef Ris Lacoste (ex Kinkead's) "has done her magic", the regional American cuisine is "even better than it was before"; in a place where "excellence is the norm", a "most romantic, delicious dinner is guaranteed."

Shamshiry [S] ▽ | 21 | 15 | 17 | $18 |
8607 Westwood Ctr. Dr. (Leesburg Pike), Vienna, VA, 703-448-8883
◪ "An incredible find – if you can find" this Persian hidden in a Vienna shopping strip; its "wonderful" flavored rice dishes and "fabulous" kebabs are "great for quick takeout" or you can join local Iranians and "enthusiastic" staff in the simple, decorative room; either way, you'll get a "huge amount of food for the buck."

Shelly's Woodroast [S] | 18 | 23 | 20 | $21 |
Congressional Shopping Ctr., 1699 Rockville Pike (Halpine Rd.), Rockville, MD, 301-984-3300
◪ Decorated like "the Northwoods brought in from the cold", this showpiece lodge on Rockville Pike generates long lines and mixed reviews; its "novel" menu of wood-roasted ("smoky") meats and fish is definitely "high gravity" (lumberjack "heavy") and short of a pricey, "full-blown dinner", some find little to eat; others are pleased by "surprisingly good food" and service "in a casual, woodsy setting."

Shiney's Kabab House [S] ⊭ ▽ | 18 | 8 | 14 | $12 |
(fka Asian Kabab House)
1108 K St., NW (bet. 11th & 12th Sts.), 202-637-9770
■ "Recommended by cab drivers" for "satisfying" kebabs wrapped in "wonderful" baked-to-order flatbreads, this Downtown Formica dive defines "cheap, cheap eats"; new management post-*Survey* has spiced up the deal with an all-you-can-eat Pakistani buffet ($4.95 for lunch, $5.95 for dinner).

Shiro-ya S   ▽ 24 | 16 | 20 | $23
2512 L St. (bet. 25th St. & Pennsylvania Ave.), 202-659-9449
◼ This "peaceful retreat" with "superfresh sushi" and an authentic Japanese menu is something of a West End neighborhood secret – aficionados swear it "blows away" the competition; but while prices may reflect the food's "quality", they're a bit steep for every day and communication "could be improved."

Silverado S   – | – | – | M
Magruder's Shopping Ctr., 7052 Columbia Pike (Evergreen Ln.), Annandale, VA, 703-354-4560
In Annandale (replacing Fritzbie's), the Great American Restaurants group has corralled another crowd-pleaser – an open-range, cowboy-themed bistro that adds SW spicing to a please-all, Contemporary American menu.

Silver Diner ◐ S   14 | 16 | 16 | $13
11806 Rockville Pike (bet. Montrose & Old Georgetown Rds.), Rockville, MD, 301-770-2828
14550 Baltimore Ave. (Cherry Ln.), Laurel, MD, 301-470-6080
12251 Silver Diner Pl. (W. Ox Rd. & Fair Lakes Pkwy.), Fairfax, VA, 22033
8101 Fletcher St. (International Dr.), McLean, VA, 703-821-5666
Potomac Mills Mall, 14375 Smoketown Rd., Dale City, VA, 703-491-7376
◼ Almost everyone likes the "modern diner concept" – a "convenient" place for a "grilled cheese and milk shake", "homestyle" cooking and gooey chocolate cake, with "lots of menu choices", late hours and a noisy ambiance that distracts "toddlers"; these '50s "flashbacks" are a fair (not great) substitute for the "real thing."

Skewers/Cafe Luna S   19 | 15 | 18 | $17
1633 P St., NW (bet. 16th & 17th Sts.), 202-387-7400
◼ Dupont Circle East Mediterranean offering just what the neighborhood wants – cheap, healthy, "hot grub when you need it", a place for "starry-eyed couples" to brunch, with easygoing management that "never kicks you out"; while its upstairs Middle Eastern restaurant and downstairs informal cafe have "separate" identities, they function in tandem as an artistic and literary hub.

Slade's S   15 | 14 | 16 | $18
7201 Wisconsin Ave. (Willow Ave.), Bethesda, MD, 301-951-8541
Montgomery Mall, 7101 Democracy Blvd. (Rte. 270), Bethesda, MD, 301-469-0690
Tysons I, 7943-B Tysons Corner Ctr. (Rtes. 7 & 123), Tysons Corner, VA, 703-760-9030

Slade's (Cont.)
Ballston Commons, 4238 N. Wilson Blvd. (N. Glebe Rd.),
Arlington, VA, 703-243-8830
◪ Though some say these "shopping mall" eateries "define
mediocrity", they're "ok in a pinch" for a burger and beer,
grilled chicken salad, "pretty good" ribs or other "standard"
American fare; patron enthusiasm depends on what else
is available ("visit only if the food court is full").

Southside 815 S   18 | 17 | 18 | $19
815 S. Washington St. (bet. Franklin & Green Sts.),
Alexandria, VA, 703-836-6222
■ "Cholesterol à la carte", but how "comforting" it is to
dig into low-country shortcake (cornbread, roast chicken,
oysters, mashed potatoes and succotash gravy) and
similar "delicious", over-the-top, "Southern-style" dishes
at this "homey" Alexandria bar off the Old Town beaten
track; minority reports of "inconsistent food" and service
are a downside.

Spices S   20 | 15 | 17 | $20
3333-A Connecticut Ave., NW (bet. Macomb &
Newark Sts.), 202-686-3833
■ In "tight" Cleveland Park quarters, this Pan-Asian
does a "good job" at the seemingly "impossible task"
of reproducing the "street food" of a "panoply" of distinctive
cuisines (including sushi); since its dark, "Tokyo"-like
premises get "crowded" and "service can be slow",
consider takeout or delivery.

Stage Door S   ▽ 14 | 13 | 16 | $19
1433 P St., NW (bet. 14th & 15th Sts.), 202-234-4050
■ "Definitely downscale", but welcome in a gritty DC
area with lots of exciting theaters and few places to eat;
this "friendly" American bistro has a lively "burgers and
bar scene", stays open late on weekends and "tries hard
to please" – bravo!

Starke's Head Hog BBQ S   19 | 10 | 18 | $15
7003 Wisconsin Ave. (Walsh St.), Bethesda, MD,
301-907-9110
■ Even if you're not a 'Skins fan, you gotta love the
hog-sized portions of "lean" juicy ribs, pulled pork and
"good" sides dished up by George and company in what
looks like a cross between a sports bar and his kitchen;
but, as you'd expect, a Dallas contingent doesn't agree:
"George tries hard, but he'll eat anything."

Star of Siam 🅂   18   14   17 $19
2446 18th St., NW (Columbia Rd.), 202-986-4133
1136 19th St., NW (bet. L & M Sts.), 202-785-2838
International Pl., 1735 N. Lynn St. (N. 19th St.), Rosslyn,
VA, 703-524-1208
✉ These "upmarket" Thais are known for "boldly" spiced
curries and not much else; one has the "best rooftop in
Adams Morgan" ("food doesn't match"), Rosslyn has a "nice
atmosphere", and Downtown DC's most "redeeming quality"
is the chance to "sit outside" for an inexpensive lunch.

State of the Union   13   17   14 $14
1357 U St. (bet. 13th & 14th Sts.), 202-588-8810
✉ "Hang out in front with Gen X intellectuals or shake
your booty in the back with DC's best DJs" at this "hip,
happening" New U place; however, most advise skipping
the Russian "gulag fare" and settling for "cool jazz" and
other live sounds, "many vodkas" and "funky decor."

Stella's 🅂   18   20   18 $22
1725 Duke St. (across from King St. Metro Station),
Alexandria, VA, 703-519-1946
■ "A new chef [Alison Swope, ex Santa Fe East] and a new
menu do wonders" for this "WWII canteen" in Alexandria;
her "mouthwatering" Southwestern and Contemporary
American cooking provides a lively contrast to the '40s
memorabilia on the walls and pleasant outdoor dining; now
"Stella" needs to invigorate the servers.

St. Elmos Cafe 🅂   15   15   15 $25
7820 Norfolk Ave. (St. Elmos St.), Bethesda, MD, 301-657-1607
✉ While this "nondescript" French bistro in Bethesda
"sometimes succeeds" in offering a "pleasant", "relaxing"
meal, it's often "more expensive than you would think"
appropriate for "undistinguished" food and service; the
"nice sidewalk cafe" is inviting, inside is "very beige."

Stone Manor 🅂   ▽ 25   27   27 $54
5820 Carroll Boyer Rd., Middletown, MD, 301-473-5454
■ Celebrating an occasion at this historic stone house
outside Frederick is "very special"; its "lovely", set-
price Contemporary American menus are crafted with
"imagination" and matched with fine wines and service;
the setting itself – a blazing fire in an elegant dining room – is
premium, as is the price.

Straits of Malaya 🅂   21   17   18 $22
1836 18th St., NW (T St.), 202-483-1483
✉ On a moonlit night, the romance of this Adams Morgan
Malaysian's rooftop terrace and the "exotic flavors and
textures" of its food can transport you to the Far East; most
other nights, you'll "eat well" if you "follow the waiter's
recommendation" and are prepared for a few glitches – that
goes for the pace and the taste; "when it's good, it's great."

Sunny Garden S | 19 | 9 | 15 | $15

1302 E. Gude Dr. (S. Law Rd.), Rockville, MD, 301-762-7477
350 Fortune Terrace (Seven Lock), Potomac, MD, 301-294-4578 ◐

◪ "Don't judge a book by its cover" or a Chinese restaurant by its overly "bright" appearance and "out-of-the-way" Rockville location; this Taiwanese, which has been a local "premier Chinese" for the past several years, insists that new owners haven't changed anything; if you "order from the Chinese menu with help from a waitress" you can judge for yourself – or try the new (unrated) Potomac location.

Sushi Chalet S | 20 | 13 | 19 | $22

Festival Shopping Ctr., 323 Muddy Branch Rd. (Great Seneca Hwy.), Gaithersburg, MD, 301-945-7373

■ When a Korean sushi shop in a Gaithersburg mall is SRO at 2:30 PM on Saturday, it's an indication that the buffet is a "real bargain" – and it is, offering some 20 kinds of sushi, salads, soups and homestyle Korean dishes for $6.96 at lunch, $14.95 at dinner; sure, it's "fast food" and the "wrong atmosphere for sushi, but what a deal."

Sushi-Ko S | 24 | 15 | 20 | $27

2307 Wisconsin Ave., NW (south of Calvert St.), 202-333-4187

■ "DC's best sushi" comes with "typical lack of ambiance" (just like in Tokyo) in Glover Park; it's "very fresh, expertly prepared" and "innovative", as are the "East meets West appetizers", daily specials and classic noodle soups; rather than choose, the area's top chefs simply put themselves in Kaz's (chef Kazuhiro Okochi) hands – you should too.

Szechuan Gallery S | ▽ 21 | 11 | 18 | $19

617 H St., NW (bet. 6th & 7th Sts.), 202-898-1180

■ "Go for the green Taiwanese menu" at this Chinatown Chinese and you "won't get hurt"; the Szechuan dishes are "tasty" too, offering "value for the price", and the "lightning quick" service is no hardship given the absence of decor.

Tabard Inn S | 22 | 22 | 20 | $29

Tabard Inn, 1739 N St., NW (bet. 17th & 18th Sts.), 202-833-2668

■ "For years", this "endearingly worn" hotel off Dupont Circle has charmed DC with its "down-at-the-heels" demeanor and "good", "simple" (albeit somewhat "pricey" and "inconsistent") Eclectic food; there's no place like it for "cocktails by the fire" or a left-wing "power lunch."

TABERNA DEL ALABARDERO | 25 | 26 | 25 | $44

1776 I St., NW (18th St.), 202-429-2200

■ The Spanish traditions of "la buena mesa" (the good table) and "gracious dining" come to life at this "elegant" K Street Madrileño; it's a "dazzling" setting for sampling the regional delights of an earthy yet refined cuisine, for pampering by "DC's most courteous waiters" and for spying "who's who in close quarters" – "if price is no object."

TACHIBANA S   25 | 15 | 19 | $26
6715 Lowell Ave. (Emerson Ave.), McLean, VA, 703-847-7771
■ "Generous slices" of very fresh fish at its "top-notch sushi bar", extremely "light tempura", "excellent udon" and sukiyaki, all "reasonably priced" and served in a welcoming atmosphere – the area's "best" Japanese "really has everything" it does down pat; and now that its McLean relocation (post-*Survey*) gives it "facilities" it lacked, there are "high hopes" for it to do even more.

Taipei/Tokyo Cafe S ∌   21 | 7 | 11 | $12
Metro Ctr. Plaza, 11510-A Rockville Pike (Nicholson Ln.), Rockville, MD, 301-881-8388
■ "Arrive hungry, leave stuffed" – it's no wonder Rockville "lives" at this Sino-Japanese storefront; everything from "Hiro's fresh sushi" to the "huge" bowls of noodle soup to tempura and veggie stir-fries are "made from scratch" with "fresh ingredients" and are a "tremendous bargain"; service (at least on the Chinese "side") and decor are definitely not why it's "always packed."

Tako Grill S   23 | 15 | 18 | $23
7756 Wisconsin Ave. (Cheltenham Rd.), Bethesda, MD, 301-652-7030
■ While this stylish Japanese slices some of Bethesda's "best" sushi, its selling point is the variety of "little stuff" (grilled fish and vegetables) along with soba and other noodle dishes that encourage sampler meals; hopefully, its post-*Survey* remodeling will ease the crowding and pressure on the sometimes "harried" help.

Tara Thai S   24 | 22 | 20 | $22
4828 Bethesda Ave. (bet. Arlington Rd. & Wisconsin Ave.), Bethesda, MD, 301-657-0488
226 Maple Ave. W. (bet. Lawyer's Rd. & Nutley St.), Vienna, VA, 703-255-2467
■ These "aquatic"-themed "Asians with atmosphere" provide a "nice meal at an affordable price" in the suburbs – a commodity so prized that "reservations are a must"; still, by most accounts, their swimmingly "fresh" fish, boldly accented Thai dishes and "competent" crew live up to the "exciting" high-tech decor.

TASTE OF SAIGON S   26 | 20 | 22 | $20
410 Hungerford Dr. (Beall Ave.), Rockville, MD, 301-424-7222
■ The area's "No. 1 Vietnamese meets all criteria" – the "extensive menu has many, many hits", the "pleasant" Rockville dining room is run by a "family" of pros and, although Grandmother Ma Tu has retired from the kitchen, the "black pepper dishes and appetizers" are still major reasons why it's way too "hard to get in."

Taste Of Thai S
| – | – | – | I |

Fairfax Circle Plaza, 9534 Arlington Blvd. (¹/₂ mi. south of Fairfax Circle), Fairfax, VA, 703-352-4494

Those willing to forgo the glossy decor of nearby Tara Thai will find the food at least "as good" and at "better prices" at this attractive, "gracious", family-run restaurant in Fairfax; we're told it has the "best pad Thai on earth", but be sure to ask about the charcoal-baked fish and other specialties.

Taverna Cretekou S
| 21 | 20 | 20 | $26 |

818 King St. (bet. Alfred & Columbus Sts.), Alexandria, VA, 703-548-8688

■ This "pretty" Greek taverna is "sometimes too small for the people who love it" – especially for festive weekend dinners or "brunch al fresco" in the arbored Old Town courtyard; credit its convincing 'opa' ambiance, with "dancing and singing by waiters", hearty homestyle cooking and a welcome that says "come hungry and don't hurry."

Teaism S
| – | – | – | M |

2009 R St., NW (Connecticut Ave.), 202-667-3827

Steeped in ancient tradition, this beautifully handcrafted Asian teahouse provides a soothing contrast to Dupont Circle coffee bars and bustle; its extensive selection of teas, made-to-order tandoori breads, kebabs, salads, sandwiches, stir-fries and luscious American desserts can be paired for an anytime snack or meal, eaten in its handsome upstairs lounge or taken home.

Tel Aviv Cafe S
| 16 | 16 | 16 | $21 |

4869 Cordell Ave. (Norfolk Ave.), Bethesda, MD, 301-718-9068

■ At the epicenter of Bethesda's "maddening crowds" is this Middle Eastern, which started out as an "open-air" cafe/carryout with "good falafel", appetizers and kosher grills; now it's action central for "Jewish singles" (Thursday night) and a place for "well-dressed suburbanites" to "be seen"; eating is no longer the point, although one Zionist quips that it all tastes like a "Palestinian plot to discredit Israeli food."

Tempo S
| 22 | 15 | 21 | $30 |

4231 Duke St. (N. Gordon St.), Alexandria, VA, 703-370-7900

◪ "An odd place" refers to the locale, "a converted Alexandria gas station", as well as the "blend of California, Italy" and the Southwest that the "different chefs" (usually the "friendly owners") bring to the menu; given the "tight space" on weekends, the neighbors are just as happy that a few surveyors think their "gem" is "just ok."

Terramar [S] 20 | 20 | 19 | $28

7800 Wisconsin Ave. (Cheltenham Dr.), Bethesda, MD, 301-654-0888

◪ The tapas served at this "congenial" Bethesda Latin are "fun to play with", "varied enough to warrant frequent visits" and supplemented by "tasty" entrees; the "airy, open", Spanish-feeling setting encourages conversation and turns lively with "entertainment on weekends"; however, some find it merely "pleasant, that's all."

T.G.I. Friday's 🌙 [S] 14 | 14 | 15 | $15

2100 Pennsylvania Ave. (21st St., NW), 202-872-4344
1201 Pennsylvania Ave., NW (1 block north of Federal Triangle Metro Station), 202-628-8443
7401 Sudley Rd. (Nicholson St.), Manassas, VA, 703-330-8333
13071 Worldgate Dr. (Elden St.), Herndon, VA, 703-787-9630
4650 King St. (N. Beauregard St.), Alexandria, VA, 703-931-4101
2070 Chain Bridge Rd. (Old Courthouse Rd.), Tysons Corner, VA, 703-556-6160
13225 Worth Ave. (across from Potomac Mills), Woodbridge, VA, 703-492-0090
12147 Rockville Pike (Twinbrook Pkwy.), Rockville, MD 301-231-9048
6460 Capitol Dr. (Greenbelt Rd.), Greenbelt, MD, 301-345-2503
14600 Baltimore Ave. (Cherry Ln.), Laurel, MD, 301-498-8443

◪ You know "what you're going to get" at these "kid-and-carnivore-friendly" fern bars – "nothing special" eats like burgers, salads and "finger food" plus "spotty service" from aggressively "cheerful" help; they're a "relatively cheap place to take relatives" (and secretaries) to lunch, though "on the Fifth Day, God didn't create them."

T.H.A.I. [S] 22 | 24 | 22 | $21

Village at Shirlington, 4029 S. 28th St. (Randolph St.), Arlington, VA, 703-931-3203

■ With its "handsome and inviting" interior, "jazzy" cuisine interpretations and attractively plated fare, Shirlington's Thai is a "beautiful presentation" of a restaurant; most are delighted to have an ethnic eatery with "real decor" and are hopeful that start-up food and service glitches "will improve."

Thai Flavor [S] ▽ 21 | 14 | 21 | $21

2605 Connecticut Ave. (Calvert St.), 202-745-2000

■ Some of its customers lost track of this "very good" Thai when it moved to a bigger space with a sidewalk cafe in Woodley Park; they're missing out on flavorful, Chinese-influenced food, an "excellent buffet" and the "nice people" who run it.

Thai Garden [S]

15 | 13 | 15 | $17

(fka Bangkok Orchid)
301 Massachusetts Ave., NE (3rd St.), 202-546-5900

◪ Congressional staffers "desperate for Thai on the Hill" and a cheap lunch buffet vote both ways on the food at this entry: "competent fare at a good price" and "eager to please" vs. "horrible" and "service is often rude"; takeout, delivery or eating on the patio is advised to avoid the "cheesy decor"; N.B. a management change in the spring of 1996 could make it blossom.

Thai Kingdom [S]

22 | 17 | 21 | $20

2021 K St., NW (bet. 20th & 21st Sts.), 202-835-1700

◪ Business-class K Street Thai with "solid" virtues, i.e. "quick", "efficient", "reasonable" and "dependable", a large menu of "well-spiced" dishes and an authentically "overdecorated" room; assessments range from "superb" to "average", with a median of "good."

That's Amore [S]

19 | 16 | 18 | $21

Danor Plaza, 150 Branch Rd. (Rte. 123), Vienna, VA, 703-281-7777
15201 Shady Grove Rd. (Research Blvd.), Rockville, MD, 301-670-9666

◪ The family-style dining "gimmick" at these "bulk Italians" works only when you "go with a big appetite, a big crowd" and "every piece of Tupperware in the house for leftovers"; even then, everyone better love garlicky, heavy-duty food and a raucous "'50s" atmosphere – in short, this deal is "not for everyone."

Thyme Square [S]

– | – | – | M

4735 Bethesda Ave. (Woodmont Ave.), Bethesda, MD, 301-657-9077

Chalk up another "promising" venture to Mark Caraluzzi (American Cafe, Bistro Bistro), whose well-designed formats for everyday eats set trends; his latest, in Bethesda, combines "healthy" dining with a "bright Pottery Barn" setting, adaptations of favorite vegetable and fish dishes from all over the world and some sinfully delicious desserts.

Tia Queta [S]

19 | 16 | 20 | $22

8009 Norfolk Ave. (Old Georgetown Rd.), Bethesda, MD, 301-654-4443

■ Somewhat off the Bethesda beaten track (and looking "tired"), this "real" Mexican is worth finding for "authentic" fish dishes, "terrific tortilla soup", "classic" mole and a very "pleasant patio"; it's also worth mentioning that the "accommodating" staff has been there "forever", is "understanding" about "messy" kids and is willing to "custom-cook anything" – but it's relatively pricey.

Tiberio
22 | 22 | 20 | $42

1915 K St., NW (bet. 19th & 20th Sts.), 202-452-1915

☑ Time has faded the roses at this K Street Northern Italian "grande dame", but the kitchen experiences "flashes of its former glory" (notably with pastas) and the dining room was just gussied up; still, an increasing number find its "old-fashioned" luxury "overpriced" even now that prices have supposedly been lowered to 1976 levels.

Tivoli
22 | 21 | 22 | $31

1700 N. Moore St. (19th St.), Rosslyn, VA, 703-524-8900

■ "Everything's right" about this "consistently excellent" Continental – "fine" food, "living room" comfort, "wonderful service" and "very impressive desserts" – only its Rosslyn "location" holds it back; nevertheless, knowledgeable party planners count on its "professionalism", good prices and parking for pre-theater, quiet business, private events and "that special dinner" for two.

Tokyo Lighthouse S
– | – | – | M

Diamond Sq. Shopping Ctr., 22 Bureau Dr. (bet. Clopper Rd. & Quince Orchard Rd.), Gaithersburg, MD, 301-977-0988

Watching tableside chefs slicing and dicing their way through your teppanyaki dinner is "great entertainment"; equally appealing is a quiet sushi lunch; in Gaithersburg, where there's a shortage of comfortable, commodious restaurants, this Japanese is a beacon.

Tomato Tango S
– | – | – | I

Olney Towne Ctr., 18115 Towne Ctr. Dr. (Spartan Rd. & Rte. 108), Olney, MD, 301-570-5247

Even though this Cal-Ital pizza and pasta place sometimes gets "crowded" and "rushed", it meets the need for casual family and business dining in Olney with "tons of pasta" at "unbelievably" low prices.

Tom Tom S
17 | 19 | 16 | $21

2333 18th St., NW (bet. Belmont St. & Kalorama Rd.), 202-588-1300

☑ In Adams Morgan, you can't beat this "electric" summer rooftop with its "hip" help, "trendy" tapas, artists at work "before your eyes", relentless music and "good beer on tap"; in winter, the action moves indoors, where it's both "artsy" and "too Melrose Place" – anyone over 30 will experience "sensory overload."

Tony & Joe's Seafood Place S
16 | 19 | 16 | $28

Washington Harbour, 3000 K St., NW (30th St.), 202-944-4545

☑ Sweeping Potomac views and a waterfront bar "mob scene" that rivals Sequoia's are the bankable assets of this Washington Harbour seafooder; the "typical" food and service are "not as impressive" as the vista, but this doesn't detract when one is "sitting outside" for an "enjoyable" brunch or a solo lunch at the bar (inside is less "fun").

Tony Cheng's Mongolian [S] | 19 | 14 | 17 | $20 |
Tony Cheng's Seafood [S]
619 H St., NW (bet. 6th & 7th Sts.), 202-842-TONY
◩ "A reliable address in Chinatown" to take tourists or teens for an "all-you-can-eat", "build-your-own" Mongolian BBQ (choose ingredients to be stir-fried, grilled or steeped tableside in hot pots); local Sinophiles who find the "novelty has worn off" head upstairs for "excellent dim sum" and Taiwanese food.

Tragara [S] | 23 | 22 | 21 | $41 |
4935 Cordell Ave. (bet. Old Georgetown Rd. & Norfolk Ave.), Bethesda, MD, 301-951-4935
■ It's "elegant" and a "bit formal", yet Bethesda's "big-bucks Northern Italian" makes "you feel like you're in Italy" and ready to enjoy "a long meal"; that's due, in part, to the "pleasant" waiters, but mostly to chef Michel Laudier's "well-prepared", "attractively presented" food – look for his breads, lobster dishes and unusual frozen sweets.

Trattoria da Franco [S] ▽ | 22 | 19 | 19 | $29 |
305 S. Washington St. (Duke St.), Alexandria, VA, 703-548-9338
◩ One of several "cozy" restaurants that preserve Old Town's "neighborhood" feel, but either you take to its "warm, hokey atmosphere", pastas with pesto and "inspired veal" or it will seem like a "poor excuse for Italian"; it's very much owner Franco Abbruzetti's place – he even holds opera nights so he can sing.

Trattu | 21 | 16 | 21 | $26 |
1823 Jefferson Pl., NW (bet. Connecticut Ave. & 19th St.), 202-466-4570
■ "Thank goodness" this "sweet" Dupont Circle Italian is "still small, still good and still a [relative] secret" – it's "crowded" enough at lunch already and if the garlicky food were "better, portions bigger" and it got a "face-lift", the price might no longer be "right."

Trumpets [S] | 23 | 19 | 21 | $28 |
1603 17th St., NW (Q St.), 202-232-4141
■ Chef David Hagedorn's gay following is proud to share the "highest-quality New American cuisine east of Dupont Circle" with everyone; just go past the bar to the "dark", "funky" back dining room where his wittily presented, "creative, delicious food" comes at a "good price"; Sunday brunch ($12.95) with unlimited champagne is a good intro.

Tsukiji [S] | – | – | – | M |
Ritchie Shopping Ctr., 785-K Rockville Pike, Rockville, MD, 301-294-9160
Walk in the door of this tiny Rockville retreat and visit Japan; it's an understated, "wonderful place for sushi and other Japanese food delights" run by a lovely "family" who will bring you tea and make you feel at home.

Tuscana West 18 | 19 | 17 | $28

1350 I St., NW (bet. 13th & 14th Sts.), 202-289-7300

◪ Weekday biz lunches at this "flashy" Downtown neo-Tuscan are "often quite good", which means the food is "not [too] exciting . . . not [too] distracting" and not marred by the "indifferent, sometimes arrogant service" one can sometimes encounter here; those who go at night for happy hour, opera night (Thursdays) and dancing and dining (weekends) have more fun.

219 [S] 20 | 22 | 21 | $31

219 King St. (Fairfax St.), Alexandria, VA, 703-549-1141

■ On one of Old Town's busiest dining streets, this "picturesque" replica of "'50s New Orleans" entices passersby; here, "good Creole cooking" can be eaten in a "romantic dungeon", a "perfect" period parlor or a people-watching heated terrace; it's also a "great jazz place" and the "best bar" in town.

Two Quail [S] 21 | 24 | 21 | $30

320 Massachusetts Ave., NE (bet. 3rd & 4th Sts.), 202-543-8030

◪ The "table in the window" of this Capitol Hill Victorian is the "ultimate for romance" (and it's not just the privacy or the view); there's something seductive about this eatery's "quirky", decorative mix of Laura Ashley and "your crazy aunt's" attic, its equally quirky American food (albeit "not as outrageous" lately) and "solicitous" staff; very few disagree.

Udupi Palace [S] – | – | – | I

1325 University Blvd. (New Hampshire Ave.), Langley Park, MD, 301-434-1431

Southern India's extensive vegetarian cuisine offers a myriad of "unusual" taste sensations even though it's prepared without meat, fish or eggs; in Langley Park, this exemplar's long menu of "cheap, fabulous" dishes makes it "paradise" for anyone with a serious interest in food; no booze or decor.

Union Street Public House [S] 18 | 19 | 18 | $20

121 S. Union St. (bet. King & Prince Sts.), Alexandria, VA, 703-548-1785

◪ Don't be fooled by the weekend "Gen X" free-for-all at the bar (and resulting "scatterbrained" service); this "model American pub" sets a "standard for decent food at decent prices" in "pleasant surroundings" with the "best steak sandwich", oyster bar and "homemade butterscotch sundaes" in town, "good tap beers" and Southern-influenced cooking – bring "out-of-towners."

Uptown Cafe S   14 | 12 | 15 | $17
3311 Connecticut Ave., NW (bet. Macomb & Newark Sts.),
202-966-7462
☑ What you see is what you get at this open-to-the-street,
"cheap French bistro" in Cleveland Park; it has a drop-by
neighborhood bar, worn surroundings and old-fashioned
"cafe fare" (crêpes, quiche, "french fries with everything")
with enough "good dishes" to make the early-bird special
worthwhile; "better than expected" if you "don't expect
much" is the bottom line.

U-topia S   17 | 19 | 19 | $21
1418 U St., NW (bet. 14th & 15th Sts.), 202-483-7669
☑ The New U's "neighborhood" restaurant is "primarily a
bar" with live music that happens to serve "interesting"
Eclectic food; the "crowd", original art and "old bike
pictures" displayed against subdued modern walls are
major decorative elements.

Vegetable Garden S   19 | 15 | 18 | $18
11618 Rockville Pike (Old Georgetown Rd. &
Nicholson Ln.), Rockville, MD, 301-468-9301
☑ This "alternative" Chinese in Rockville makes a "good
effort" at presenting "healthy", "inexpensive" vegetarian
food in "relaxing" surroundings; since there are "so few
vegetarian eateries", it seems churlish to complain about
one of the area's best and most "creative", but "some
dishes taste distressingly the same" – "bland."

Veneziano S   21 | 17 | 20 | $30
2305 18th St., NW (Kalorama Rd.), 202-483-9300
■ "Fresh", authentically prepared food and "professional
service" keep patrons "happy" at this "middling" Northern
Italian; it's "relatively unknown" outside Adams Morgan
(largely due to the parking hassle), but its $13.95 early-bird/
late-supper menu, pasta and fagioli soup at lunch and more
than 200 grappas reward a visit.

VIDALIA   25 | 22 | 23 | $40
1990 M St., NW (bet. 19th & 20th Sts.), 202-659-1990
☑ Whether DC is "still a Southern town" is debatable, but it
certainly has an appetite for contemporary Dixie-accented
food in sophisticated, business-oriented surroundings;
possibly the "best" of the "sorta-Southern" contingent
has settled into a "well-appointed", "attentively" run, step-
down space on M Street "where what they do with onions"
(and "the check") "will bring tears to your eyes."

Vienna's Grille ◐ S
▽ 19 | 14 | 15 | $18

146 Maple Ave. E. (bet. Park & Center Sts.), Vienna, VA, 703-255-0800

■ Cajun-Creole food plus live music and a dance floor sounds like a winning combo for this 'New Orleans in Vienna' complex; throw in an impressive list of beers, a kitchen that has the "spice level" right (if not the "side dishes"), lots of discounts and nice people, and it adds up to a place that surveyors hope "stays open."

Vietnam S
▽ 22 | 13 | 21 | $19

4924 St. Elmos St. (Carter Ave.), Bethesda, MD, 301-656-2280

■ One of several new Vietnamese options in Bethesda comes in a "plain" wrapper and does a "very good" job with a long menu of grills, rice dishes, curries and pho; recommended choices include the "outrageous" special pancake, soups and appetizers.

Village Bistro S
24 | 16 | 20 | $25

Colonial Village, 1723 Wilson Blvd. (Quinn St.), Arlington, VA, 703-522-0284

■ A "gem", a "sleeper", a "surprise on Wilson Boulevard" – only our savvy surveyors would've found this "outstanding" French bistro in a "nondescript strip mall" (which houses several other worthwhile eateries); the "food has DC sophistication, but the restaurant has local warmth and prices"; ergo it's often "packed."

Vincenzo
21 | 20 | 19 | $35

(fka Trattoria "al Sole")

1606 20th St., NW (bet. Q St. & Connecticut Ave.), 202-667-0047

■ Recasting "the best of Old Vincenzo's at reasonable prices", one of DC's top Italians is now a "gracious, refined" setting for "exceptional seafood", delicate housemade noodles and regional pastas and entrees; there's also a "divine" private dining room that hosts classy events; its latest (post-*Survey*) format retains the trattoria pricing and menu diversity that "improved" it last year.

Virginia Beverage Co. S
– | – | – | M

607 King St. (bet. St. Asaph & S. Washington Sts.), Alexandria, VA, 703-684-5397

There's a "wild and woolly beer selection" at Old Town's "fine new microbrewery" – an "upscale" King Street attraction that "feels like Seattle" (home of pioneering brewpubs); early reports suggest that diners stick with basics, like the "great club sandwich and homemade potato chips", since the "hot" stuff can "leave you cold"; P.S. check out the single-malt scotch and bourbon list.

Vivace Enoteca S 18 16 19 $23
2311 M St., NW (bet. 23rd & 24th Sts.), 202-833-3227
▣ This enterprising West End Italian has many interesting "concepts" – it's a "wine bar", a "sports bar", an after-work hangout featuring Italian tapas (half-portion entrees and "appetizers ordered as a meal") and a staff that "really makes an effort" to mix "service and speed"; but its ideas "need to be developed" and aren't helped by the "post-Armageddon decor."

Vox Populi 21 19 19 $19
800 Connecticut Ave., NW (H St.), 202-835-2233
▣ Along with breakfast cappuccino, "great" salads and light French fare, there are "good celebrity-gazing possibilities" at this near-the-White-House, "daytime cafe/buffet"; the tone (politics and biz) is "quite likable", the servers "super friendly and helpful" – and the price "a bit too expensive" for what it is.

Warehouse Bar & Grill S 22 20 21 $26
214 King St. (bet. Fairfax & Lee Sts.), Alexandria, VA, 703-683-6868
■ "One of Old Town's best" cooks Creole-Cajun seafood and steaks, looks like its parent (the "original" R.T.'s as "rendered by Disney") and has one of the neatest piano bars around; its "loyal following" (whose caricatures are on the wall) has no problem with the menu's "predictable twists", the "noise" or "waits" when ensconced in a "window table."

West End Cafe S 20 19 19 $29
1 Washington Circle Hotel, NW (bet. New Hampshire Ave. & 23rd St.), 202-293-5390
■ Prized for "business lunches" and before or after Kennedy Center, this gardenlike West End room's hostess ("always a laugh") and the "best piano player in town" make it "*the* place to go" for dinner after the show; an "inventive" Contemporary American menu, a Ken-Cen shuttle and an antipasto lunch buffet ($8.50) are further recommendations.

WILLARD ROOM S 23 27 24 $46
Willard Hotel, 1401 Pennsylvania Ave., NW (bet. 14th & 15th Sts.), 202-637-7440
■ A "great room", restored to its former Beaux Arts glory, where "one expects Teddy Roosevelt to come striding in"; now, as then, it's DC's premier "big event" setting, with "excellent" Contemporary French food and exemplary service; try the "innovative tasting menu with perfect wines to match" or go for "high tea."

Willow Grove Inn S
▽ 23 | 23 | 24 | $40

Willow Grove Inn, 14079 Plantation Way (off Rte. 15, 1 mi. north of Orange), Orange, VA, 540-672-5982

■ When visiting Charlottesville and Monticello, this "romantic" antebellum mansion is a lovely stop; its Regional American "country home cooking", "natural" garden setting, "nice" manners – even the "scraped paint" and occasional misses – lend it a "quaint" charm.

Woo Lae Oak S
24 | 17 | 19 | $24

River House, 1500 S. Joyce St., Arlington, VA, 703-521-3706

◪ As "in Seoul", this Arlington Korean offers a range of "authentic", fiery eating possibilities – "cook your own" BBQ, bi bim bap (grilled meat and vegetables), noodle dishes, casseroles and real kimchi; one fares best in this "remote", "Hot Shoppes"–like location "with Korean friends for guides" since English is not always "spoken here."

Wurzburg-Haus
20 | 16 | 18 | $22

Red Mill Shopping Ctr., 7236 Mancaster Mill Rd. (Shady Grove Rd.), Rockville, MD, 301-330-0402

■ The wholesome, "hearty" food and rollicking "rathskeller" atmosphere at this Rockville German could fit a "cold winter night" mood; it's not the best (and not nearby), but "you could do a lot wurst" – and, for a relatively modest tab, you'll eat more than your fill.

Xing Kuba S
21 | 21 | 21 | $31

2218 Wisconsin Ave., NW (Calvert St.), 202-965-0665

◪ In a great-looking, neo-deco Glover Park setting, diners "test pilot" a "clever menu" of fusion food inspired by Asian, Latino and Southwestern "flavors" and techniques; sometimes the "psychedelic" ideas pan out and "sometimes it's just odd food" that looks as "attractive" as the staff, the space and many of the customers.

Yin Yang S
– | – | – | I

2323 18th St., NW (bet. Kalorama & Belmont Rds.), 202-319-1111

They're cheap, fast, tasty and light – so it's small wonder that Pan-Asian noodle houses are very 'in' these days, doubly so this trendy entry in Adams Morgan whose piquant salads and noodle bowls come in a deliberately unfinished industrial-feeling space (like NYC's SoHo); streetside seating provides diners with an excellent view of the passing parade.

Yosaku [S] 21 | 14 | 20 | $25

4712 Wisconsin Ave., NW (bet. Chesapeake & Davenport Sts.), 202-363-4453

■ Near movies and shopping, this trusty Upper Northwest Japanese "never fails" to provide "fine", "fresh" sushi and "delicious" noodle soups and cooked dishes along with a sense of "peace"; it's a "good value" ("especially at lunch") – try it once, you'll "go a lot."

Zed's [S] 19 | 11 | 17 | $18

3318 M St., NW (bet. 33rd & 34th Sts.), 202-333-4710

◩ Although DC Ethiopians cluster in Adams Morgan, many consider this "shabby" storefront in Georgetown (near the Key Bridge) to be "peerless"; reputedly "used by the embassy" for official dining, it makes "authentic injera" (using the proper grain, "teff") and "better seasoned dishes" with many vegetarian choices; "if you like" spicy finger food, it's "cheap eats."

TYPES OF CUISINE

Afghan
Kabul Caravan
Panjshir
Paradise

African
Meskerem
Red Sea
Zed's

American (Contemporary)
American Grill
Aquarelle
Bistro
Bistro Bistro
Bistro 2015
Bleu Rock Inn
Cafe Bethesda
Cafe on M
Cafe Promenade
Calasia
Carlyle Grand Cafe
Cashion's Eat Place
Chardonnay
Cities
Coeur de Lion
Dean & DeLuca
Elysium
Eye St. Cafe
Felix
Fern St. Bistro
Flint Hill Public Hse.
4 & 20 Blackbirds
Greenwood's
Inn/Little Wash.
Jefferson
Lafayette
Market St. B&G
Melrose
Metro Center Grille
Morrison-Clark Inn
Mrs. Simpson's
New Heights
Nora
Occidental Grill
Old Angler's Inn
Oval Room
Perry's
Pesce
R.C., The Grill
Roof Terrace
Ruppers
Seasons
701
1789
Silverado
Stage Door
Stella's
Stone Manor
Tabard Inn

Thyme Square
Trumpets
Two Quail
Vidalia
West End Cafe
Willard Room
Willow Grove Inn

American (Regional)
America
Crisfield
Georgia Brown's
Inn/Little Wash.
Kinkead's
Morrison-Clark Inn
O'Donnell's
Old Angler's Inn
1789
Shelly's Woodroast
Stone Manor
Vidalia
Virginia Bev. Co.
Willow Grove Inn

American (Traditional)
America
Artie's
B & C
Bardo Rodeo
Belmont Kitchen
Bilbo Baggins
Bistro Bistro
Cafe Deluxe
Calvert Grille
Capitol City Brewing
Carlyle Grand Cafe
Cashion's Eat Place
Cedar Knoll Inn
Chadwick's
Chart House
Cheesecake Factory
Clyde's
Cowboy Cafe
Dixie Grill
Easby's Buffet
Evans Farm Inn
Fedora Cafe
Fleetwood's
Gadsby's Tavern
Garrett Park Cafe
Gulf Coast Kitchen
Hard Rock Cafe
Hard Times Cafe
Herb's
Hogate's
Houston's
Inn at Glen Echo
J. Paul's
King Street Blues
Kramerbooks

Coffee Shops/Diners
Bob & Edith's Diner
C.F. Folks
Florida Ave. Grill
Luna Grill
Metro 29
Silver Diner

Continental
Baron's
Bilbo Baggins
Eurogrill
Falls Landing
Jockey Club
Lafayette
Lite 'n' Fair
Lite 'n' Fair/BV
Normandie Farms
Nova Europa
R.C., The Grill
R.C., The Restaurant
River Club
Tivoli
Two Quail

Cuban
Havana Cafe

Delis
Cafe Mozart
Krupin's
Lite 'n' Fair
Lite 'n' Fair/BV
Parkway Deli

Dim Sum
China Chef
China Inn
Fortune
Four Rivers
Good Fortune
Hunan Lion II
Hunan Number One
Mr. Yung's
Sunny Garden
Tony Cheng's Seafood

Eclectic
C.F. Folks
Cities
Fern St. Bistro
Greenwood's
Planet X
Savory
State of the Union
Tabard Inn
Tempo
Thyme Square
Trumpets
Two Quail
U-topia
Xing Kuba

Ethiopian
Meskerem
Red Sea
Zed's

French
Au Pied du Cochon
Bistro Francais
Bistrot Lepic
Cafe Parisien
Cafe Riviera
Gerard's Place
Jean-Michel
La Bergerie
La Bonne Auberge
La Brasserie
La Chaumiere
La Colline
La Cote d'Or Cafe
La Ferme
La Fourchette
La Madeleine
La Miche
La Mirabelle
L'Auberge Chez Francois
L'Auberge Provencale
Lavandou
Le Caprice
Le Gaulois
Le Lion D'Or
Le Paradis
Le Refuge
Le Rivage
Lespinasse
Le Vieux Logis
Maison Blanche
Provence
St. Elmos Cafe
Willard Room

French Bistro
Au Pied du Cochon
Bistro Francais
Bistro Le Monde
Bistrot Lepic
Cafe Parisien
Cafe Riviera
Gerard's Place
La Brasserie
La Chaumiere
La Colline
La Cote d'Or Cafe
La Fourchette
La Madeleine
La Miche
Lavandou
Le Bon Cafe
Le Caprice
Le Gaulois
Le Paradis
Le Refuge
Les Halles
Patisserie Cafe Didier

St. Elmos Cafe
Uptown Cafe
Village Bistro
Vox Populi

French (Contemporary)
Citronelle
Gerard's Place
Jean-Michel
Le Caprice
Le Refuge
Lespinasse
Maison Blanche
Provence
Willard Room

German
Cafe Berlin
Cafe Mozart
Wurzburg-Haus

Greek
Aegean Taverna
Ambrosia
Athenian Plaka
Mykonos
Taverna Cretekou

Hamburgers
Artie's
Capitol City Brewing
Carlyle Grand Cafe
Chadwick's
Clyde's
Cowboy Cafe
Hard Rock Cafe
Herb's
Houston's
J. Paul's
Martin's Tavern
Mick's
Mike's American
Montgomery's Grille
Nathan's
Old Ebbitt Grill
Planet Hollywood
Polly's Cafe
Slade's
Stage Door
T.G.I. Friday's
Union St. Public Hse.
Virginia Bev. Co.

Indian/Pakistani
Aangan
Aaranthi
Aditi
Aroma
Bombay Bistro
Bombay Club
Bombay Dining
Bombay Palace
Cafe New Delhi
Cafe Taj
Connaught Place

Delhi Dhaba
Food Factory
Haandi
India Kitchen
Maharaja
Shiney's Kabab House
Udupi Palace

Indonesian
Melati
Sabang
Sarinah Satay House

Italian
(N=Northern; S=Southern;
N&S=Includes both)
Arucola (N&S)
BeDuCi (N&S)
Bei Tempi (N)
Bertolini's (N&S)
Bertucci's (N&S)
Bice (N)
Buon Giorno (N&S)
Cafe Milano (N)
Cafe Mileto (S)
Café Oggi (N&S)
"Ciao baby" Cucina (N&S)
Da Domenico (N&S)
Donatello (N&S)
Duca Di Milano (N)
Ecco Cafe (N&S)
Faccia Luna (N&S)
Filomena Ristorante (N&S)
Galileo (N)
Generous George's (N&S)
Geranio (N&S)
Goldoni (N)
Il Borgo (N&S)
Il Cigno (N)
Il Pizzico (N&S)
Il Radicchio (N&S)
Il Ritrovo (S)
I Matti (N&S)
I Ricchi (N)
Landini Brothers (N&S)
La Panetteria (N&S)
La Tomate (N&S)
Listrani's (N&S)
Luigino (N)
Mare E Monti (N&S)
Nathan's (N)
Notte Luna (N&S)
Obelisk (N)
Otello (N&S)
Paolo's (N&S)
Pappa-Razzi (N&S)
Parioli (N&S)
Pasta Plus (N&S)
Petitto's (N&S)
Pines of Florence (N&S)
Pines of Rome (N&S)
Pirandello (N&S)
Pizza de Resistance (N&S)

Positano (S)
Primi Piatti (N&S)
Radio Free Italy (N&S)
Red Tomato Cafe (N&S)
Renato (N&S)
Ristorante Capri (N&S)
Sesto Sento (N)
Tempo (N&S)
That's Amore (N&S)
Tiberio (N)
Tivoli (N&S)
Tomato Tango (N&S)
Tragara (N)
Trattoria da Franco (N&S)
Trattu (N&S)
Tuscana West (N&S)
Veneziano (N)
Vincenzo (N&S)
Vivace Enoteca (N)

Japanese
Appetizer Plus
Atami
Benkay
Genji
Ginza's
Hinode
Hisago
Ichiban
Kawasaki
Makoto
Mama Wok
Matuba
Miyagi
Nulbom
Sam Woo
Shiro-ya
Sushi-Ko
Tachibana
Taipei/Tokyo Cafe
Tako Grill
Tokyo Lighthouse
Tsukiji
Yosaku

Kebabs
Cafe Rose
Food Factory
Hautam Kebobs
Kabob Bazaar
Mediterranean Blue
Moby Dick
Paradise
Persepolis
Shamshiry
Shiney's Kabab House
Skewers/Cafe Luna
Tel Aviv Cafe

Korean
Ichiban
Jin-ga
Nulbom
Sam Woo

Sushi Chalet
Woo Lae Oak

Kosher
Royal Dragon

Latin/S. American
Argentine Grill
Cafe Atlantico
Chicken Place
Coco Loco
Crisp & Juicy
El Caribe
El Pollo Rico
Granja de Oro
Havana Cafe
Lauriol Plaza
Terramar
Xing Kuba

Mediterranean
Bacchus
B & C
BeDuCi
Cafe Promenade
Cedar Knoll Inn
Eye St. Cafe
Il Ritrovo
Lebanese Taverna
Medditeranean Blue
Mediterranee
Notte Luna
Ozio
Pasha Cafe
Skewers/Cafe Luna
Tel Aviv Cafe
Tom Tom

Mexican
El Gavilan
El Tamarindo
Enriqueta's
La Lomita
Lauriol Plaza
Mi Rancho
Tia Queta

Middle Eastern
Bacchus
Dar Es Salaam
Kabob Bazaar
Kazan
Lebanese Taverna
Mediterranean Blue
Moby Dick
Nizam's
Pasha Cafe
Skewers/Cafe Luna
Tel Aviv Cafe

Moroccan
Dar Es Salaam

Persian
Cafe Rose
El Caribe

NEIGHBORHOOD LOCATIONS

WASHINGTON, D.C.

Capitol Hill
America
Bistro Le Monde
B. Smith's
Burrito Brothers
Cafe Berlin
Fatt Daddy's
La Brasserie
La Colline
La Lomita
Le Bon Cafe
Monocle
Red River Grill
Thai Garden
Two Quail

Chinatown/Convention Center/Penn Quarter
Bertolini's
Bice
Cafe Atlantico
Capitol City Brewing
Capital Grille
China Inn
Coco Loco
Dean & DeLuca
Eat First
Full Kee
Haad Thai
Hard Rock Cafe
Hunan Chinatown
Jaleo
Luigino
Metro Center Grille
Mr. Yung's
Pho
Rupperts
701
Szechuan Gallery
Tony Cheng's Seafood

Columbia Road/ Adams Morgan
Argentine Grill
Belmont Kitchen
Bua
Burrito Brothers
Cashion's Eat Place
Cities
El Tamarindo
Felix
Florida Ave. Grill
Grill from Ipanema
Il Radicchio
I Matti
La Fourchette
Lauriol Plaza

Lebanese Taverna
Meskerem
Miss Saigon
Mo Bay Cafe
Perry's
Red Sea
Saigonnais
Star of Siam
Straits of Malaya
Tom Tom
Trumpets
Veneziano
Yin Yang

Downtown
Benkay
Bombay Club
Burma
Cafe Mozart
Cafe Promenade
Chardonnay
Coeur de Lion
Dean & DeLuca
Dixie Grill
Fran O'Brien's
Georgia Brown's
Gerard's Place
Herb's
Jefferson
Lafayette
Les Halles
Lespinasse
Maison Blanche
Morrison-Clark Inn
Notte Luna
Occidental Grill
Old Ebbitt Grill
Oval Room
Planet Hollywood
Red Sage
Shiney's Kabab House
Tuscana West
Vox Populi
Willard Room

Dupont Circle/Dupont East/Dupont South
Arizona
Bacchus
BeDuCi
Bistro 2015
Burrito Brothers
Burro
Cafe Asia
Calif. Pizza Kit.
C.F. Folks
City Lights of China

NEARBY VIRGINIA

SPECIAL FEATURES AND APPEALS

Breakfast

(All major hotels
and the following)
Au Pied du Cochon
B & C
Bob & Edith's Diner
Cafe Parisien
Dean & DeLuca
Firehook Bakery
Kramerbooks
Krupin's
La Brasserie
La Colline
La Madeleine
Le Bon Cafe
Louisiana Express
Martin's Tavern
Old Ebbitt Grill
Parkway Deli
Patisserie Cafe Didier
Pho Cali
Silver Diner
Teaism

Brunch

(Best of many)
America
Aquarelle
Artie's
Austin Grill
Belmont Kitchen
Bilbo Baggins
Bistro
Bistro Bistro
Bistro 2015
Bleu Rock Inn
Bombay Club
B. Smith's
Calvert Grille
Carlyle Grand Cafe
Cashion's Eat Place
Cedar Knoll Inn
Citronelle
Clyde's
Coppi's
Felix
Filomena Ristorante
Flint Hill Public Hse.
4 & 20 Blackbirds
Gabriel
Gadsby's Tavern
Georgia Brown's
Inn at Glen Echo
Jaleo
Kinkead's
Kramerbooks
Mediterranean Blue
Melrose
Mike's American

Morrison-Clark Inn
Mrs. Simpson's
New Heights
Old Angler's Inn
Paolo's
Pappa-Razzi
Polly's Cafe
R.C., The Grill
R.C., The Restaurant
Roof Terrace
Santa Fe East
Seasons
Sequoia
Tabard Inn
Taverna Cretekou
Trumpets
Union St. Public Hse.
West End Cafe

Buffet Served

(B = brunch; L = lunch;
D = dinner)
Aangan (L)
Aaranthi (L)
Aroma (B)
Athenian Plaka (B)
Balalayka (L)
Benkay (L)
Bistro 2015 (B)
Bombay Bistro (B,L)
Bombay Club (B)
Bombay Dining (L)
Cafe Dalat (L)
Cafe Mileto (L)
Cafe New Delhi (B)
Cafe Promenade (B)
Cafe Taj (L)
"Ciao baby" Cucina (L)
Cintra (B)
Coco Loco (L)
Connaught Place (L)
Delhi Dhaba (B)
Easby's Buffet (L,D)
El Tamarindo (L)
Evans Farm Inn (L)
Fedora Cafe (B)
Filomena Ristorante (B,L)
Gabriel (L)
Gangplank (B)
Generous George's (L)
Georgia Brown's (B)
Guapo's (L)
Hogate's (B,L)
India Kitchen (B,L)
Maharaja (L)
Metro Center Grille (L)
Normandie Farms (B)
Persepolis (L)
Phillips Flagship (B,L,D)
Phillips Seafood (B)

Radio Free Italy (L)
R.C., The Grill (B,L)
R.C., The Restaurant (L)
Shiney's Kabab House (L,D)
Stella's (B)
Sushi Chalet (L,D)
Thai Garden (L)
Tony & Joe's (B)
Virginia Bev. Co. (B)

Business Dining
Aquarelle
Artie's
Bacchus
Bice
Bistro
Bombay Club
Cafe Atlantico
Cafe Promenade
Capital Grille
Carlyle Grand Cafe
Chardonnay
Citronelle
Elysium
Galileo
Gerard's Place
Goldoni
Hisago
Jefferson
Jin-ga
Jockey Club
Kinkead's
La Colline
Lafayette
Le Lion D'Or
Lespinasse
Luigino
Maison Blanche
Melrose
Monocle
Morrison-Clark Inn
Morton's of Chicago
Occidental Grill
Old Ebbitt Grill
Oval Room
Palm, The
Prime Rib
Primi Piatti
Provence
R.C., The Grill
R.C., The Restaurant
Red Sage
Ruth's Chris
Sam & Harry's
Seasons
701
Taberna del Alabardero
Tivoli
Tragara
Vidalia
Vincenzo
Willard Room

124

Caters
(Best of many)
Aditi
Bacchus
Balalayka
Bombay Club
B. Smith's
Cafe Bethesda
Cafe Parisien
Cafe Rose
C.F. Folks
Citronelle
City Lights of China
Connaught Place
Dean & DeLuca
Duangrat's
Fern St. Bistro
Germaine's
Greenwood's
Hard Times Cafe
Il Radicchio
Krupin's
La Madeleine
Lebanese Taverna
Le Bon Cafe
Listrani's
Lite 'n' Fair
Louisiana Express
Old Glory BBQ
Parkway Deli
Pasha Cafe
Patisserie Cafe Didier
Peking Gourmet Inn
Primi Piatti
Provence
Radio Free Italy
Raku
Red Hot & Blue
Rockland's
Sam Woo
Sea Catch
701
Shiro-ya
Silver Diner
Starke's
Sushi-Ko
Tako Grill
Tara Thai
Taste of Saigon
Taverna Cretekou
Tel Aviv Cafe
Trumpets
Vidalia
Vox Populi
Zed's

Dancing/Entertainment
(Check days, times and
performers for entertainment;
D = dancing)
Alamo (mariachi)
Alamo/VA (bands)

Andalucia (Spanish guitar)
Balalayka (guitar/singer)
Bistro Bistro (jazz)
Bistro 2015 (piano)
Bombay Club (piano)
B. Smith's (jazz)
Cafe Promenade (varies)
Coco Loco (D/bands)
Coeur de Lion (jazz/piano)
Cowboy Cafe (bands)
Da Domenico (opera)
Dar Es Salaam (belly dancing)
Dixie Grill (jazz)
Duangrat's (Thai dance)
Duca Di Milano (D/bands)
El Caribe (guitar)
Elysium (piano)
Evans Farm Inn (piano)
Fatt Daddy's (jazz)
Felix (D/DJ/varies)
Fleetwood's (varies)
Fran O'Brien's (piano)
Gadsby's Tavern (lute/violin)
Galaxy (Vietnamese band)
Hard Rock Cafe (bands)
Havana Cafe (DJ/guitar)
Herb's (singing)
I Matti (comedy)
Jefferson (piano/jazz)
King Street Blues (blues/jazz)
Kinkead's (piano)
Melrose (D/varies)
Muer's Seafood (jazz/piano)
Normandie Farms (D/piano)
Ozio (D/DJ)
Paolo's (jazz)
Pappa-Razzi (jazz/opera)
Petitto's (opera)
Planet X (varies)
R.C., The Grill (piano)
R.C., The Restaurant (D/jazz)
River Club (D)
State of the Union (varies)
Terramar (Latin guitar)
Thai Flavor (varies)
Tony & Joe's (varies)
Trattoria da Franco (piano)
219 (jazz)
U-topia (blues/Brazilian jazz)
Vivace Enoteca (opera)
West End Cafe (piano)
Willard Room (piano)
Yin Yang (D/DJ)

Delivers*/Takeout

(Nearly all Asians, coffee shops, delis, diners & pizzerias deliver or do takeout; here are some best bets; D = delivery, T = takeout)
Aangan (D,T)
Aaranthi (T)

Aditi (T)
Aegean Taverna (T)
Alamo (T)
Ambrosia (T)
America (T)
Appetizer Plus (T)
Aroma (T)
Asia Nora (T)
Athenian Plaka (T)
Austin Grill (T)
Bacchus (T)
Balalayka (D,T)
Bangkok St. Grill (T)
Bei Tempi (T)
Belmont Kitchen (D,T)
Benkay (T)
Bertucci's (T)
Bice (T)
Bistro Bistro (D,T)
Bistro Francais (T)
Bistro Le Monde (T)
Bistrot Lepic (T)
Blue & Gold (T)
Blue Point Grill (T)
Bombay Bistro (T)
Bombay Club (T)
Bombay Dining (T)
Bombay Palace (T)
Burro (D,T)
Cactus Cantina (T)
Cafe Asia (D,T)
Cafe Bethesda (T)
Cafe Deluxe (T)
Cafe Mozart (D,T)
Cafe New Delhi (D,T)
Café Oggi (T)
Cafe Parisien (T)
Cafe Rose (D,T)
Cafe Taj (D,T)
Cheesecake Factory (T)
Chicken Place (T)
Clyde's (T)
Connaught Place (T)
Cottonwood Cafe (T)
Cowboy Cafe (D,T)
Crisfield (D,T)
Da Domenico (T)
Dar Es Salaam (T)
Dean & DeLuca (D,T)
Duca Di Milano (T)
Enriqueta's (D,T)
Evans Farm Inn (T)
Falls Landing (T)
Fedora Cafe (T)
Felix (D,T)
Fern St. Bistro (T)
Filomena Ristorante (T)
Fran O'Brien's (T)
Gabriel (T)
Georgetown Seafood (T)
Georgia Brown's (T)
Germaine's (T)

125

Dessert & Ice Cream

(Besides Baskin-Robbins, Ben & Jerry's, Bob's Famous, Haagen-Dazs, Jeffrey's, Steve's, Thomas Sweet, Swensen's, I Can't Believe It's Yogurt)

Dining Alone

(Other than hotels)

Coco Loco
Gabriel
Georgetown Seafood
Il Radicchio
I Matti
Jaleo
Kinkead's
Kramerbooks
La Madeleine
Luigino
Makoto
Melrose
Morrison-Clark Inn
Music City Roadhouse
Notte Luna
Perry's
Pesce
Pizzeria Paradiso
Raku
Red Sage
701
Sushi-Ko
Tachibana
Vivace Enoteca
Vox Populi

Family Style
Arucola
Evans Farm Inn
Music City Roadhouse
That's Amore

Fireplaces
Bilbo Baggins
Bleu Rock Inn
Chadwick's
Chart House
Dixie Grill
Elysium
Evans Farm Inn
Falls Landing
4 & 20 Blackbirds
Gangplank
Geranio
Inn/Little Wash.
Jefferson
La Chaumiere
La Ferme
La Madeleine
La Mirabelle
L'Auberge Chez Francois
L'Auberge Provencale
Le Gaulois
Mike's American
Monocle
Normandie Farms
Old Angler's Inn
Polly's Cafe
Potowmack Landing
R.C., The Grill
Red Sage
Ruth's Chris
Santa Fe East

Sea Catch
1789
219
Willow Grove Inn

Health/Spa Menus
(Most places cook to order to
meet any dietary request; call
in advance to check; almost
all health-food spots, Chinese,
Indian and other ethnics have
health-conscious meals, as
do the following)
Asia Nora
Bistro 2015
Cashion's Eat Place
Greenwood's
Melrose
Morrison-Clark Inn
Nora
Old Angler's Inn
Planet X
Seasons
Thyme Square
Trumpets
Vegetable Garden
Zed's

Historic Interest
(Year Opened)
1750 Alamo/VA*
1753 L'Auberge Provencale
1778 Willow Grove Inn
1792 Gadsby's Tavern*
1800 Bilbo Baggins
1800 Santa Fe East
1817 Pappa-Razzi*
1856 Music City Roadhouse
1860 Old Angler's Inn
1860 1789*
1865 Morrison-Clark Inn*
1867 Martin's Tavern*
1887 Tabard Inn
1890 Ruppert's
1904 Two Quail
1910 4 & 20 Blackbirds
1931 Normandie Farms
(* Building)

Hotel Dining
ANA Hotel
  Bistro
Capitol Hilton
  Fran O'Brien's
Carlton
  Lespinasse
Channel Inn
  Pier 7
Doubletree Park Terr. Hotel
  Chardonnay
Embassy Row Hotel
  Bistro 2015

127

Four Seasons Hotel
    Seasons
Georgetown Inn
    Cafe Riviera
Hay-Adams Hotel
    Lafayette
Henley Park Hotel
    Coeur de Lion
Holiday Inn/Governor's House
    Herb's
Hyatt/Reston
    Market St. B&G
Inn at Little Washington
    Inn/Little Wash.
Jefferson Hotel
    Jefferson
Latham Hotel
    Citronelle
L'Auberge Provencale
    L'Auberge Provencale
Loew's L'Enfant Plaza
    American Grill
Marriott at Metro Center
    Metro Center Grille
Mayflower Hotel
    Cafe Promenade
Morrison-Clark Inn
    Morrison-Clark Inn
Morrison House Hotel
    Elysium
Park Hyatt Hotel
    Melrose
Radisson-Barcelo
    Gabriel
Ritz-Carlton (DC)
    Jockey Club
Ritz-Carlton/Pentagon City
    Grill, The
Ritz-Carlton/Tysons II
    Restaurant, The
Sheraton Premiere
    Baron's
Stratford Motor Lodge
    Cafe Rose
Tabard Inn
    Tabard Inn
Westin Hotel
    Cafe on M
Willard Hotel
    Willard Room
Willow Grove Inn
    Willow Grove Inn

"In" Places
Bistro Francais
Cafe Atlantico
Cafe Milano
Cashion's Eat Place
Coco Loco
Felix
Germaine's
Jaleo
Rupperts

128

Sesto Sento
Sushi-Ko
Tel Aviv Cafe

Jacket Required
Baron's
Jockey Club
Lafayette
L'Auberge Chez Francois
L'Auberge Provencale
River Club
1789
Tragara

Late Late – After 12:30
(All hours are AM)
Ambrosia (2)
Au Pied du Cochon (24 hrs.)
Bistro Francais (4)
Bob & Edith's Diner (24 hrs.)
Burrito Brothers (3)*
Cafe Rose (1)
Carlyle Grand Cafe (1)
Chadwick's (1)
Coppi's (1)
Dynasty (1:30)
El Gavilan (1)
El Tamarindo (3)*
Full Kee (3)
Full Key (2)
Good Fortune (2)
Hard Rock Cafe (1)
Hunan Number One (1:45)
Il Ritrovo (2)
Kramerbooks (24 hrs.)
Meskerem (2)
Metro 29 (3)
Mo Bay Cafe (5:30)
Mr. Yung's (1)
Music City Roadhouse (1)
Old Ebbitt Grill (1)
Planet Hollywood (1)
Planet X (1)
Polly's Cafe (2)
Raku (2)
Sequoia (1)
Seven Seas (1)
Sunny Garden (1)
Tel Aviv Cafe (1)
T.G.I. Friday's (1)
Thai Flavor (3)
Vienna's Grille (1)
Virginia Bev. Co. (1)
(* Check locations and nights)

Meet for a Drink
America
Artie's
Bistro Bistro
Blue & Gold
Bombay Bistro
B. Smith's
Cafe Atlantico
Cafe Milano

Carlyle Grand Cafe
"Ciao baby" Cucina
Clyde's
Coco Loco
Fedora Cafe
Gabriel
Georgia Brown's
Gulf Coast Kitchen
Jaleo
Jockey Club
Kinkead's
Lespinasse
Montgomery's Grille
Old Ebbitt Grill
Oval Room
701
Trumpets
West End Cafe

Noteworthy Newcomers
Bangkok St. Grill
Bertolini's
Bistro Lepic
Bombay Bistro
Bombay Curry Co.
Bugaloo Creek
Cafe Atlantico
Cafe Deluxe
Cafe Mileto
Cafe Riviera
Calasia
Cashion's Eat Place
Cintra
Fatt Daddy's
Felix
Fran O'Brien's
Galaxy
Goldoni
Greenwood
Grillfish
Il Ritrovo
Jin-ga
Lespinasse
Luna Grill
Malik
Mediterranee
Memphis BBQ
Oodles Noodles
Ozio
Raku
Red River Grill
Ristoranti Capri
Shelly's Woodroast
Silverado
Stage Door
Sushi Chalet
Teaism
Tel Aviv Cafe
T.H.A.I.
Thyme Square
Uptown Cafe
Virginia Bev. Co.

Vivace Enoteca
Yin Yang

Offbeat
Au Pied du Cochon
Bistro Francais
Bob & Edith's Diner
C.F. Folks
Cowboy Cafe
Florida Ave. Grill
Hibiscus Cafe
Trumpets

Outdoor Dining
(G = Garden; P = Patio;
R = Rooftop; S = Sidewalk;
T = Terrace; W = Waterside)
Aangan (P)
Aegean Taverna (P)
America (S)*
Argentine Grill (S)
Aroma (P)
Arucola (P)
Athenian Plaka (P)
Bacchus (P)*
BeDuCi (S)
Belmont Kitchen (P)
Bertolini's (S)*
Bice (P)
Bistro (G)
Bistro Bistro (P,S)*
Bistro 2015 (P)
Bleu Rock Inn (T)
Blue Point Grill (P)
Bombay Bistro (P)*
Bombay Club (P)
Bua (P)
Busara (G)
Cactus Cantina (S)
Cafe Berlin (P)
Cafe Bethesda (P)
Cafe Deluxe (P)
Cafe Milano (P)
Cafe Mileto (P)
Cafe New Delhi (P)
Cafe Parisien (S)
Cafe Taj (P)
Capitol City Brewing (T)*
Carlyle Grand Cafe (P)
Cashion's Eat Place (S)
C.F. Folks (P)
Chadwick's (P)*
Chardonnay (G)
Chart House (P)
Chesapeake Seafood (P)
Clyde's (P,W)*
Coco Loco (P)
Cottonwood Cafe (P)
Crystal Thai (T)
Dean & DeLuca (P)*
Donatello (T)
Duangrat's (P)
Duca Di Milano (T)

Parties & Private Rooms

(Any nightclub or restaurant charges less at off hours; * indicates private rooms available; best of many, excluding hotels)

Alamo*
America*
Bacchus*
Bice*
Bilbo Baggins*
Bistro Le Monde*
Bleu Rock Inn*
Blue & Gold*
B. Smith's*
Busara*
Cactus Cantina*
Cafe Milano*
Capital Grille*
Carlyle Grand Cafe
Chadwick's*
Chardonnay*
"Ciao baby" Cucina*
Cintra*
Cities*
Citronelle*
Clyde's*
Coco Loco*
Coeur de Lion*
Cowboy Cafe*
Da Domenico*
Dar Es Salaam*
Duangrat's*
Duca Di Milano*
Ecco Cafe*
Enriqueta's*
Evans Farm Inn*
Falls Landing*
Felix*
Fleetwood's*
Fortune*
4 & 20 Blackbirds*
Gabriel*
Galaxy*
Galileo*
Gangplank
Generous George's*
Geranio*
Germaine's
Good Fortune*
Guapo's*
Hibiscus Cafe*
I Matti*
King Street Blues*
Kinkead's*
La Bergerie*
La Chaumiere*
La Colline*
La Ferme*
L'Auberge Chez Francois
Le Gaulois*

Le Lion D'Or*
Le Rivage
Les Halles*
Le Vieux Logis*
Luigino*
Meskerem*
Monocle*
Montgomery's Grille*
Morrison-Clark Inn*
Morton's of Chicago*
Mrs. Simpson's*
Nora*
Normandie Farms*
Old Ebbitt Grill*
Oval Room*
Palm, The*
Paolo's*
Peking Gourmet Inn*
Primi Piatti*
R.C., The Grill*
R.C., The Restaurant*
Red Hot & Blue
Rupperts*
Ruth's Chris*
Sam & Harry's*
Santa Fe East*
Sea Catch*
701*
1789*
Stone Manor*
Straits of Malaya*
Tabard Inn*
Taberna del Alabardero*
Taste Of Thai*
That's Amore*
Tivoli*
Tony & Joe's*
Tragara*
219*
Two Quail*
Union St. Public Hse.*
Vidalia*
Willow Grove Inn*
Xing Kuba*

People-Watching

America
Belmont Kitchen
B. Smith's
Cactus Cantina
Cafe Atlantico
Cafe Milano
Carlyle Grand Cafe
Cashion's Eat Place
C.F. Folks
Cities
Coco Loco
Dean & DeLuca
Filomena Ristorante
Galileo
Georgia Brown's
Germaine's
I Ricchi

Maison Blanche
Makoto
Market St. B&G
Melrose
Obelisk
Oval Room
Pho Cali
Red River Grill
Rupperts
701
1789
St. Elmos Cafe
Stone Manor
Taberna del Alabardero
Tivoli
Trattu
Uptown Cafe
West End Cafe
Willard Room
Willow Grove Inn
Yosaku

Pubs
Blue & Gold
Chadwick's
Clyde's
Houston's
Inn at Glen Echo
J. Paul's
King Street Blues
Martin's Tavern
Nathan's
Old Ebbitt Grill
Polly's Cafe
R.T.'s
Southside 815
Union St. Public Hse.

Quiet Conversation
Bombay Club
Chardonnay
Coeur de Lion
Elysium
Jefferson
Lafayette
Le Caprice
Melrose
Morrison-Clark Inn
Obelisk
R.C., The Grill
R.C., The Restaurant
Seasons
1789
Tivoli
Vincenzo
Willard Room

Raw Bars
Chart House
Clyde's
Georgetown Seafood
J. Paul's
Kinkead's
Legal Sea Food

Old Ebbitt Grill
Perry's
Sea Catch

Reservations Essential
Calasia
Citronelle
Coeur de Lion
Duca Di Milano
Geranio
Gerard's Place
Germaine's
La Bergerie
La Bonne Auberge
Lafayette
L'Auberge Chez Francois
L'Auberge Provencale
Le Lion D'Or
Maison Blanche
Morton's of Chicago
Nora
Palm, The
Prime Rib
Provence
R.C., The Restaurant
Rupperts
Saigonnais
Stone Manor
Taberna del Alabardero

Reservations Not Accepted
(Check for larger parties)
Alamo/VA
Ambrosia
Arucola
Austin Grill
Bangkok St. Grill
Bertucci's
Bilbo Baggins
Bombay Bistro
Bugaboo Creek
Cafe Deluxe
Calif. Pizza Kit.
Calvert Grille
Capitol City Brewing
Chadwick's
Clyde's
Crisfield
Dixie Grill
Enriqueta's
Fatt Daddy's
4 & 20 Blackbirds
Generous George's
Georgetown Seafood
Hard Rock Cafe
Hard Times Cafe
Havana Cafe
Hibiscus Cafe
King Street Blues
Luna Grill
Mare E Monti
Mick's

Outback Steakhouse
Ozio
Paolo's
Pasha Cafe
Perry's
Persepolis
Pesce
Pho Cali
Radio Free Italy
R.T.'s Seafood
Saigon Gourmet
Shamshiry
South Austin Grill
Southside 815
Tel Aviv Cafe
T.G.I. Friday's
That's Amore
Tomato Tango
Tony Cheng's Mongolian
Uptown Cafe
Wurzburg-Haus

Romantic Spots
Bleu Rock Inn
Bombay Club
Chardonnay
Citronelle
Coeur de Lion
Inn/Little Wash.
L'Auberge Chez Francois
Le Refuge
Provence
River Club
Saigonnais
Stone Manor
Two Quail

Saturday Dining
(B = brunch; L = lunch;
best of many)
Aangan (L)
Aaranthi (L)
Aditi (L)
Alamo/VA (L)
Ambrosia (L)
America (B,L)
American Grill (L)
Aroma (B)
Artie's (L)
Arucola (L)
Atami (L)
Athenian Plaka (L)
Au Pied du Cochon (L)
Austin Grill (B)
Balalayka (L)
Bangkok Vientiane (L)
Bei Tempi (L)
Belmont Kitchen (B)
Benjarong (L)
Bertolini's (L)
Bertucci's (L)
Bilbo Baggins (B,L)
Bistro (B,L)

Bistro Bistro (L)
Bistro Francais (B,L)
Bistrot Lepic (L)
Bistro 2015 (L)
Blue Point Grill (L)
Bob & Edith's Diner (L)
Bombay Bistro (B)
Bombay Dining (L)
Bombay Palace (L)
B. Smith's (B,L)
Bua (L)
Bugaboo Creek (L)
Burrito Brothers (L)
Burro (L)
Busara (L)
Cactus Cantina (B,L)
Cafe Asia (L)
Cafe Berlin (L)
Cafe Dalat (L)
Cafe Deluxe (L)
Cafe Milano (L)
Cafe Mileto (L)
Cafe Mozart (L)
Cafe New Delhi (L)
Cafe on M (L)
Cafe Parisien (L)
Cafe Promenade (L)
Cafe Rose (L)
Cafe Saigon (L)
Cafe Taj (L)
Calif. Pizza Kit. (L)
Calvert Grille (B,L)
Cambodian (L)
Capitol City Brewing (L)
Carlyle Grand Cafe (L)
Cedar Knoll Inn (L)
Chadwick's (L)
Chardonnay (L)
Charlie Chiang's (L)
Cheesecake Factory (L)
Chesapeake Seafood (L)
Chicken Place (L)
China Canteen (L)
China Chef (L)
China Inn (L)
Cintra (L)
Citronelle (L)
City Lights of China (L)
Clyde's (B)
Coco Loco (L)
Coeur de Lion (B,L)
Connaught Place (B,L)
Cottonwood Cafe (L)
Cowboy Cafe (L)
Crisfield
Crisp & Juicy (L)
Crystal Thai (L)
Dean & DeLuca (L)
Delhi Dhaba (L)
Dixie Grill (L)
Duangrat's (L)
Dusit (L)

Persepolis (L)
Pesce (L)
Petitto's (L)
Phillips Flagship (L)
Pho (L)
Pho Cali (L)
Pho 95 (L)
Pho 75 (L)
Pilin Thai (L)
Pines of Florence (L)
Pines of Rome (L)
Pirandello (L)
Pizzeria Paradiso (L)
Planet Hollywood (L)
Planet X (L)
Polly's Cafe (B)
Positano (L)
Potowmack Landing (L)
Queen Bee (L)
Rabieng (L)
Radio Free Italy (L)
Raku (L)
R.C., The Grill (L)
R.C., The Restaurant (L)
Red Hot & Blue (L)
Red River Grill (L)
Red Sea (L)
Red Tomato Cafe (L)
Renato (L)
Rio Grande Cafe (L)
Ristorante Capri (L)
Rockland's (L)
R.T.'s (L)
R.T.'s Seafood (L)
Sabang (L)
Saigon Gourmet (L)
Saigon Inn (L)
Saigonnais (L)
Sala Thai (L)
Sam Woo (L)
Santa Fe East (L)
Sarinah Satay House (L)
Savory (L)
Sea Catch (L)
Sequoia (B)
Seven Seas (L)
Shamshiry (L)
Shelly's Woodroast (L)
Shiney's Kabab House (L)
Silver Diner (L)
Skewers/Cafe Luna (L)
Slade's (L)
South Austin Grill (B,L)
Southside 815 (L)
Spices (L)
Star of Siam (L)
Starke's (L)
St. Elmos Cafe (L)
Stone Manor (L)
Sunny Garden (L)
Sushi Chalet (L)
Szechuan Gallery (L)

Tabard Inn (B)
Tachibana (L)
Taipei/Tokyo Cafe (L)
Tara Thai (L)
Taste of Saigon (L)
Taste Of Thai (L)
Taverna Cretekou (L)
Teaism (L)
Tel Aviv Cafe (L)
T.G.I. Friday's (B,L)
T.H.A.I. (L)
Thai Flavor (L)
Thai Garden (L)
Thai Kingdom (L)
Thyme Square (L)
Tia Queta (L)
Tiberio (L)
Tokyo Lighthouse (L)
Tomato Tango (L)
Tony & Joe's (L)
Tony Cheng's Mongolian (L)
Trattoria da Franco (L)
Tsukiji (L)
219 (L)
Union St. Public Hse. (L)
Uptown Cafe (L)
U-topia (B)
Vegetable Garden (L)
Veneziano (L)
Vienna's Grille (L)
Vietnam (L)
Virginia Bev. Co. (B,L)
Warehouse B&G (L)
West End Cafe (L)
Woo Lae Oak (L)
Wurzburg-Haus (L)
Xing Kuba (B)
Zed's (L)

Sunday Dining
(B = brunch; L = lunch;
D = dinner; plus all hotels
and most Asians)
Aangan (B,D)
Aaranthi (D)
Aditi (L,D)
Aegean Taverna (L,D)
Alamo/VA (L,D)
America (B,L,D)
Andalucia (D)
Appetizer Plus (D)
Argentine Grill (B,D)
Aroma (B,D)
Artie's (B,D)
Atami (D)
Athenian Plaka (B,L,D)
Au Pied du Cochon (L,D)
Austin Grill (B,D)
Bacchus (D)
Balalayka (L,D)
Bangkok St. Grill (L,D)
Bangkok Vientiane (L,D)

Thai Flavor (L,D)
Thai Garden (L,D)
Thai Kingdom (L,D)
That's Amore (D)
Tia Queta (D)
Tom Tom (B,D)
Tragara (D)
Trattoria da Franco (L,D)
Trumpets (B,D)
219 (B,D)
Two Quail (D)
Union St. Public Hse. (B,D)
Uptown Cafe (B,L,D)
U-topia (B,D)
Veneziano (D)
Vienna's Grille (L,D)
Vietnam (L,D)
Virginia Bev. Co. (B,L,D)
Warehouse B&G (B,L,D)
West End Cafe (L,D)
Xing Kuba (B,D)
Yin Yang (L,D)
Yosaku (D)
Zed's (L,D)

Singles Scenes
Artie's
Austin Grill
Bardo Rodeo
Bistro Bistro
Bua
Cafe Atlantico
Cafe Milano
"Ciao baby" Cucina
Coco Loco
Dixie Grill
Fedora Cafe
Felix
Fleetwood's
Grill from Ipanema
Gulf Coast Kitchen
Jaleo
J. Paul's
King Street Blues
Montgomery's Grille
Polly's Cafe
Raku
Sequoia
Sesto Sento
South Austin Grill
Stella's
Tel Aviv Cafe
Tom Tom
Tony & Joe's
Trumpets
Tuscana West
U-topia

Sleepers
(Good to excellent food, but
little known)
Bombay Dining (MD)
Cafe New Delhi (VA)

Cafe Rose (VA)
Cafe Taj (VA)
Chardonnay
China Canteen (MD)
Cintra (VA)
Connaught Place (VA)
Fern St. Bistro (VA)
Full Key (MD)
Genji (VA)
Granja de Oro (VA)
Hautam Kebobs (MD)
Il Borgo (VA)
Il Ritrovo (MD)
India Kitchen (MD)
Kabul Caravan (VA)
Kawasaki
Le Paradis (MD)
Makoto
Malik
Mama Wok
Mare E Monti (MD)
Miyagi (VA)
Nulbom (MD)
Pasta Plus (MD)
Pho
Pho Cali (VA)
Pho 95 (MD)
Shamshiry (VA)
Shiro-ya
Sushi Chalet (MD)
Szechuan Gallery
T.H.A.I. (VA)
Thai Flavor
Tsukiji (MD)
Vietnam (MD)
Willow Grove Inn

Teflons
(Gets lots of business, despite
so-so food, i.e. they have
other attractions that prevent
criticism from sticking)
America
Au Pied du Cochon
Bardo Rodeo (VA)
Bertolini's
Capitol City Brewing
Chadwick's
Dixie Grill
Evans Farm Inn (VA)
Fleetwood's (VA)
Hard Rock Cafe
Hogate's
Kramerbooks
Phillips Flagship
Pines of Florence
Planet Hollywood
Potowmack Landing (VA)
Silver Diner
Slade's
T.G.I. Friday's

Smoking Prohibited
(May be permissible at bar or outdoors)
Aangan
Appetizer Plus
Aroma
Asia Nora
Bacchus
Balalayka
B & C
Benjarong
Bertucci's
Bombay Bistro
Bombay Dining
Burro
Cafe Bethesda
Cafe Dalat
Cafe Mileto
Cafe Parisien
Cafe Saigon
Calasia
Calif. Pizza Kit.
Carlyle Grand Cafe
C.F. Folks
Chardonnay
Chicken Place
Cowboy Cafe
Crisfield
Crisp & Juicy
Crystal Thai
Dean & DeLuca
Delhi Dhaba
Easby's Buffet
Eat First
Elysium
Firehook Bakery
Food Factory
Foong Lin
4 & 20 Blackbirds
Four Rivers
Full Kee
Full Key
Gadsby's Tavern
Good Fortune
Haandi
Hautam Kebobs
Hinode
House of Chinese
Hunan Lion II
Inn/Little Wash.
Jean-Michel
Kazan
Krupin's
La Madeleine
La Miche
L'Auberge Chez Francois
L'Auberge Provencale
Lebanese Taverna
Le Bon Cafe
Ledo Pizza
Le Paradis
Le Vieux Logis

Lite 'n' Fair
Los Chorros
Louisiana Express
Luna Grill
Maharaja
Mama Wok
Matuba
Mediterranee
Mi Rancho
Moby Dick
Morrison-Clark Inn
Mrs. Simpson's
Nam's
Nora
Obelisk
Oodles Noodles
Paradise
Parioli
Parkway Deli
Pasha Cafe
Pho 95
Pho 75
Pizzeria Paradiso
Planet X
Queen Bee
Rabieng
Raku
Red Tomato Cafe
Renato
Rockland's
Roof Terrace
R.T.'s Seafood
Sabang
Saigon Inn
Sala Thai
Sam Woo
Shamshiry
Stone Manor
Sushi Chalet
Tachibana
Taipei/Tokyo Cafe
Tako Grill
Tara Thai
Teaism
Terramar
T.G.I. Friday's
Thyme Square
Tia Queta
Tomato Tango
Tragara
Tsukiji
Vegetable Garden

Teas
(See also *Coffeehouses* & *Dessert* Indexes)
Aquarelle
Cafe Promenade
Coeur de Lion
Elysium
Jefferson
Lafayette

Lespinasse
Melrose
Morrison-Clark Inn
Patisserie Cafe Didier
R.C., The Grill
R.C., The Restaurant
Seasons
Teaism
Willard Room

Transporting Experiences
Bombay Club
Dar Es Salaam
Duangrat's
Gadsby's Tavern
Hisago
Inn/Little Wash.
Jin-ga
Morrison-Clark Inn
Sarinah Satay House
Shelly's Woodroast
Taverna Cretekou

Visitors on Expense Accounts
Aquarelle
Asia Nora
Bice
Bombay Club
Capital Grille
Citronelle
Elysium
Galileo
Gerard's Place
Hisago
Inn/Little Wash.
Jefferson
Jockey Club
Kinkead's
La Bergerie
Lafayette
L'Auberge Chez Francois
Le Lion D'Or
Lespinasse
Makoto
Melrose
Morrison-Clarke Inn
Morton's of Chicago
New Heights
Nora
Obelisk
Old Angler's Inn
Oval Room
Palm, The
Prime Rib
Primi Piatti
Provence
R.C., The Grill
R.C., The Restaurant
Red Sage
Rupperts
Ruth's Chris
Sam & Harry's

Seasons
701
1789
Stone Manor
Taberna del Alabardero
Vidalia
Willard Room

Wheelchair Access
(Check for bathroom access;
almost all hotels and chains
plus the following best bets)
America
Andalucia
Artie's
Athenian Plaka
Bacchus*
B & C
Bei Tempi
Bilbo Baggins
Bistro Bistro
Bleu Rock Inn
Blue & Gold
Blue Point Grill
Bombay Bistro
Bombay Club
Bombay Dining
Bombay Palace
B. Smith's
Buon Giorno
Busara
Cactus Cantina
Cafe Bethesda
Cafe Deluxe
Cafe Milano
Cafe Mileto
Cafe New Delhi
Café Oggi
Cafe Taj
Cajun Bangkok
Calasia
Calvert Grille
Capitol City Brewing
Capital Grille
Carlyle Grand Cafe
Cedar Knoll Inn
Chardonnay
Chart House
Cheesecake Factory
Cities
Clyde's*
Coco Loco
Coppi's
Cottonwood Cafe
Crisfield
Da Domenico
Dar Es Salaam
Dean & DeLuca
Duangrat's
Duca Di Milano
Dynasty
Ecco Cafe

Wine & Beer Only

Winning Wine Lists

Worth a Trip

White Post
  L'Auberge Provencale

Young Children

(Besides the normal fast-food places; * indicates children's menu available)

Austin Grill*
Cactus Cantina*
Cafe Deluxe*
Cafe Promenade*
Calvert Grille*
Chart House*
Clyde's*
Crisfield*
Evans Farm Inn*
Faccia Luna
Generous George's*
Guapo's
Hard Rock Cafe
Hard Times Cafe*
La Lomita*
Lebanese Taverna
Ledo Pizza*
Mare E Monti*
Mick's*
Music City Roadhouse
Normandie Farms*
Old Glory BBQ
Outback Steakhouse*
Paolo's*
Phillips Flagship*
Phillips Seafood*
Radio Free Italy*
Red Hot & Blue*
Rio Grande Cafe
Roof Terrace
Shelly's Woodroast*
Silver Diner*
South Austin Grill*
T.G.I. Friday's*
Tokyo Lighthouse*

Baltimore

Baltimore's Favorites

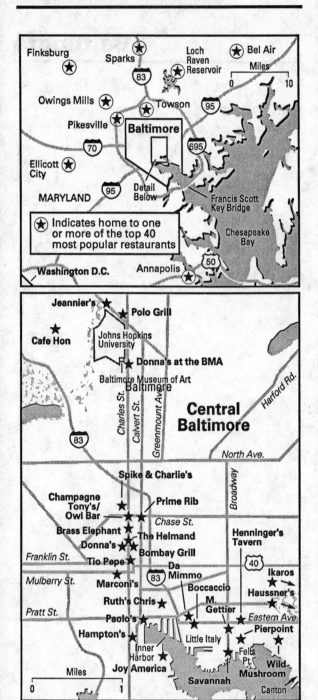

Finksburg

Sparks

83

Loch Raven Reservoir

Bel Air

Miles

0   10

Owings Mills

Towson

95

Pikesville

70

Baltimore

695

Ellicott City

95

MARYLAND

Detail Below

Francis Scott Key Bridge

★ Indicates home to one or more of the top 40 most popular restaurants

Chesapeake Bay

Washington D.C.

Annapolis

50

Jeannier's

Polo Grill

Cafe Hon

Johns Hopkins University

Donna's at the BMA

Baltimore Museum of Art

Baltimore

Central Baltimore

Harford Rd.

Charles St.

Calvert St.

Greenmount Ave.

83

North Ave.

Broadway

Spike & Charlie's

Champagne Tony's/ Owl Bar

Prime Rib

Chase St.

Brass Elephant

The Helmand

Henninger's Tavern

40

Donna's

Bombay Grill

Franklin St.

Tio Pepe

Da Mimmo

Ikaros

Mulberry St.

Marconi's

83

Boccaccio

Haussner's

Ruth's Chris

M. Gettier

Eastern Ave.

Pratt St.

Paolo's

Pierpoint

Hampton's

Little Italy

Inner Harbor

Joy America

Fells Pt.

Wild Mushroom

Savannah

Canton

Miles

0   1

Baltimore's Most Popular Restaurants

Each of our reviewers has been asked to name his or her five favorite restaurants. The 40 spots most frequently named, in order of their popularity, are:

1. Tio Pepe
2. Prime Rib
3. Polo Grill
4. Linwood's
5. Milton Inn
6. Hampton's
7. M. Gettier
8. Brass Elephant
9. Helmand
10. Haussner's
11. Spike & Charlie's
12. Ruth's Chris
13. Joy America
14. Boccaccio
15. Outback Steakhouse
16. Pierpoint
17. Tersiguel's
18. Donna's at BMA
19. Marconi's
20. Savannah
21. Rudys' 2900
22. Jeannier's
23. Chart House
24. Wild Mushroom
25. Peerce's Plantation
26. Champagne Tony's
27. Puffin's
28. Cafe Troia
29. Due
30. Henninger's Tavern
31. Northwoods/A
32. Donna's
33. California Pizza Kitchen
34. Hersh's Orchard Inn
35. Red Hot & Blue
36. Ikaros
37. Paolo's
38. Da Mimmo
39. Cafe Hon
40. Bombay Grill

It's obvious that most of the restaurants on the above list are among the most expensive, but Baltimore diners love a bargain. Were popularity calibrated to price, we suspect that a number of other restaurants would join the above ranks. Thus, we have listed over 140 "Best Buys" on pages 156 and 157.

A = Annapolis.

Top Ratings*

Top 40 Food Ranking

28 Prime Rib
27 Inn at Perry Cabin/A
Chester River Inn/A
Rudys' 2900
Hampton's
Milton Inn
M. Gettier
Northwoods/A
Linwood's
26 Tio Pepe
Polo Grill
Pierpoint
25 Tersiguel's
Joy America
Boccaccio
Helmand
Henninger's Tavern
Savannah
24 La Piccola Roma/A
Brass Elephant

Josef's Country Inn
Orchard Market/Cafe
Peter's Inn
Treaty of Paris/A
Due
Purple Orchid
Antrim 1844
Matsuri
Spike & Charlie's
Szechuan Best
Ruth's Chris
Da Mimmo
Banjara
23 Wild Mushroom
Stone Mill Bakery/Ecole
Jeannier's
Cafe Troia
Thai Landing
Narrows/A
Puffin's

Top Spots by Cuisine

Top American
24 Treaty of Paris/A
23 Narrows/A
Marconi's
21 Hersh's Orchard Inn
Harryman House

Top American (New)
27 Chester River Inn/A
Hampton's
Milton Inn
Linwood's
26 Polo Grill

Top Breakfast†
23 Cafe Normandie/A
21 Morning Edition
Donna's
18 Cafe Hon
Woman's Ind. Exchange

Top Brunch
27 Hampton's
26 Polo Grill
Pierpoint
25 Savannah
24 Treaty of Paris/A

Top Business Lunch
27 Linwood's
26 Polo Grill
25 Savannah
24 La Piccola Roma/A
Brass Elephant

Top Chinese
24 Szechuan Best
23 Jumbo Seafood
22 Hunan Manor
Joey Chiu's
Szechuan

---

* Excluding restaurants with low voting.
† Other than hotels
A = Annapolis.

Top Continental
- **27** Inn at Perry Cabin/A
  - Rudys' 2900
  - Northwoods/A
- **26** Tio Pepe
- **24** Brass Elephant

Top Crab Houses
- **21** Cantler's Riverside/A
  - Crab Claw/A
  - Harris' Crab Hse./A
- **20** Gunning's (Dorsey Rd.)
  - Jimmy's Famous Seafood

Top Family Dining
- **21** Cantler's Riverside/A
- **20** Red Hot & Blue
- **19** Tomato Palace
- **18** Loco Hombre
  - Friendly Farms

Top French
- **27** M. Gettier
- **25** Tersiguel's
- **23** Jeannier's
  - Cafe Normandie/A
- **21** Martick's

Top Hotel Dining
- **27** Hampton's/
  - Harbor Court Hotel
- **26** Polo Grill/
  - Inn at the Colonnade
- **24** Treaty of Paris/
  - Maryland Inn/A
- **21** Windows/
  - Renaissance Harborpl.
- **19** Berry & Elliot's/
  - Hyatt Regency

Top Indian
- **24** Banjara
- **23** Bombay Grill
- **22** Mughal Garden
- **20** Akbar

Top Italian
- **25** Boccaccio
- **24** La Piccolo Roma/A
  - Due
  - Da Mimmo
- **23** Cafe Troia

Top Japanese
- **24** Matsuri
- **21** Jpn.
  - Kawasaki
  - Nichi Bei Kai
  - Sushi-Ya

Top Newcomers/Rated
- **25** Joy America
  - Savannah
- **23** Wild Mushroom
- **21** Cafe Zen
- **19** Nacho Mama's

Top Newcomers/Unrated
- daniel's
- OPA
- Ruby Lounge
- Saigon
- Sotto Sopra

Top Seafood
- **26** Pierpoint
- **23** Narrows/A
  - O'Leary's/A
- **22** Faidley's
- **21** Hoang's

Top Steakhouses
- **28** Prime Rib
- **24** Ruth's Chris
- **22** McCafferty's
- **20** Outback Steakhouse
- **—** Lewnes' Steakhouse/A

Top Vegetarian
- **23** Wild Mushroom
  - Puffin's
  - Thai
- **21** Margaret's Cafe
- **18** One World Cafe

Top Worth a Trip
- **28** 208 Talbot/
  - St. Michaels, MD
- **27** Inn at Perry Cabin/
  - St. Michaels, MD
  - Chester River Inn/
  - Kent Narrows, MD
  - Imperial Hotel/
  - Chestertown, MD
- **24** Antrim 1844/
  - Taneytown, MD

Top 40 Decor Ranking

29 Inn at Perry Cabin/A
Hampton's
28 Antrim 1884
27 Milton Inn
Brass Elephant
26 Linwood's
25 Prime Rib
Champagne Tony's
Polo Grill
Pavilion at the Walters
Joy America
Treaty of Paris/A
Haussner's
24 King's Contrivance
Windows
Tersiguel's
Peerce's Plantation
Boccaccio
23 Narrows/A
Savannah

Rudys' 2900
Carrol's Creek Cafe/A
Tio Pepe
22 Donna's at BMA
Harry Browne's/A
Joey Chiu's
Due
M. Gettier
Henninger's Tavern
Northwoods/A
Berry & Elliot's
Helmand
21 Middleton Tavern/A
Chart House
One World Cafe
Ruth's Chris
Windows on the Bay
Rusty Scupper
Cafe Normandie
La Piccola Roma/A

Top Outdoor

Bay Cafe
Cantler's Riverside/A
Carrol's Creek Cafe/A
Chart House
Cheesecake Factory
Donna's at BMA
Lista's
McGarvey's/A

Middleton Tavern/A
Paolo's
Peerce's Plantation
Pier 500
River Watch
Rusty Scupper
Sanders' Corner
Victor's

Top Rooms

Antrim 1884
Brass Elephant
Donna's at BMA
Hampton's
Haussner's
Inn at Perry Cabin/A

Linwood's
Lista's
Milton Inn (Hearth Room)
Pavilion at the Walters
Polo Grill
Prime Rib

Top Views

Bamboo House (Harborplace)
Bay Cafe
Berry & Elliot's
Carrol's Creek Cafe/A
Chart House
Hampton's
Inn at Perry Cabin/A

Joy America
Michael Rork's/A
Peerce's Plantation
Piccolo's
Pier 500
Victor's
Windows

Top 40 Service Ranking

28	Hampton's	Woman's Ind. Exchange
27	Prime Rib	Chester River Inn/A
26	Inn at Perry Cabin/A	Da Mimmo
	Milton Inn	Treaty of Paris/A
25	Rudys' 2900	**22** Helmand
	Linwood's	Orchard Market/Cafe
	Northwoods/A	King's Contrivance
	Antrim 1844	Due
24	Polo Grill	La Piccola Roma/A
	Tersiguel's	Haussner's
	M. Gettier	Hunan Manor
	Boccaccio	Ruth's Chris
23	Marconi's	Sushi-Ya
	Brass Elephant	**21** Pierpoint
	Banjara	Thai Landing
	Peerce's Plantation	Jeannier's
	Savannah	Joey Chiu's
	Tio Pepe	Narrows/A
	Joy America	Windows
	Harry Browne's/A	Henninger's Tavern

Best Buys

Top 100 Bangs For The Buck

This list reflects the best dining values in our *Survey*. It is produced by dividing the cost of a meal into the combined ratings for food, decor and service.

1. One World Cafe
2. Woman's Ind. Exchange
3. Jimmy's (Fells Pt.)
4. GlasZ Cafe
5. Ethel & Ramone's
6. Desert Cafe
7. Adrian's Book Cafe
8. Canopy
9. Chick & Ruth's Delly/A
10. Margaret's Cafe
11. Peter's Inn
12. Attman's Delicatessen
13. Faidley's
14. Cafe Hon
15. Baugher's
16. PaperMoon Diner
17. Nacho Mama's
18. Duda's
19. Double T Diner
20. Bajara
21. Cafe Zen
22. Bel-Loc Diner
23. Field's Pharmacy
24. New Towne Diner
25. Morning Edition Cafe
26. Al Pacino Cafe
27. Louie's Bookstore Cafe
28. Orchard Market/Cafe
29. Ledo Pizza
30. Helmand
31. Szechuan Best
32. Hunan Manor
33. Bombay Grill
34. Cafe Manet
35. Bill Bateman's Bistro
36. Silver Diner
37. Gunning's (Dorsey Rd.)
38. Sanders' Corner
39. Ban Thai
40. Mughal Garden
41. Szechuan
42. Cafe Tattoo
43. Thai
44. Tomato Palace
45. Jumbo Seafood
46. Donna's
47. Akbar
48. Crease
49. Bangkok Place
50. Thai Landing
51. Peerce's Gourmet
52. Alonso's
53. Friendly Farms
54. Wharf Rat
55. Bandaloops
56. Wild Mushroom
57. Matsuri
58. Kisling's
59. Amicci's
60. Tully's
61. Metropol
62. John Steven
63. Bertucci's
64. Adam's Rib/A
65. Red Hot & Blue
66. Ikaros
67. Pavilion at the Walters
68. Hull St. Blues
69. Bare Bones
70. Hunt Valley Szechuan
71. Sushi-Ya
72. Bamboo House
73. Ralphie's Diner
74. Regi's
75. California Pizza Kitchen
76. Strapazza
77. Charred Rib
78. Joey Chiu's
79. Mama Lucia
80. Donna's at BMA
81. Ransome's Harbor Hill Cafe
82. Bertha's
83. No Way Jose
84. Great Amer. Melting Pot
85. Loco Hombre
86. Jerry D's Saloon
87. Mick's
88. Burke's
89. Haussner's
90. Corner Stable
91. McGarvey's/A
92. Acropolis
93. Griffin's/A
94. T.G.I. Friday's
95. Jilly's
96. Swallow at the Hollow
97. Puffin's
98. River Watch
99. Henninger's Tavern
100. Kawasaki

A = Annapolis

Additional Good Values
(A bit more expensive, but worth every penny)

Angler/A

Bowman

Braznell's

Cafe Bretton

Cafe du Vin/A

Cafe Sophie/A

Ciao Bella

Claddagh Pub

Di Pasquale's

El Taquito Mexicano

Fazzini's

Frazier's

Giolitti/A

Grand Palace

Hampton Tea Room

Hoang's

Holly's/A

Jenning's

J. Patrick's

Kelly's

Kelsey's

Luigi Petti

Mai Thai

Nam Kang

New No Ja Di

Nick's

OPA

Perring Place

Purim Oak

Rams Head/A

Riordan's/A

Saigon

Saigon Palace/A

Samos

Schultz's Crab House

Silver Spring Mining Co

Sunset

Surfin' Bull

Sushi Cafe

Tenosix

Thai Orient

Thames St. Tavern

Vito's Cafe

Wing Wah

Ze Mean Bean

Zorba's

Alphabetical
Directory
of Restaurants

Baltimore

F | D | S | C

Acropolis [S] — 18 | 11 | 18 | $16
4714-8 Eastern Ave. (Oldham St.), 410-675-3384
◩ At this Greektown icon, cheapskates with "big appetites" overdose on "more than enough" Greek food in "ethnically comforting" surroundings (translation: "zero decor"); picky eaters fuss about "old mutton" dressed as lamb.

Adrian's Book Cafe [S] — 17 | 18 | 16 | $11
714 S. Broadway (bet. Lancaster & Aliceanna Sts.), 410-732-1048
■ A "cozy" bookstore cafe in "manic" Fells Point with "creative" snacks, "killer" sweets and enough books to "scare off the skateboarders"; be prepared to "linger."

Akbar [S] — 20 | 15 | 19 | $16
823 N. Charles St. (bet. Madison & Read Sts.), 410-539-0944
3541 Brenbrook Dr. (Liberty Rd.), Randallstown, 410-655-1600
Columbia Marketplace, 9400 Snowden River Pkwy., Columbia, 410-381-3600
■ This "cave-like Indian classic" in Mt. Vernon and its suburban sibs "continue to win converts to Indian food" despite stiff competition from Mughal Garden and Bombay Grill; go for the "reliable" standards, "attentive" help and "bargain" lunch buffets.

Alonso's 🌙[S] — 16 | 8 | 14 | $12
415 W. Coldspring Ln. (bet. Charles St. & Roland Ave.), 410-235-3433
■ Attractive "barflies, huge [1 lb.] hamburgers" and great pizza lure "aging preppies" to this "funky, unkempt" Roland Park "nabe cave"; it's a perennial winner of Baltimore's "best burger" and best "late-night-drunk" place awards – a "barbaric tribute to red meat."

Al Pacino Cafe [S] — 19 | 10 | 14 | $12
609 S. Broadway (bet. Fleet & Aliceanna Sts.), 410-327-0005
Belvedere Sq., 542 E. Belvedere Ave. (York Rd.), 410-323-7060
900 Cathedral St. (Read St.), 410-962-8859
Lake Forest Village, 6084 Falls Rd. (Lake Ave.), 410-377-3132
Festival at Woodholme, 1809 Reisterstown Rd. (Hooks Ln.), Pikesville, 410-653-6868
513 Baltimore Pike (Rte. 24), Bel Air, 410-638-8057
■ Pizza "diversity" with a Middle Eastern spin at these no-frills (BYOB) brick ovens is "something to be desired" – their "cramped", "carry-out" atmosphere is not; don't miss the sharm el-sheq pizza with a side of baba ghanoush.

Amicci's S   21 | 15 | 18 | $17
231 S. High St. (bet. Stiles & Fawn Sts.), 410-528-1096
2903 O'Donnell St. (S. Linwood Ave.), 410-675-3207
■ "Fun" and "trendy", these "rock 'n' roll Italians" feature red-sauced pasta and seafood cooked by youthful "singing chefs"; the scene is "cramped but cute" in Little Italy, Canton is "more roomy" and "relaxed."

Anastasia S   ▽ 13 | 14 | 13 | $22
2501 Boston St. (O'Donnell St.), 410-276-7000
■ You can avoid parking problems by sailing to this Canton anchorage, but dock only for the noisy bar scene and "nice view"; according to most reviewers, as a seafooder, it's an impostor.

Angelina's S   19 | 12 | 17 | $19
7135 Harford Rd. (Rosalie Ave.), 410-444-5545
■ A "softball"-sized "mound of fantastic lump crabmeat" puts this dimly lit, North Baltimore Irish-Italian bar on the gastronomic map; but don't expect its legendary crab cake to come with much in the way of atmosphere – or to come cheap.

ANTRIM 1844 S   24 | 28 | 25 | $52
Antrim 1844 Country Inn, 30 Trevanion Rd. (Rte. 140), Taneytown, 410-756-6812
■ An excursion to this "magnificent restoration" an hour northwest of Baltimore evokes the "age of innocence" with an "imaginative", multicourse Contemporary American meal and "breathtaking" setting; equally breathtaking pricing, however, makes some reviewers decide to "go there once, not twice."

A-1 Crab Haven ●S   17 | 11 | 17 | $19
1600 Old Eastern Ave. (Back River Neck Rd.), 410-657-6000
■ "Affluent suburbanites" frequent this "comfortable", aptly named East Baltimore seafooder for top-quality steamed crabs (in season), spicy steamed shrimp and Greek salad; you get what you pay for seafood-wise and vice versa.

Attman's Delicatessen S   20 | 8 | 14 | $10
1019 E. Lombard St. (bet. Lloyd & Watson Sts.), 410-563-2666
■ The "last of the real Lombard Street delis" is still hanging in there, although the premises and neighborhood have been "declining rapidly" for years; mavens report that the "kibitzing has slipped, but the corned beef hasn't"; N.B delivery advised.

Backfin S
10 | 6 | 11 | $16

1116 Reisterstown Rd. (Sudbrook Ln.), Pikesville, 410-484-7344
☑ Though capable of producing a "respectable" crab cake ("at times"), this "Pikesville crab dive" draws some of this *Survey*'s worst reports: "no decor or ambiance", "an anomaly in seafood city" and "two-for-one coupons have kept it afloat."

Bamboo House S
20 | 19 | 19 | $19

Harborplace, Pratt St. Pavilion (Light St.), 410-625-1191
Yorktowne Plaza Shopping Ctr., 26 Cranbrook St. (York Rd.),
Cockeysville, 410-666-9550
■ "Tasteful" settings, "unthreatening" Chinese food and Joey Chiu's "professional" oversight keep these "pretty" old-timers evergreen; add a sensational view (Harborplace) for the "best lunch in the Inner Harbor."

Bandaloops
19 | 19 | 18 | $17

1024 S. Charles St. (Cross St.), 410-727-1355
■ A "cheerful" SoBo "hangout for serious drinkers" and "interesting characters", this American with "artsy but not bizarre help" also draws "a big weekday lunch crowd" since you can hear yourself talk; its "relaxed" manners and eclectic bar food let you drop by in "dress up" or sweats.

Bangkok Place S
21 | 13 | 19 | $16

5230 York Rd. (bet. Cold Spring Ln. & Woodbourne Ave.),
410-433-0040
■ "Daily special curries" are the "best bet" at this "well-established" North Baltimore Thai; it's "not fancy, but a good deal" and fine for a family fill-up or "dinner before the Senator" movie theater.

Banjara S
24 | 19 | 23 | $16

1017 S. Charles St. (bet. Hamburg & Cross Sts.), 410-962-1554
■ The "wonderful aroma of spices" fills this Federal Hill storefront leading Baltimore's burgeoning Indian parade; the "flavorful", fairly priced dishes taste even better because you're treated like their "most important customer."

Ban Thai
19 | 12 | 18 | $14

340 N. Charles St. (Mulberry St.), 410-727-7971
■ This "predictable" Thai won't win any creative-cooking prizes; what it offers instead is a pleasant place to talk business Downtown and "good, plentiful food for the price"; but don't be fooled by its quiet demeanor — regulars swear that some of the dishes pack such a punch "you won't know what hit you."

Bare Bones **S**   18 | 15 | 17 | $16 |
617 S. Frederick Ave. (½ mi. north of Shady Grove Rd.),
Gaithersburg, 301-948-4344
St. John's Plaza, 9150 Baltimore Nat'l. Pike (1 light west of
Rte. 29), Ellicott City, 410-461-0770
■ Bones are "all that's left" when rib lovers leave these
"decently priced", family-style rib joints – and, happily,
their recent remodeling doesn't interfere with the pleasure
of messy eating; some go mostly for "Monday night football"
and the "rowdy fun" that results when the "beer selection is
better than the food."

Baugher's **S**   16 | 11 | 17 | $11 |
289 W. Main St. Ext. (Rtes. 31 & 32), Westminster, 410-848-7413
■ A "relic" of "deep-fried" "country cooking" at "1940s
prices" sums up this "folksy" Carroll County farmstand/
restaurant with "crusty" servers and "farm-fresh fruit", pies
and ice cream; be prepared to contend with "busloads" of
pilgrims seeking "comfort."

Bay Cafe **◐S**   14 | 17 | 13 | $17 |
2809 Boston St. (Linwood Ave.), 410-522-3377
▨ "Wonderful sunsets", "awesome" shrimp salad
sandwiches and doing the "meat market mambo" are the
attractions at Canton's "beach" on the bay; but even if
you're not an "Xer or boater", this dockside watering hole
is worthwhile for a drink; and the "wonderful" view can
help you forget the "indifferent" seafood, "absurdly slow
service" and crowds.

Bel-Loc Diner **◐S**   11 | 12 | 14 | $9 |
Corner of Loch Raven Blvd. & Joppa Rd., East Towson,
410-668-2525
▨ "A real diner from the old days" with "burnt eggs", "gravy
from a barrel" and "cheap, bland food"; it's staffed by
"female commandos" (as "bitter as the coffee") and
frequented, sooner or later, by virtually everyone who
passes this NE Baltimore County intersection; it's also
"one of the last places left to play jukebox warfare" or go
for "3 AM munchies."

Berry & Elliot's **S**   19 | 22 | 19 | $24 |
Hyatt Regency Baltimore, 300 Light St. (bet. Pratt &
Conway Sts.), 410-605-2835
▨ With the harbor lights twinkling, the "magnificent view" is
the main draw at this Contemporary American hotel dining
perch popular with "out-of-towners and conventioneers";
although some say the steak and seafood are "surprisingly
good" accompaniments, the consensus is "go for the
view, not the food."

Bertha's 🅂
18 | 17 | 16 | $17

734 S. Broadway (Lancaster St.), 410-327-5795

■ It's "hard to resist" this "salty" old Fells Point "institution" with its "great waterfront atmosphere", legendary "seafood, jazz and beer", "serious afternoon tea" (by reservation) and indefinable "charm"; despite the "hype" and quips ("gone flabby, losing its mussels"), "everyone goes and loves it."

Bertucci's 🅂
17 | 16 | 16 | $15

8130 Corporate Pl. (bet. Honeygo & Perry Hall Blvds.), Perry Hall, 410-931-0900
Owings Mills Mall, Owings Mills Blvd. at I-795, Owings Mills, 410-356-5515
1818 York Rd. (Ridge Rd.), Timonium, 410-561-7000
12 Bel Air S. Pkwy. (Rte. 24), Bel Air, 410-569-4600
Snowden Sq., 9081 Snowden River Pkwy. (Robert Fulton Dr.), Columbia, 410-312-4800

See Washington, DC, Alphabetical Directory.

Bill Bateman's Bistro ◗🅂
18 | 15 | 15 | $14

7800 York Rd. (Cross Campus Dr.), Towson, 410-296-2737

■ Bill Bateman's "gut-stuffing" formula — "no flash, little cash, heart-stopping ribs" and "wings to fly for" plus "beer in a frosted mug" — makes this a "family dining" place as well as a "college hangout and sports bar"; credit the "open spaces", "perky" help and irresistible appeal of "great unhealthy" eats; "if the food doesn't kill you, the noise will."

Birds of a Feather
– | – | – | E

1712 Aliceanna St. (Broadway), 410-675-8466

Serious eaters flock to this quaint, "intimate" Fells Point bar for wild fowl, game and Contemporary American fare "cooked to perfection" in a "very professional" kitchen headed by the owners' son, a Michael Rork (ex Hampton's) disciple; write-ins tap it for "future greatness", not to mention the "best scotch selection in Baltimore."

Bo Brooks Crab House 🅂
20 | 9 | 16 | $20

5415 Belair Rd. (Frankford Ave.), 410-488-8144

■ All a "crab house needs are mallets, brown paper", cold beer and a reliable source of "big, sweet" crabs in and out of season — which explains why this "windowless factory" in NE Baltimore rates as one of the best; its "other seafood" is "acceptable", but the "uniquely Baltimore" steamed crab "experience" should not be missed.

BOCCACCIO 🅂
25 | 24 | 24 | $34

925 Eastern Ave. (bet. Exeter & High Sts.), 410-234-1322

■ Baltimore's top Italian strikes many as the kind of "classy", "aloof", "can't loosen your belt at the table" restaurant they'd find in New York; nevertheless, the "great pastas and seafood", "outstanding veal chop", well-chosen Northern Italian wines and "romantic" setting compel admiration: a "real treasure in Little Italy."

Bombay Grill S   23 19 21 $18
2 E. Madison St. (N. Charles St.), 410-837-2973
Cafe Bombay S
114 E. Lombard St. (Calvert St.), 410-539-2233
Bombay Peacock Grill S
*10005 Old Columbia Pike (Eden Brook Dr.), Columbia,
410-381-7111*
■ Even if Indian food is normally "not your thing", the
"excellent", subtly spiced food, refined surroundings and
"rajah" treatment at one of Baltimore's best Indians could
sway you; aficionados "can't go wrong here" and biz
lunchers swear by the "quiet-for-conversation" settings
and "truly delicious" bargain buffets; check out the dosas
(S. Indian crêpes) and mod take on the classics at the
newish Downtown cafe.

Bowman S   18 16 18 $19
9306 Harford Rd. (bet. Java Rd. & Puddy Hill), 410-665-8600
☑ This Parkville North hub scores a bull's-eye with regulars
for its crab cakes and light fare served on the "dark" bar
side; "a charming older crowd" goes for the "step above
church supper" fare dished out in the "small" dining room;
it's one of those "likable", "good value for your dollar"
places that every neighborhood needs; N.B. try the comedy
club downstairs after dinner.

BRASS ELEPHANT S   24 27 23 $33
924 N. Charles St. (bet. Read & Eager Sts.), 410-547-8480
■ A "ritzy" backdrop for anything from a "stockbroker"
dinner to a TV shoot, this Downtown Edwardian showplace's
"lovely" Northern Italian and Mediterranean-Continental
menu and service let you go "first class" without paying
"ridiculous prices" – particularly if you take advantage of
the $8 lunch or $19.95 pre-theater deals or go for a light
bite in the "fabulous marble bar" upstairs.

Brasserie S   ▽ 20 18 17 $18
*Pomona Sq., 1700 Reisterstown Rd. (Naylors Ln.),
Pikesville, 410-484-0476*
☑ It's not clear why this Pikesville Northern Italian is often
"empty"; it's "roomy, comfortable, quiet and easy to park"
nearby – it even has "decent", "reasonably" priced food;
perhaps it's the "unlikely location" in a shopping mall, plus
the somewhat dispiriting atmosphere and only "fair service."

Braznell's Caribbean Kitchen S ▽ 19 15 16 $17
1623 E. Baltimore St. (Broadway), 410-327-2445
☑ Alfred and Esme Braznell cook up a fiery Caribbean storm
at their low-rent Downtown location just like they would
back home in Trinidad – slowly and "superbly"; a "real
survivor in a tough area", it's a "decent place to get your
goat" or "hang out" and "eat in the bar."

Burke's Cafe ◐ [S] 13 | 11 | 14 | $13
36 Light St. (Lombard St.), 410-752-4189
◪ A "dark, sleazy" "dinosaur" lazing on prime Downtown corner real estate; it's a "love it, hate it" deal with onion rings "the size of inner tubes", "greasy" burgers, steak and beer – "no fad foods or California bull" – and "good comedy" upstairs, if not always good service.

Cacao Lane [S] 18 | 18 | 17 | $20
8066 Main St. (Tiber Alley), Ellicott City, 410-461-1378
◪ Reeking of "Old Ellicott City charm", this rustic little eatery "fits in well" with the historic surroundings; the "please-everyone" Continental menu, weekend music and multilevel outdoor deck please most, but there are those who grouse about "inept service" and "wait in vain for the flavor of the food to match that of the setting."

Caesar's Den [S] 21 | 16 | 21 | $26
223 S. High St. (Stiles St.), 410-547-0820
■ This Southern Italian's food tastes "home cooked", it treats customers "like family" and the "cute paintings" and "close tables" give it a "cozy", "romantic" air; go for "consistency", not nuova cucina – it's a Little Italy "classic."

Cafe Bretton ▽ 24 | 16 | 22 | $28
849 Baltimore-Annapolis Blvd. (McKinsey Rd.), Severna Park, 410-647-8222
■ In Europe, it's not unusual for a "small, family-owned" restaurant to use produce from its "own garden" to add fresh flavor to its countrified food; but in a "suburban backwater" north of Annapolis it's noteworthy – so is this French-Continental's "good value" and "attempts to please."

Cafe Hon [S] 18 | 16 | 17 | $12
1002 W. 36th St. (bet. Roland Ave. & Falls Rd.), 410-243-1230
■ "Working hard in its new ['95] space to be homey" and not run short of either chicken salad or "folksy" help, this old-time American supplies an "eclectic mix" of Hampden blue collars and university types with "cheap", "normal" food; it's rapidly become "everyone's favorite for meetings and brunch" (not to mention breakfast and lunch), raising concerns that it's becoming too popular.

Cafe Manet 19 | 11 | 15 | $13
1020 S. Charles St. (Cross St.), 410-837-7006
◪ "Quirky" Continental carryout (with a handful of tables and "extremely casual" service) near the Cross Street Market comes in handy for "picnics at the harbor", an "after-work wind down", below-$10 wines and take-home dinners; some marvel that "warm-up food can taste so good", others "don't agree."

Café Pangea S　　　　　　– | – | – | I
4007 Falls Rd. (bet. 40 & 41st Sts.), 410-662-0500
An engaging mix of gingerbread architecture, cyberspace
access, exotic coffees, interesting wines and sophisticated
snacks draws cybernauts, oenophiles, caffeine heads, TV
news teams (headquartered nearby) and the curious to
this Hampden cafe and wine bar; check out your E-mail at
one of the sleek computer booths or settle into the sofa
for an old-fashioned chat.

Cafe Tattoo　　　　　　15 | 10 | 15 | $12
4825 Belair Rd. (Moravia Rd.), 410-325-7427
☑ A "smoky" bar with many beers, "loud bands", "good
chili", "great ribs" and a "tattoo parlor" upstairs – this
roadhouse also has "fantastic burritos and peanut butter
pie" and what those who don't dig the "wit" or the "rough
crowd" call an "unfriendly atmosphere"; nevertheless, it
"fits well in B'more."

Cafe Troia　　　　　　23 | 20 | 21 | $28
*28 W. Allegheny Ave. (Washington Ave.), Towson,
410-337-0133*
☑ Since this Towson Italian became the "rage", admirers
bemoan the expansion that sometimes "overwhelms" its
"excellent" kitchen and "cordial" staff and prices it "not
for every day"; still, most remain enthusiastic about the
"sophisticated" food and ambiance that feels "like Italy."

Cafe Zen S　　　　　　21 | 17 | 18 | $14
438 E. Belvedere Ave. (York Rd.), 410-532-0022
☑ Senator moviegoers flock to this dressed-up Chinese
serving good "traditional" fare enlivened by sushi and a
couple of "unusual" dishes; it gets points for "trying to
be fresh in an area that needs freshness" and for giving
vegetarians interesting things to eat, but not for being "a
little slow" at night.

Candle Light Inn S　　　　　　18 | 20 | 20 | $24
1835 Frederick Rd. (Rolling Rd.), 410-788-6076
☑ "The established Catonsville restaurant" for anniversaries
and family occasions pairs a colonial setting with "chart-
topping" chicken cordon bleu and chocolate mousse; the
"pleasant" atmosphere and covered porch make it a "nice
little getaway" for "conservative" diners – and we hear the
new chef (early '96) is serving some "new food."

Canopy, The S　　　　　　16 | 7 | 12 | $8
*5820 Johnnycake Rd. (Ingleside Ave.), 410-744-2188
Roberts Field Shopping Ctr., 721 Hanover Pike (North
Woods Trail), Hampstead, 410-239-4089*

Canopy, The (Cont.)

5 Vernon Ave., NW (Ritchie Hwy.), Glen Burnie, 410-768-1719
9319 Baltimore Nat'l Pike (Chatham Rd.), Ellicott City,
410-465-5718
607 E. Main St. (Chartley Dr.), Reisterstown, 410-526-4229
Peddlers Sq. Shopping Ctr., 2030 Liberty Rd. (Monroe Ave.),
Eldersburg, 410-549-2880
Festival, 8125-P Ritchie Hwy. (Jumpers Hole Rd.),
Pasadena, 410-647-7722
140 Village Shopping Ctr., Westminster, 410-848-7443

■ Known for "great roast beef sandwiches", messy ribs and fresh-cut fries, these "quick pit stops" serve simple, tasty "fast food" in spartan, self-service settings that are impervious to kids; they're Bawlmer's home-grown answer to BBQ, though a minority labels them the pits – period.

Captain Harvey's 〔S〕 〔17〕〔13〕〔17〕〔$23〕

11510 Reisterstown Rd. (Nicodemus Rd.), Reisterstown,
410-356-7550

◪ "Decor is not available" at this Reisterstown destination – "seafood is all that counts" here; the steady clientele is "never let down" by the "old-fashioned" menu (shellfish, sandwiches, steak) and motherly ("sometimes surly") waitresses, but if you're not a part of the local scene, it'll seem "mediocre all the way around."

Champagne Tony's/Owl Bar 〔S〕 〔20〕〔25〕〔19〕〔$25〕

The Belvedere, 1 E. Chase St. (N. Charles St.), 410-347-0888

◪ There is no more "elegant" dining room or atmospheric bar than these "wonderfully restored" "Baltimore classics" in The Belvedere; young see and "be seens" lap up salads and designer pizzas in the "beer hall" and "more varied" types seek neo-Italian dishes and "crackling" fires in CT; both venues suffer from "staff turnover" (notably, the summer '96 departure of the chef responsible for the above food rating) and "erratic" fare; N.B. take advantage of valet parking or park on site.

Chapps Kosher Oriental 〔S〕 ▽ 〔14〕〔12〕〔14〕〔$16〕

Pomona Sq., 1700 Reisterstown Rd. (Naylors Ln.),
410-653-3198

■ It may be a bit difficult to imagine "good" Chinese food cooked "with a Jewish flair", but this Pikesville kosher Chinese does it; it also manages to produce convincing versions of the real thing without shrimp, shellfish or pork.

Charred Rib 〔S〕 〔18〕〔12〕〔16〕〔$15〕

2010 York Rd. (Timonium Rd.), Timonium, 410-561-0735

■ "Forget the tacky decor" – one goes to this dark, smoky Timonium bar for "falling off the bone", "melt in your mouth" ribs, fries and fellowship; an occasional salad has been sighted, but don't let that spoil your "high cholesterol" fun.

Chart House 🅂   19 | 21 | 19 | $28
Pier 4, 601 E. Pratt St. (Marketplace St.), 410-539-6616
See Washington, DC, Alphabetical Directory.

Cheesecake Factory   19 | 18 | 17 | $20
Harborplace, Pratt St. Pavilion (South St.), 410-234-3990
See Washington, DC, Alphabetical Directory.

Chiapparelli's 🅂   19 | 16 | 19 | $21
237 S. High St. (Fawn St.), 410-837-0309
◪ This Little Italy Italian defines the genre with its "great",
garlicky salad, "heavy" pastas and veal and "family-like"
atmosphere; maybe it's "outdated", but it's a beacon for
tourists and the faithful because it remains, comfortably,
the "same as always."

Ciao Bella 🅂   ▽ 21 | 20 | 23 | $20
236 S. High St. (bet. Stiles & Fawn Sts.), 410-685-7733
■ When family owners take "pride in their work" (as they
do here), you can taste it in the pastas and "homemade"
sauces and tell it by the "royal treatment" you get; although
many seemingly similar "Little Italy restaurants are not
worth their price", its clientele thinks this one is.

City Lights 🅂   14 | 18 | 15 | $18
Harborplace, Light St. Pavilion, 2nd fl. (Pratt St.), 410-244-8811
◪ Panoramic city skyline and harbor views from its terrace
keep this Harborplace stalwart "in business"; otherwise,
the American food is "overpriced" and "ordinary" and it
seems like the "staff is always new" – however, given the
alternatives, it's "ok" for lunch.

CJ's   15 | 10 | 15 | $18
*10117 Reisterstown Rd. (Painters Mill Rd.), Owings Mills,
410-363-6694*
◪ When Owings Mills locals don't want to drive "for
midweek crabs", they dock at this "cramped", "noisy",
"smoky", "dark" seafood shack; the place offers plenty
of finfare choices, but as most regulars will tell you,
it's best to eat steamed crabs, crab soup or possibly
pizza – and "nothing else."

Claddagh Pub   ▽ 21 | 16 | 21 | $17
Canton Sq., 2918 O'Donnell St. (Curley St.), 410-522-4220
■ Youthful "Irish charm" fills this Emerald Isle–themed
pub in Canton that offers neighborly vibes and "perfect
for the '90s food"; virtually everything from the "upscale"
bar grub and the "build your own burger" Saturday lunch
special ($2.95) to the "great" black Angus steaks and
"excellent" mashed potatoes (before 6 PM) gets the nod.

Clyde's   17 | 21 | 18 | $21
*10221 Wincopin Circle, Columbia, 301-596-4050, (DC)
410-730-2829*
See Washington, DC, Alphabetical Directory.

Corner Stable S 19 11 15 $15
9942 York Rd. (Church Ln.), Cockeysville, 410-666-8722
■ *Cheers*-like Cockeysville BBQ satisfies meat cravings with some of Baltimore County's "best" baby back ribs and garlic-salted fries; but ribs aren't the only reason it's packed – this "dark" bar and its "no-nonsense waitressing" generate so much atmosphere, "you can't be sad in here"; N.B. other locations share the name, but they ain't the same.

Crack Pot S 16 11 15 $18
Ravenwood Shopping Ctr., 8102 Loch Raven Blvd. (Taylor Ave.), 410-828-1095
☑ TV ads haven't changed much about this dark, "smoky" bar near Parkville; as always, it "desperately needs to remodel" and serves "pretty good" seafood "for the price"; neighborhood "old-timers" treat it like their "retirement village", while others come to "experience" crabs (in season) and "quintessential", if "pedestrian", Baltimore.

Crease, The S 16 15 16 $14
523 York Rd. (bet. Allegheny & Pennsylvania Aves.), Towson, 410-823-0395
☑ Unless you play lacrosse, or follow it intently, you may not understand this "preppy" Towson sports bar's goal, which is to give postgraduate jocks a place to drink beer, swap stories and fill up on a "smorgasbord" of "khaki" (i.e. fried) bar food; it scores with "good burgers and chicken" for a "fast dinner before the movies."

Crossroads – – – E
Cross Keys Inn, 5100 Falls Rd. (Northern Pkwy. & Cold Spring Ln.), 410-435-0101
Given the lack of restaurants in the Uptown area, the reopening of this Contemporary American hotel dining room is good news indeed; it's where Roland Park matrons lunch and business deals are done in an atmosphere of quiet civility; don't miss the serious Sunday brunch.

Dalesio's of Little Italy S 20 19 20 $28
829 Eastern Ave. (Albemarle St.), 410-539-1965
☑ An "intimate" townhouse in Little Italy offering Northern Italian–inspired pastas and seafood and its signature "spa cuisine"; surveyors split on service and whether one finds "Italy in Baltimore" or a plate of "yesteryear's Italiana fare."

Da Mimmo S 24 20 23 $37
217 S. High St. (Stiles St.), 410-727-6876
☑ Does the "limo pickup from hotels", the "glitz", the lobster-stuffed pasta or even the "veal chop of infamy" justify the cost of a meal at this small, crowded Little Italy restaurant?; that depends on one's pocketbook and appetite for luxury ingredients – many think it "doesn't get any better" than this; P.S. the cost escalates sharply if one succumbs to the waiter's "polished sell" of the "expensive" specials.

daniel's S   – | – | – | E |
(fka Tabrizi's)
1026 S. Charles St. (bet. Cross & Hamburg Sts.),
410-752-3810
Susan Daniel has reinvented her "innovative" South
Baltimore restaurant, Tabrizi's, to celebrate Chesapeake
cuisine and international seafood; this involved a major
gentrification of the atrium-lit dining room, filling the
courtyard with greenery and glittering lights, and installing a
new chef trained at the Culinary Institute of America; the
rest of the staff remains – as does her high-profile following.

Desert Cafe ⊄   20 | 17 | 19 | $12 |
1605-07 Sulgrave Ave. (Newbury St.), 410-367-5808
■ If ever there was a spot for a rainy afternoon or coffee
and sweets at night, it's this "romantic, four-table hideaway
in Mt. Washington"; by most accounts, the "whole earth"
Middle Eastern nibbles are "worth a try", the atmosphere
"relaxing" and the falafel a must – now "if only they'd take
the calories out of those wonderful desserts."

Di Pasquale's Cafe   ∇ 17 | 15 | 16 | $10 |
8 W. Cross St. (bet. S. Charles & Hanover Sts.),
410-347-0585
■ It's little bigger than a food stall in the nearby Cross
Street Market, yet this sunny corner of Italy builds an
"excellent porketta sandwich" and other mouth-filling
subs; every day there's a homey hot special to nourish
all the briefcases who wish it weren't "only open for
Monday–Friday lunch."

Di Vivo's S   – | – | – | M |
801 Eastern Ave. (President St.), 410-837-5500
Notwithstanding its garish exterior, this blockbuster Little
Italy addition pulls a lively mix of happy eaters with its
spacious setting highlighting wonderful city skyline views,
on-site parking, a giant pastry showroom, wood-burning
pizza oven, perky salads and improved versions of red-
sauced Italian favorites; locals already love it, tourists
will be impressed.

DONNA'S AT THE BMA S   22 | 22 | 19 | $21 |
Baltimore Museum of Art, Art Museum Dr. (N. Charles St.),
410-467-3600
■ No food could "match the art" or rival the BMA's "tree-
rimmed sculpture garden", which is the backdrop of this
"contempo" museum cafe; nevertheless, this Donna sib
produces fresh, modern American food that tastes like it
was "made from scratch" yet "does not distract" from the
"elegant" surroundings; service remains problematic and
reservations are a good idea.

Donna's Coffee Bar S   21 19 18 $17
2 W. Madison St. (N. Charles St.), 410-385-0180
22 W. Allegheny Ave. (York Rd.), Towson, 410-828-6655

Donna's at Bibelot
*Festival at Woodholme, 1819 Reisterstown Rd. (1 block
north of Hooks Ln.), Pikesville, 410-653-6939*

Donna's at UMMS
*University of Maryland, 22 S. Greene St. (Baltimore St.),
410-328-1962*

Donna's Espress
Calvert & Centre Sts., 410-539-1858 (carryout only; Mon.-Fri.)
■ Donna Crivello "found a niche and filled it nicely" with
"light designer fare" — roasted veggies, fresh salads, great
bread — and "minimalist", "pose or die" surroundings; but
someone should "tell those folks to wear less black" and
lighten up; her newish niche, The Ruby Lounge, is next door.

Dotson's BBQ S⊘   – – – I
*7317 Furnace Branch Rd. (bet. Baltimore-Annapolis Blvd.
& Ritchie Hwy., off Rte. 10), Glen Burnie, 410-768-2784*
■ BBQ fiends often won't tell you when they find the "real"
thing — they want to keep those succulent, mouthwatering
ribs and chicken for themselves; once you try this "great",
little-known pit/carryout in Glen Burnie, you'll probably
feel the same way; P.S. "insiders" take their food to the
"screened-in spot across the street."

Double T Diner ⬤S   14 13 17 $11
6300 Baltimore Nat'l Pike (Rolling Rd.), 410-744-4151
1 Mountain Rd. (Ritchie Hwy.), Glen Burnie, 410-766-9669
◪ Only at this colorful diner near Catonsville that grew
(and grew) can you find "Peking duck on Belgian waffles . . .
24 hours a day", hundreds of other "dizzying" choices,
"Day-Glo desserts", "caustic" waitresses and a chance to
see the "face of Maryland" — all for loose pocket change;
N.B. the Double T on Ritchie Highway is a "too new" relation
and the one on Rte. 40E ain't no kin.

Duda's Tavern ⬤   20 16 19 $14
1600 Thames St. (Bond St.), 410-276-9719
■ One of the few "genuine" waterfront bars left in Fells
Point, this "corner" local is so small that its "gargantuan"
subs, "great salads" and terrific burgers nearly fill the
place; the kitchen is even smaller (and therefore "slow"),
giving customers plenty of time to sample the 150 beers.

Due S   24 22 22 $29
25 Crossroads Dr. (McDonough Rd.), Owings Mills, 410-356-4147
■ This "uptown" trattoria in Owings Mills brings an "earthy"
Tuscan "touch" to the "imaginative bistro cuisine", "posh"
surroundings and "accommodating" dining approach
popularized at its sister Linwood's; many consider it "almost
as good" as its sib, though a few claim they're "due" more.

Elkridge Furnace Inn ▽ 21 | 25 | 18 | $21

5745 Furnace Ave. (Washington Blvd.), Elkridge, 410-379-9336

■ Not many people realize that this picture-perfect wedding venue, a "delightfully restored" 18th-century property near BWI, serves weekday lunch and dinner; it's one of those "well-intentioned" places that produces a "pleasant" meal even when the Continental food and service fall short of the "lovely setting"; BYOB – liquor license expected soon.

El Taquito Mexicano – | – | – | I

1744 Eastern Ave. (Broadway), 410-563-7840

This low-rent Mexican functions as a community center for Eastern Fells Point's Central American enclave, offering authentic chile rellenos, rolled tacos and other typical dishes; artists, students and adventurous diners join them for a bargain tour – "this is good" and "cheap."

Ethel & Ramone's Cafe [S] 18 | 20 | 18 | $11

1615 Sulgrave Ave. (bet. Newbury St. & Kelly Ave.), 410-664-2971

■ "Tucked away" in Mt. Washington is a "cute, little, funky" place to "sip tea, eat pastry" (or healthy light fare), "chat and get warm"; it's very much a family affair, run by very talkative Ramone (aka Jeff), his wife, Ethel (aka Jane), and their son, who was recently installed in an "expanded" kitchen whipping out 'New Age' California cuisine.

Faidley's Seafood 22 | 11 | 15 | $11

Lexington Market, 400 W. Lexington St. (Paca St.), 410-727-4898

■ A "standup" crab cake at this city market raw bar is a "Baltimore experience not to be missed" – well "worth the risky location" and "dumpster" smells; this is one eatery with no "yuppie pretensions" – just "excellent value" and the "freshest" seafood and coldest beer in town; it'll "bring out the hon'" in you.

Fazzini's Italian Kitchen [S] ▽ 22 | 9 | 20 | $12

Cranbrook Shopping Ctr., 578 Cranbrook Rd. (York Rd.), Cockeysville, 410-667-6104

◪ If you live or work in Cockeysville, chances are you've stopped by this "bare bones", strip stop Italian for "fresh", "delicious" carryout on your way home; it's also handy for a "cheap" pizza or a bring-the-kids, midweek dinner.

Field's Pharmacy [S] 16 | 9 | 13 | $10

1401 Reisterstown Rd. (Walker Ave.), Pikesville, 410-486-3375

■ This "classic" drugstore lunch counter is still a Pikesville "place to eat and greet" and see what life "was like 35 years ago"; there aren't many places left offering old-fashioned shrimp salad, grilled-cheese sandwiches, milk shakes, "gravy and fries" and "great snowballs in summer", but "you could die waiting" to be served.

Fisherman's Wharf S
19 | 15 | 17 | $21

Dulaney Valley Shopping Ctr., 826 Dulaney Valley Rd.
(Fairmont Ave.), Towson, 410-337-2909
◪ A "huge selection" of moderately priced seafood and a
kitchen ready to prepare it "your way" explain why this
Towson fish house is a favorite "everyday spot for dinner";
its "unlikely" commercial setting and dishes that sometimes
"lack flavor" keep it from being more; don't overlook the
"interesting specials" or the light bar menu.

Fishery, The S
▽ 22 | 16 | 21 | $25

1717 Eastern Ave. (Broadway), 410-327-9340
■ "Maybe Baltimore's best seafood secret" is the "good
selection" of Spanish and Chesapeake seafood dishes
served in delightfully "tacky", Mediterranean-feeling
surroundings and the "personal touches that make you feel
welcome" at this Fells Point Iberian; note, however, that it
may be "erratic."

Foster's S
– | – | – | M

606 S. Broadway (Fleet St.), 410-558-3600
Reopened in June '96 following another ownership change,
this Fells Point yuppie stronghold now covers the latest
trendy bases with cigars, microbrews on tap, a casual raw
bar, sushi, seasonal American fare and billiards upstairs.

Frazier's S
14 | 11 | 15 | $15

857 W. 33rd St. (Elm Ave.), 410-889-1143
919 W. 36th St. (Roland Ave.), 410-662-4914
◪ Hampden has "changed over the years", but not this
knotty pine "basement bar" or the picnic tables out back, the
classic "beware of frozen peas" American menu or the $9.95
Sunday night dinners (for two!); the new location (36th St.) is
"charmless" and finding its legs.

Friendly Farms S
18 | 11 | 19 | $15

17434 Foreston Rd. (Mt. Carmel Rd.), Upperco, 410-239-7400
◪ The "groaning" board of farm food at this "Presbyterian
picnic" in Upperco could cap a pleasant, inexpensive family
outing – that is, if you're up for "serious fill 'em up", pass
the bowls eating (a bit "like the Army") and no alcohol; the
"lovely" grounds and duck pond will amuse the kids and
you'll find some of the best crab cakes around.

Gabler's S
▽ 23 | 19 | 19 | $21

2200 Perryman Rd. (Old Philadelphia Rd.), Aberdeen,
410-272-0626
■ Fame hasn't spoiled the "restful" atmosphere of this
crab joint near Aberdeen; its "unrivaled", "wonderful
setting" takes one back to the "old days on the shore"
when the crabs were plump and flavorful and life seemed
to stand still; since times have changed, however, be sure
to reserve ahead.

Germano's Trattoria [S] 23 | 19 | 21 | $30
(fka Petrucci)
300 S. High St. (Fawn St.), 410-752-4515
■ "Gutsy" Tuscan-style fare, "festive", art deco, poster-filled surroundings and "Germano himself" (a "gem" of a host) keeps this trattoria a Little Italy "favorite" despite rising prices and occasional "disappointments"; unless you opt for half portions, you won't need to eat for a week.

Gibby's [S] 18 | 14 | 16 | $20
22 W. Padonia Rd. (I-83), Cockeysville, 410-560-0703
■ "Jammed" into this nautical fish place is a "finny feast" of "fresh seafood, plainly served" to what seems like all of Timonium; whereas food-wise it's a "great" place to celebrate crab in all its glorious guises, the atmosphere would be much improved if the "bar noise" and smoke didn't creep in.

GlasZ Cafe [S] 21 | 20 | 16 | $11
6840 Falls Rd. (Lake Ave.), 410-377-9060
◪ Besides "great coffee", "attractive desserts", "gourmet sandwiches and salads" and "eclectic, interesting" prepared foods, this tiny, "stylish" Falls Road "self-serve" cafe and carryout is also a "place to be seen"; but it's "not very user-friendly" and "quite expensive for takeout."

Grand Palace [S] ▽ 25 | 15 | 23 | $16
5721 Ritchie Hwy. (Church St.), 410-636-8333
■ "Amazingly good" daily dim sum explains the full parking lot outside this ordinary-looking Brooklyn Park Chinese; inside, it's "homey, warm" and filled with Asian-Americans eating what may be some of the best Cantonese food "outside of San Francisco."

Great American Melting Pot 15 | 14 | 16 | $15
(aka Gampy's)
904 N. Charles St. (Read St.), 410-837-9797
◪ If you're brave enough to venture Downtown "after hours", this "tatty" venue is *the* place to "see who is out and about"; the "colorful atmosphere" and "freak show" are the main draws; the "novelty" bar food is mostly (perhaps only) an attraction "in the middle of the night."

Gunning's Crab House [S] 18 | 10 | 16 | $21
3901 S. Hanover St. (Jeffrey St.), Brooklyn, 410-354-0085
■ The site of one of South Baltimore's old-time, "down-home", "blue-collar" crab houses; although the Gunnings moved on, it's still a destination for "messy as you want" steamed crab and seafood eating that draws faces (like Cal Ripkin) and just plain folks, too; P.S. since "crabs are the main thing", check on availability before you go.

Gunning's Seafood 🟥   20 | 13 | 18 | $15
7304 Parkway Dr. (off Dorsey Rd., Rte. 176), Dorsey,
410-712-9404
◼ "Exiled" to a "small strip mall" near BWI Airport, the
Gunnings keep on steaming crabs and clams, frying green
peppers (and "everything else") and serving them along
with all manner of seafood in a "helpful", no-fuss way;
if you want "great crabs", come here – if you want
atmosphere, go elsewhere.

HAMPTON'S 🟥   27 | 29 | 28 | $52
Harbor Court Hotel, 550 Light St. (bet. Conway & Lee Sts.),
410-234-0550
◼ Rated tops in decor and service (and No. 3 for food) in
Baltimore, this most "luxurious" hotel dining room never
fails to "impress" guests; it has the "best of everything" –
from the harbor lights view to the "refined" appointments,
pampering service, Contemporary American menu and
fine wines; especially now that the kitchen has settled in
(after a chef change), it's worth the "splurge."

Hampton's of Towson 🟥   ▽ 21 | 20 | 22 | $25
Hampton House, 204 E. Joppa Rd. (Goucher Blvd.),
Towson, 410-821-8888
◼ An "older set" dines and dances at this comfortable,
"friendly" apartment house dining room with a lovely view
overlooking Towson; while the Continental-American menu
holds few surprises, it's priced for everyday dining and the
piano bar hosts a "nice" crowd.

Hampton Tea Room ⊭   ▽ 16 | 22 | 19 | $16
Hampton Mansion, 535 Hampton Ln. (Dulaney Valley Rd.),
Towson, 410-583-7401
☑ This aptly named, "sweet" old Towson historic site feels
like you're sipping tea or sherry and nibbling sandwiches in
your great aunt's parlor – if she lived in a "historic mansion"
and entertained her "blue-haired" friends en masse; limited
hours (Tuesday–Saturday, lunch) and menu.

Harryman House 🟥   21 | 20 | 20 | $25
340 Main St. (1¼ mi. north of Franklin Blvd.), Reisterstown,
410-833-8850
◼ It's a little "drafty", but what else would you expect
when the middle room of this "woody" charmer is a log
cabin dating from the 1790s?; the "great bar" (with lots of
beers) and rustic dining rooms (with American "light fare
or full dinners") are where Reisterstown locals "socialize",
antique hunters lunch and lovers come when they "don't
want to be seen."

Harvey's S
19 | 18 | 19 | $21

Greenspring Station, 2360 W. Joppa Rd. (Falls Rd.),
Brooklandville, 410-296-9526

▣ The problem with this contemporary "neighborhood
fixture" and its please-everyone California and spa menus —
and ability to accommodate everything from a "short
business meeting" to a casual family snack — is that it gets
"monotonous" (also "uneven") because people go so much;
it's best "outdoors in the summer" with live music; N.B.
there's a carryout/gourmet shop next door.

HAUSSNER'S
19 | 25 | 22 | $23

3242 Eastern Ave. (Clinton St.), 410-327-8365

▣ "Worth a trip" for its "unique", floor-to-ceiling art
and kitsch, "stag bar", "gruff" waitresses and the
experience, if not the actual eating, of its German and
Old Maryland food, this vast Highlandtown "landmark"
is a Baltimore tourist's "must"-see; be sure to take
home a strawberry shortcake.

HELMAND, THE S
25 | 22 | 22 | $20

806 N. Charles St. (bet. Read & Madison Sts.),
410-752-0311

■ Imagine a restaurant with food that's inoffensively spicy,
"health-conscious", vegetarian-friendly and "affordable",
then add an "intimate", ethnic, modern setting and really
"helpful" help; even if it didn't do "amazing things with
pumpkin", this Mt. Vernon Afghan would be a winner;
N.B. be careful at night.

HENNINGER'S TAVERN
25 | 22 | 21 | $24

1812 Bank St. (bet. Ann & Wolfe Sts.), 410-342-2172

■ Not only is this "classic" Fells Point tavern a great
neighborhood watering hole with top-notch bar food, its
tiny back room is "sort of elegant", very "civilized" and
serves "excellent" Contemporary American–Continental
food; the no-reserving policy often makes it tough to get a
table on weekends.

Hersh's Orchard Inn S
21 | 19 | 21 | $29

1528 E. Joppa Rd. (½ mi. west of Loch Raven Blvd.), East
Towson, 410-823-0384

▣ Nostalgia isn't the only reason for this suburban steak
and seafood stronghold's staying power; its Cadillac
clientele never tire of the clubby ambiance, lively lounge,
"iceberg lettuce salad", "military" precision of the service or
the "great family" that honors *their* reservations — it doesn't
seem "stuffy" to them.

Hoang's Seafood Grill & Sushi Bar S   21 | 16 | 19 | $20
1619 Sulgrave Ave. (Kelly Ave.), 410-466-1000
6805 York Rd. (Regester Ave.), 410-377-2500 (takeout and delivery only) 🚫

■ This "professionally" run Mt. Washington Asian's menu sweeps from Tokyo to Thailand, making stops in Korea, China and Vietnam for "beautifully presented", fresh-tasting food; despite occasional sputters, it's a "great" engine for an edible tour of the Orient, as is the York Road carryout (be sure to try one of the Vietnamese meal-in-a-bowl phos).

Holy Frijole   – | – | – | I
908 W. 36th St. (Roland Ave.), 410-235-2326
The tasty Mexican eats at this hot Hampden hole for the multipierced and tattooed are not its main attraction; if you can squeeze into this narrow corner slot, the colorful, modern decor – walking as well as on the walls – will command your attention.

Hull St. Blues Cafe S   19 | 18 | 19 | $18
1222 Hull St. (bet. Fort Ave. & Cuba St.), Locust Point, 410-727-7476
■ In a "scrubbed-step neighborhood" near Fort McHenry, this "charming but erratic" pub-plus gets citywide attention for its "heart attack brunch", "cheap bar food" and "simple American favorites" served in the "dressier dining room"; be sure to leave room for the homemade desserts.

Hunan Manor S   22 | 20 | 22 | $18
7091 Deepage Dr. (off Snowden River Pkwy. at corner of Carved Stone Rd.), Columbia, 410-381-1134
■ "Really good" multiregional Chinese with the ability to attractively accommodate a large group as well as a briefcase lunch or family dinner while satisfying a range of tastes – it does "wonderful vegetarian dishes" and things "not on the menu"; in Columbia, where such amenities are scarce, it's "popular" and "business-minded."

Hunt Ridge S   15 | 13 | 18 | $18
Yorkridge Shopping Ctr., Ridgely Rd. at York Rd., Lutherville, 410-252-2122
☑ "Comfortable" Towson shopping strip standby catering to a seasoned clientele with the sounds and "generous" bites of the '50s, '60s and '70s; if you "stick with" a "favorite" from the seafood-strong American menu, you'll do alright.

Hunt Valley Szechuan S   20 | 17 | 18 | $18
9 Schilling Rd. (York Rd.), Hunt Valley, 410-527-1818
☑ A "nice enough Chinese restaurant" in terms of food and decor, its multiregional menu and sushi are just what most Hunt Valley diners have come to expect; only a few wonder how food can be "hot 'n' spicy" and "still lack flavor" and whether the usually "polite" servers were having a bad day.

Ikaros S $\boxed{21}\boxed{16}\boxed{19}\boxed{\$18}$
4805 Eastern Ave. (bet. Oldham & Ponca Sts.), 410-633-3750
☑ For many Baltimoreans, this "Highlandtown haunt" is
synonymous with "you'll never leave hungry" portions of
inexpensive Greek food and being treated "like family"
while you feast; the rest insist there's "better, cheaper"
Aegean food, "without the wait", nearby.

Jeannier's $\boxed{23}\boxed{19}\boxed{21}\boxed{\$29}$
*Broadview Apts., 105 W. 39th St. (University Pkwy.),
410-889-3303*
■ Some occasions demand a "classic" béarnaise and
genteel, "take your mom" surroundings, while others call for
"great" onion soup, gumbo or a soft-crab sandwich in a
casual, "hand-holding" cafe; at this Uptown apartment-
house French, all of the above (plus light fare) are "made
with care", fairly priced and served by "college types."

Jenning's Cafe ◑ $\boxed{\triangledown \ 17}\boxed{11}\boxed{15}\boxed{\$14}$
808 Frederick Rd. (Ingleside Ave.), Catonsville, 410-744-3824
■ Food-wise, this 1950s relic is a "fat-o-rama" with
possibly the best fried chicken, fried oyster sandwiches
and cheeseburgers extant; you can blow your cholesterol
count in "very Baltimore" company at this "smoky" old
bar in Catonsville.

Jerry D's Saloon ◑◗S $\boxed{18}\boxed{10}\boxed{14}\boxed{\$15}$
7808 Harford Rd. (bet. Taylor & Linwood Aves.), 410-665-0525
☑ "Best bar dining – bar none" or big drinks, big steaks and
"bar food that plays at being homemade" – however you
slice it, this "expanded" Parkville saloon serves a lot of food
"for the price", threatening your waist but not your wallet.

Jilly's S $\boxed{14}\boxed{11}\boxed{14}\boxed{\$14}$
1012 Reisterstown Rd. (Waldron Ave.), Pikesville, 410-653-0610
*Enchanted Forest Shopping Ctr., 10030 Baltimore Nat'l
Pike (Bethany Ln.), Ellicott City, 410-461-3093*
☑ "If you're looking for a place to watch an O's game",
meet friends, get some ribs or a shrimp salad sandwich
(or "see your boss with the other woman"), this Pikesville
"dump" will do; everyone complains about the Styrofoam,
the servers, the sonics and the smoke – and everyone goes;
P.S. its Ellicott City upstart also hosts "neighborly" fun.

Jimmy's S⊅ $\boxed{16}\boxed{12}\boxed{18}\boxed{\$9}$
801 S. Broadway (Lancaster St.), 410-327-3273
■ In a town that takes justifiable pride in its diner "dives",
this Fells Point "grease pit" stands out; whether you go for
one of Baltimore's cheapest morning-after breakfasts ("with
draft beer"), Sunday AM sightings, a pork chop lunch or
simply to observe the "gritty" Damon Runyonesque scene,
you "gotta love it."

Jimmy's Famous Seafood ◐ [S] 20 | 10 | 17 | $22
6526 Holabird Ave. (bet. Dundalk Ave. & Broening Hwy.), 410-633-4040
■ Steamed "crabs are a tradition" at this massive "Dundalk seafood hall for blue collars" (it's also frequented by an "old-time" Bawlmer crowd); many picky pickers consider its steamed crabs the best "seasoned", its Greek salad impossible to finish and its shrimp and finfare a "dream"; the help is down-to-earth.

Joey Chiu's Greenspring Inn 22 | 22 | 21 | $22
10801 Falls Rd. (Greenspring Valley Rd.), Brooklandville, 410-823-1125
■ Although this Brooklandville Chinese takes the same "pretty place with pretty food" approach to ethnic dining as its Baltimore sibs (Bamboo House), it deserves separate mention for its "predictable but very well prepared food, good sushi" and for giving customers a chance to "need their best bib and tucker."

John Steven, Ltd. ◐ [S] 21 | 19 | 17 | $18
1800 Thames St. (Ann St.), 410-327-5561
■ American sushi and steamers in the bar are only one side of this "hard-working" Fells Point tavern's gastronomy – its "patio possibilities" extend to "ambitious" Contemporary American fare; but what really packs the joint is a "genuine" waterfront atmosphere that persists even though the "local riffraff" are outnumbered by "yuppies."

Josef's Country Inn [S] 24 | 20 | 21 | $27
2410 Pleasantville Rd. (Rte. 152), Fallston, 410-877-7800
◪ A "country drive" and a flashback to the "good old days" of "fräulein-served" German-Continental dining are the major attractions of this Harford "getaway"; the older dining rooms are "noisy, crowded" and kitschy, but we hear that a "back room" done up as a Victorian library is a "delight."

JOY AMERICA CAFE [S] 25 | 25 | 23 | $35
American Visionary Art Museum, 800 Key Hwy. (Covington St.), 410-244-6500
◪ Despite concerns that its pricey "tall food" would be too visionary for Baltimore, this "cutting edge" American, open for only a few months at the time of this *Survey*, garnered Top 20 ratings for food and service and Top 10 for decor; its minimalist decor, harbor views and the folk art museum in which it's housed are well worth a look.

J. Patrick's ◐ [S] ⊅ ▽ 18 | 17 | 16 | $14
1371 Andre St. (Fort Ave.), 410-244-8613
◪ A "congenial" place to celebrate St. Patrick's Day or listen to traditional Irish bands, this Locust Point pub's Irish-American menu is a "little more varied than bar food" and can be eaten in a "nice dining room"; but boisterous boozing is its main thing.

Jpn. [S] 21 | 17 | 19 | $22
(fka Shogun)
316 N. Charles St. (bet. Saratoga & Pleasant Sts.), 410-962-1130
■ "Asian food buffs" give this Charles Street sushi "master" points for its shoes-off tea room, "high standards" and non-sushi items like seafood teriyaki and yakitori.

Jumbo Seafood [S] 23 | 18 | 21 | $18
48 E. Sudbrook Ln. (Old Court Rd.), Pikesville, 410-602-1441
■ When "jumbo" portions of some of the area's "best" Chinese food are served in "too small" Pikesville premises, the result is "long lines" and a brisk carry-out trade; at this very popular Asian, the menu doesn't stray far from the standards, but the kitchen prepares "unusual" specials and is "very accommodating with special requests."

Kaufmann's Tavern [S] ▽ 19 | 15 | 18 | $20
329 Gambrills Rd. (Rte. 175), Gambrills, 410-923-2005
■ "Seafood the way it should be done" – in timeworn, "after-the-game" simplicity; this "nice place in nowhere land" proves that if you steam a great crab and "treat patrons like gold", the world will come to you.

Kawasaki 21 | 19 | 20 | $22
413 N. Charles St. (bet. Franklin & Mulberry Sts.), 410-659-7600
■ "Despite the Chesapeake Bay", Baltimore lacks the rarefied sushi found in LA or NYC; but that doesn't mean "cold fish addicts" can't get "good", "fresh" sushi at this "steady" Charles Street Japanese (especially when it's not "pressured") or that less "daring" appetites can't find a "nice selection" of tempura, teriyaki and noodle-based entrees.

Kelly's ◐ [S] ▽ 23 | 15 | 20 | $15
2108 Eastern Ave. (bet. Duncan & Chester Sts.), 410-327-2312
■ This may be the "finest neighborhood bar" in a great bar town, not to mention its serving some of the "most perfectly seasoned", best-quality steamed crabs in Crab City (and very good everyday grub, too); but its real specialty is "fun times" – only Kelly and Mary Sheridan could pull off karaoke in an East Baltimore Irish pub.

Kelsey's [S] ▽ 17 | 16 | 16 | $18
Normandy Shopping Ctr., 8480 Baltimore Nat'l Pike (Center Ave.), Ellicott City, 410-418-9076
◪ A "good neighborhood saloon" in an area near Ellicott City lacking one, this "comfortable" storefront offers "steak value", burgers and "great" french fries along with a "bountiful" shrimp salad sandwich and American entrees to a suburban clientele that has "just discovered" it; in their view, "service could improve."

KING'S CONTRIVANCE S   23 | 24 | 22 | $32
*10150 Shaker Dr. (bet. Rtes. 29 & 32), Columbia,
410-995-0500*
☑ Though the Continental food and service sometimes seem to be "coasting", this "magnificent" Victorian mansion remains "the place for private parties in Columbia" (the dining rooms aren't "private enough for romance"); the "pre-theater special" is the "only way to go" to Merriweather events.

Kisling's Tavern ◗S   18 | 12 | 16 | $14
2100 Fleet St. (Chester St.), 410-327-5477
☑ Bay fries and blaring sports TV mark this "reliable way station on a Fells Point pub crawl" frequented by "youngish" types; while beer is the name of its game, the "finger food" is "cheap", comes in "substantial quantities" and affords "occasional pleasant surprises"; "grouchy" help and grunge go with the territory.

La Scala S   – | – | – | E
411 S. High St. (Eastern Ave.), 410-783-9209
A relaxed, contemporary Italian meal in this well-appointed Little Italy row house is a bit like dining at a friend's home; staffers, who clearly want patrons to like them and their food, create a cozy, inclusive atmosphere in a space that's way too small for secrets.

La Tesso Tana S   22 | 19 | 18 | $29
Abarcrombie Badger Bed & Breakfast, 58 W. Biddle St. (Cathedral St.), 410-837-3630
■ With "reservations necessary" before a "BSO or Lyric event", this "cozy" step-down "treasure" across from the Meyerhoff displays its "romantic" potential when unrushed; at such times, the "rich" Italian cuisine is a "masterful" prelude to whatever you have planned and "tight" seating could be turned into an advantage.

Ledo Pizza S⇦   17 | 10 | 15 | $12
1020-40 W. 41st St. (Falls Rd.), 410-243-4222
Snowden Ctr., 6955 Oakland Mills Rd. (Snowden River Pkwy.), Columbia, 410-381-1270
Park Plaza, 552 E. Ritchie Hwy. (Baltimore-Annapolis Blvd.), Severna Park, 410-544-3344
11321 York Rd. (Shawan Rd.), Hunt Valley, 410-785-5336
405 N. Center St. (Cranberry St.), Westminster, 410-857-3500
2657-A Old Annapolis Rd. (Rte. 175), Hanover, 410-551-0220
See Washington, DC, Alphabetical Directory.

Liberatore's Bistro S   21 | 19 | 20 | $29
Timonium Corporate Ctr., 9515 Deereco Rd. (Padonia Rd.), Timonium, 410-561-3300
Freedom Village Shopping Ctr., 6300 Georgetown Blvd. (Liberty Rd.), Eldersburg, 410-781-4114

Liberatore's Bistro (Cont.)

New Town Village Ctr., 9712 Groffs Mills Dr.
(Lakeside Blvd.), Owings Mills, 410-356-3100

■ "Chubby cherubs" may be an incongruous backdrop for doing lunchtime deals, but Timonium briefcase toters seem to take it in stride; in the evening, this "office park" Northern Italian's "luxuriant" civility, "excellent" traditional menu and easy parking seem more in keeping with its status as the "suburban place to go" – ditto at its other locations.

LINWOOD'S S   27 26 25 $35

25 Crossroads Dr. (McDonough Rd.), Owings Mills, 410-356-3030

■ Linwood Dame "got it together" at this "stylish" Owings Mills Contemporary American; his food is "imaginative", the help is "accommodating" and the room is "hopping" with "heavy-hitters" reminiscent of the "old Pimlico Hotel"; a few wish it weren't quite so "mink"-lined, but no one can deny it's a real "value at lunch."

Lista's S   15 20 16 $19

Brown's Wharf, 1637 Thames St. (bet. Broadway & Bond St.),
410-327-0040

◪ At Margaritaville on the Fells Point waterfront, the atmosphere is so "zippy" most don't notice the "faux" SW decor, "fake" Tex-Mex fare and flawed service – especially if they're seated at a patio table, listening to live music and watching the ships go by; call it "partying" with a "price tag."

Loco Hombre S   18 15 16 $17

413 W. Coldspring Ln. (bet. Charles St. & Roland Ave.),
410-889-2233

◪ This "colorful" Roland Park Tex-Mex isn't big enough to seat its many amigos – that's not surprising given the college neighborhood and "very good yuppie Mexican cuisine" (i.e "greaseless", gringoized and "overspiced"); the artwork is 'with it', which is more than you can always say for the help.

Louie's Bookstore Cafe ◑S   17 20 14 $14

518 N. Charles St. (bet. Franklin & Centre Sts.), 410-962-1224

◪ Baltimore's "Left Bank" runs up Charles Street to this bookstore/cafe where "artists and musicians serve playful Eclectic food and excellent desserts" to "diverse" types who go for "stimulation" (books, music, art, people-watching and conversation) as much as for sustenance and who shrug philosophically that "when the service is good, the food is so-so" and vice versa; N.B. be careful at night.

Luigi Petti ◑S   19 17 19 $20

1002 Eastern Ave. (Exeter St.), 410-685-0055

◪ It's easy to "love this place in the summer" when you're eating some of the "best gnocchi in Little Italy" or a "good red sauce" staple on the terrace; it's less enjoyable inside when there are "interminable waits" or the food tastes like "they stopped trying"; petti-good or petti-bad – it's a toss-up.

Mai Thai S   ▽ | 20 | 14 | 18 | $17 |
1032 Light St. (bet. Cross & Hamburg Sts.), 410-539-5611
■ South Baltimore foodies can't understand why more people don't know about their "secret" Thai, an offshoot of the Thai Restaurant in Waverly, since the traditional dishes are well-prepared and "not very hot" and the hospitality is usually "great too"; perhaps it's because the white tablecloths and chandeliers belie the "inexpensive" tab.

Mama Lucia S | 17 | 11 | 15 | $14 |
Valley Ctr., 9616 Reisterstown Rd. (Greenspring Valley Rd.), Owings Mills, 410-363-0496
☑ When you cash in your "coupon" at this "shopping center Italian", you'll "doggie-bag tomorrow's dinner"; the double-sized portions of "hearty" pastas, pizza and subs help offset the "mediocre surroundings" and some misses in the menu; carryout is another way to deal with the "cheesy" decor.

Manor Tavern S | 19 | 20 | 18 | $24 |
15819 Old York Rd. (Manor Rd.), Monkton, 410-771-8155
☑ "A great spot in horse country for a burger", a full American-Continental meal in formal candlelight or mingling with the "horsey set" in the rustic bar; but some feel this atmospheric coach stop could be improved by teaching the "college kids" to "pace a meal."

MARCONI'S | 23 | 18 | 23 | $26 |
106 W. Saratoga St. (bet. Park Ave. & Cathedral St.), 410-727-9522
■ They say that "if you're not a Baltimorean, you don't understand" this "Old Maryland" "townhouse treasure" however much you relish the "fabulous" lobster Cardinale, fried eggplant, creamed spinach and "chocolate sundae without equal", the courtliness of the "shuffling waiters" and the fact that it "retains its old-time dowdiness" and "time-warp" prices – nevertheless, you should go.

Margaret's Cafe S | 21 | 21 | 19 | $14 |
909 Fell St. (bet. Thames & Wolfe Sts.), 410-276-5605
■ Margaret Footner's "spare", "healthy and hip" Fells Point cafe is hailed as a "gem" and her customers look upon her "innovative, light", vegetarian-minded cooking as an "eating adventure" and shrug off an occasional "disappointment" and the "eccentric" help; they even "support local artists" whose works hang in the nonprofit gallery upstairs.

Martick's | 21 | 17 | 17 | $24 |
214 W. Mulberry St. (bet. Park Ave. & Howard St.), 410-752-5155
☑ Straining the envelope of "quirkiness", Morris Martick holds court (at his "whim") in his family's "run-down" Baltimore speakeasy (no sign, light or doorknob – ring the "buzzer" above the door) with his "unique" French food and "early aircraft carrier" decor; "on a good night it can be lots of fun, on a bad night it's a disaster"; but neither the restaurant nor the neighborhood is for timid souls.

Matsuri
24 | 17 | 19 | $18

1105 S. Charles St. (Cross St.), 410-752-8561

■ "Baltimore's hippest sushi bar", and probably its best Japanese restaurant, packs a lot of excellent eating into a smart-looking, "closet"-like space in South Baltimore; be sure to go beyond the "artistic" raw fish offerings to the wonderful noodle dishes and robatayaki (grills) – and be prepared for an "agonizing wait."

McCabe's S
– | – | – | M

3845 Falls Rd. (Cox St.), Hampden, 410-467-1000

"Known for perfect burgers, great crusted fries" and "exceptional bar food", this "tiny local pub in Hampden" recently reopened to citywide applause; diverse local diners "sit at the bar" – the best place to soak up the "atmosphere."

McCafferty's S
22 | 21 | 20 | $31

1501 Sulgrave Ave. (Newbury St.), 410-664-2200

■ If you "don't eat red meat", it could be because you've never succumbed to the "great beef" and lamb served in "chummy" comfort at this Mt. Washington "testosterone" palace; Montana meat, "delicious garlic mashed potatoes", "personalized service", football memorabilia and plenty of polished wood are just a few of the disparate elements that come together here.

Metropol Cafe & Gallery S
20 | 20 | 16 | $18

1718 N. Charles St. (Lafayette St., 1 block north of Penn Station), 410-385-3018

◪ Although it can be a "neat place to visit for art and a cup of joe", "innovative" smoked seafood, veggies and "great desserts", people forget about this cafe/culturama unless "there's a good flick at the Charles"; perhaps better service would help, not to mention a safer location.

M. GETTIER
27 | 22 | 24 | $37

505 S. Broadway (bet. Eastern Ave. & Fleet St.), 410-732-1151

■ Michael Gettier runs his "superb" restaurant like its counterpart in a small French country town, handcrafting each "wonderful, imaginative" dish from "the best" ingredients and ensuring that it's properly served; the result is near unanimous acclaim – now if only he could find an equally "intimate", "romantic" space in a less "seedy" neighborhood (take advantage of valet parking).

Michael's ◑ S
18 | 15 | 16 | $20

2119 York Rd. (Gerard Ave.), Timonium, 410-252-2022

◪ There's no mystery about this Timonium pub's popularity – it has "location" and "excellent" crab cakes as well as a raw bar, "good happy hour" grub and lots of attractive customers playing the singles game or the "19th hole" (or both); consequently, the "expanded" premises can't seem to accommodate the crowds.

Mick's S   16 | 16 | 16 | $16
Towson Commons, 425 York Rd. (bet. Pennsylvania &
Chesapeake Aves.), Towson, 410-825-0071
See Washington, DC, Alphabetical Directory.

Miller's Delicatessen S   13 | 9 | 10 | $12
Greenspring Shopping Ctr., 2849 Smith Ave. (Sanzo Rd.),
Pikesville, 410-602-2233
☑ When deli mavens want a corned beef fix, chicken soup
or a "good Reuben", they're willing to endure "standing
on line and being yelled at" in this relocated cafeteria-style
entry in Pikesville; P.S. dining at its prior premises was
really a "desperation measure."

MILTON INN S   27 | 27 | 26 | $44
14833 York Rd. (bet. Hunt Valley Mall & Belfast Rd.),
Sparks, 410-771-4366
■ "The quiet charm of a country inn", tuxedoed cosseting,
"consistently excellent" Regional American food and the
"crackling fires" of the hearth room "make any celebration
perfect" at this old stone mansion and earn it a Top 10 slot
for food; be sure to bring a designated driver – it uncorks
some of the area's finest wines.

Minato S   – | – | – | M
(fka CoChin)
800 N. Charles St. (Madison St.), 410-332-0332
Replacing CoChin in its brick-walled Mt. Vernon basement,
this thoroughgoing Japanese touches all of that cuisine's
bases – sushi, sashimi, hot and cold noodle dishes, yakitori
and tiny grilled tidbits are just some of the possibilities; N.B.
care advised at night.

Morgan Millard S   18 | 18 | 18 | $20
4800 Roland Ave. (bet. Upland & Elmhurst Rds.),
410-889-0030
☑ Where Roland Park "matrons lunch" while "preppies"
crunch numbers and assorted neighborhood "50-year-olds
go to feel young"; this "arts 'n' crafts" restaurant in a historic
building specializes in "home cooking outside of the home",
has had a recent "Southern reincarnation" and remains
as "sleepy" as ever.

Morning Edition Cafe S   21 | 20 | 14 | $15
153 N. Patterson Park Ave. (Fayette St.), 410-732-5133
☑ Heroic patience is rewarded with "delicious fresh-baked
breads, muffins" and "brunch offerings" at this "Vermont"-
feeling "haven in the Highlandtown war zone"; "clearly,
the servers are better artists than waiters", but the "Jerry
Garcia" vibes and the "entire Sunday paper" should help
pass the time

Mo's Crab & Pasta Factory　　　19 | 14 | 16 | $22
502 Albemarle St. (Eastern Ave.), 410-837-1600 ◐ S

Mo's Fisherman's Exchange
Satyr Hill Shopping Ctr., 2025 E. Joppa Rd. (Satyr Hill Rd.),
Parkville, 410-665-8800 ◐ S

Mo's Fisherman's Wharf Inner Harbor
219 President St. (Stiles St.), 410-837-8600 ◐ S

Mo's Seafood Factory
7146 Ritchie Hwy. (Furnace Branch Rd.), Glen Burnie,
410-768-1000 ◐ S
2403 Belair Rd. (Mountain Rd.), Fallston, 410-893-6666 S
■ Doggie bags the size of shopping bags indicate these
seafood factories don't skimp on portions; here, you'll find
a big catch of "very fresh" seafood cooked "101 ways"
(mostly garlicky and "rich") but not much finesse, causing
some to carp about "too much" of a not so good thing.

Mt. Washington Tavern S　　　15 | 17 | 14 | $18
5700 Newbury St. (Sulgrave Ave.), 410-367-6903
◪ Bashing this Mt. Washington brew hole and its clientele
is a cottage industry – "Beavis and Butt-head with bank
accounts", "lacrosse nirvana: bring a jock", "very J. Crew";
nevertheless, hundreds of surveyors find a "nice niche in the
sun room" or go to "meet friends", rating the "surroundings
more enjoyable than the service" or "fair" "tavern fare."

Mughal Garden S　　　　　22 | 17 | 20 | $18
920 N. Charles St. (bet. Read & Eager Sts.), 410-547-0001
■ The "third jewel in the Little India crown"; reviewers laud
this "roomy", "cheerful" Charles Street Indian for its "great
vindaloos and curries", "American portions", "tasteful
decor" and, especially, for its "superb" midday spread –
"calling it another lunch buffet is like calling the Taj Mahal
another tomb", "there's so much food at Sunday brunch
you'll go home and go back to sleep."

Nacho Mama's ◐ S　　　　　19 | 19 | 19 | $14
2907 O'Donnell St. (Linwood Ave.), 410-675-0898
■ "Tex-Mex with a sense of humor" in a happening area
is the short of it; the rest of the story is this Canton hangout
mixes Elvis kitsch, "chips in a hubcap", Texas chili and other
"good, hearty, unpretentious feed" to come up with a "good
place for a guy to meet his brother for dinner" – that is, "if
they can get in the door."

Nam Kang ◐ S　　　　　　－|－|－| _⏌
2126 Maryland Ave. (Charles St.), 410-685-6237
Write-ins draw attention to this Little Korea community
center with a comprehensive Korean menu plus "good
sushi" and other Asian dishes; it's a good place to expand
your vocabulary with words like bulgoki (marinated sliced
beef) and kimchi (spicy fermented cabbage).

Nates & Leons [S] – | – | – | M
300 W. Pratt St. (Howard St.), 410-234-8100
Nostalgia for overstuffed corned beef sandwiches, chicken salad and banana cream pie, along with a savvy regard for Convention Center, Oriole Park and Inner Harbor traffic, prompted the revival of this legendary deli on prime turf; early returns range from "needs more practice" and "better food" to "fun place."

New No Da Ji [S] 19 | 11 | 17 | $17
2501 N. Charles St. (25th St.), 410-235-4846
◪ The bargain "all-u-can-du" sushi buffet, which "ranges from fair to excellent depending on when you go", lures an "eclectic collection" of "adventurous" students and suits to this Charles Street Asian, but it's the "superior Korean part of the menu" that turns them into regulars; P.S. this place has "no charisma, no charm" and "not a great location" (i.e. "always lock your car").

New Orleans Cafe – | – | – | M
322 N. Charles St. (bet. Saratoga & Mulberry Sts.), 410-727-6317
Gumbo fiends head to this Charles Street storefront for a local sampler of Louisiana music and eats; here, le bon temps roule in a laid-back way that makes tourists feel as comfortable as the hip types who used to frequent this weekend evening hot spot when it was Profusions.

New Towne Diner ◐ [S] 14 | 14 | 16 | $11
11316 Reisterstown Rd., Reisterstown, 410-654-0066
◪ In Reisterstown (on the site of Twin Kiss), this phoenix-like diner proves that if you give folks "lots of food at a fair price", "tolerate" their kids and position a mouthwatering bakery as they come in the door, you'll have to double your size in a year; critics cite "too long lines" and "bland food."

Nichi Bei Kai [S] 21 | 18 | 21 | $23
1524 York Rd. (Seminary Ave.), Lutherville, 410-321-7090
Columbia Market Pl., 9400 Snowden River Pkwy. (Oakland Mills Rd.), Columbia, 410-381-5800
◪ The enduring popularity of Japanese slice 'n' dice shows, like these suburban samurais, irritates purists – the lunch specials at the "decent sushi bars" are more their style; but hey, as long as you provide a "good dinner at a reasonable price", what's wrong with making "food fun"?

Nick's Inner Harbor Seafood – | – | – | I
Cross Street Market, 1065 S. Charles St. (Cross St.), 410-685-2020
Construction workers rub elbows with young professionals over an inexpensive bite and a brew at this much-expanded fish stall in the Cross Street Market; most nights, it's a "happy-hour happening" with hundreds swarming the sushi bar, lobster bar, raw bar, beer bar, and soup and crab cake station – so if you want to sit, go before 5 PM.

No Way Jose S   16 | 14 | 15 | $15
1041 Marshall St. (Cross St.), 410-752-2837

☑ Where twentysomethings fill up on "good, greasy" (translation: "authentic") Tex-Mex "before a night out in Federal Hill", this border cafe near the Cross Street Market is also known for its margarita-fueled bar scene; note that the kitchen really loves to play with fire – watch out for the killer-spiced wings and BBQ.

Obrycki's S   20 | 14 | 18 | $25
1727 E. Pratt St. (bet. Broadway & Regester St.), 410-732-6399

☑ Whether this venerable Baltimore crab house is everything "it's cracked up to be" is the question; naysayers list "poor quality", "seafood dishes swimming in butter", "bad attitude", "horrendous waits" and "chancy" 'hood; still, the fans smile "have had my best crabs here."

Ocean Pride   18 | 10 | 15 | $19
1534 York Rd. (bet. Seminary Rd. & Bellona Ave.), Lutherville, 410-321-7744

☑ "Great crabs and cold beer – what else do you need to know" about this Lutherville crab joint?; possibly that it's "willing to be flexible", has one of the "best raw bars" and cream of crab soup around and doesn't promise more than it can deliver.

One World Cafe S   18 | 21 | 17 | $10
904 S. Charles St. (E. Henrietta St.), 410-234-0235

■ This atmospheric Federal Hill bean bar with veggie fare is variously described as a "great black bean burrito coffee place", a "stop by and check out the local artwork place", a "hang out, read a book, watch the crowd, listen to the music, relax and enjoy the atmosphere" place – you get the drift.

OPA ◖S   – | – | – | M
1911 Aliceanna St. (Wolfe St.), 410-522-4466

An "Inner Harbor transplant" (Taverna Athena's stepchild) brings a "nice Greek menu" and festive spirit to Fells Point; here, you'll find 'Athenian pasta' and lots of seafood besides the "fresh Greek salad" and lamb that locals used to have to contend with tourists to enjoy.

Orchard Market & Cafe S   24 | 18 | 22 | $18
8815 Orchard Tree Ln. (Joppa Rd.), East Towson, 410-339-7700

■ "Hidden in the suburbs", where it "doesn't get enough credit" for bringing "delicious" Persian food, "extraordinary hospitality" and "striking decor" within reach of families "on a budget" (in addition to "parking at the door" and a "BYOB bonus"); if you've never tried the rich, flavorful cuisine of Persia, this ethnic market and cafe will be a "treat."

Orient [S] ▽ 22 | 17 | 18 | $17
319 York Rd. (bet. Chesapeake Ave. & Towsontown Blvd.), Towson, 410-296-9000
■ It's ostensibly Chinese, but the "very fresh" sushi is a big seller at this "dependable", tastefully turned out Towsonite; the "huge portions of unadorned sushi" and possibly the "best California roll in town" more than satisfy such yens; P.S. there are "wonderful eggplant dishes" for those otherwise inclined.

OUTBACK STEAKHOUSE [S] 20 | 16 | 19 | $21
Perry Hall Sq., 4215 Ebenezer Rd. (Belair Rd.), 410-529-7200
Tollgate Plaza, 615 Belair Rd. (Rte. 24), Bel Air, 410-893-0110
See Washington, DC, Alphabetical Directory.

Pacific Rim [S] ▽ 17 | 15 | 18 | $20
9726 York Rd. (Padonia Rd.), Cockeysville, 410-666-2336
◪ The Pacific Rim in Cockeysville stretches from Southeast Asia to New Orleans – an "eclectic mix" reflected in the "creative" menu and designer decor; reactions vary from "great sushi" to "new name, old food."

Palermo's Grill 20 | 18 | 18 | $21
Padonia Park Plaza, 106 W. Padonia Rd. (Broad St., off I-83), Timonium, 410-252-0600
◪ In keeping with the generous spirit of namesake Steve Palermo, portions are sized large and "extra large" at this sports-themed Italian-American bar and grill in Timonium; but notwithstanding the "nice-looking" surroundings, "pleasant" help and "decent prices", the call is just "ok" ("good bar, but the restaurant needs help").

Paolo's [S] 20 | 19 | 18 | $22
Harborplace, 301 Light St. Pavilion (Pratt St.), 410-539-7060 ◐
Towson Commons, 1 W. Pennsylvania Ave. (York Rd.), Towson, 410-321-7000
See Washington, DC, Alphabetical Directory.

PaperMoon Diner ◐ [S] 13 | 19 | 12 | $11
227 W. 29th St. (bet. Howard & Remington Sts.), 410-889-4444
◪ "Weird and wacky" (in a "dicey area", too) Remington comfort-food station that's strictly for "young, zany, late-night snackers" and "slackers" – smokers preferred; unless you're into "headless Barbie Dolls", "Pez dispensers", "stale desserts", "Soviet-style service" and questionable housekeeping, this place is not for you.

PAVILION AT THE WALTERS [S] 22 | 25 | 20 | $21
600 N. Charles St. (Centre St.), 410-727-2233
■ There is no more "elegant" backdrop for a business or special occasion lunch than the "quiet, formal", skylit atrium of the Walters Art Gallery; but its Contemporary American food, while "very good", "will never find a permanent place in the museum" and the help is sometimes "condescending"; lunch and weekend brunch only.

Peerce's Gourmet S 21 | 14 | 17 | $16 |
9624 Deereco Rd. (Padonia Rd.), Timonium, 410-561-2233
■ This American "overachiever in a culinary wasteland" on
Deereco Road, an offshoot of the "real Peerce's" (Peerce's
Plantation) and Josef's Country Inn, offers "excellent carry-
out" and eat-in lunch options ranging from a "roasted veg
sandwich", soups and "great specials" to a comprehensive
Sunday brunch buffet.

PEERCE'S PLANTATION S 23 | 24 | 23 | $31 |
12460 Dulaney Valley Rd. (Loch Raven Dr.), Phoenix,
410-252-3100
☑ The tradition of "Sunday drives to the country" for family
celebrations may be "better than the Continental food", but
that doesn't diminish this lovely Loch Raven Reservoir
overlook's appeal; for many, being served "seafood in puff
pastry" by a "personable" waiter defines fine dining the
"way it used to be."

Perring Place S ▽ 23 | 16 | 22 | $20 |
Perring Crossing, Perring Pkwy. (McLean Blvd.), 410-661-0630
■ "Good eats at a good price" draws crowds anywhere, so
it's hardly surprising that a Northeast suburban strip mall
location hasn't hurt this fixture's bottom line; long ago, word
of its old-fashioned "comfort food", "huge slab servings"
and "friendly" folks spread in the neighborhood – since
then it's been a local "favorite."

Peppermill ●S 17 | 15 | 19 | $19 |
Heaver Plaza, 1301 York Rd. (Greenridge Rd.), Lutherville,
410-583-1107
☑ In a Lutherville office building, this unimpressive old
trouper plays to a mature ("blue-haired") audience that
"goes here frequently to see all their friends"; management
sees no reason to change the "wholesome" American menu
or "hire a decorator" – after all, the place is always full.

Peter's Inn ⌂ 24 | 19 | 20 | $14 |
504 S. Ann St. (Eastern Ave.), 410-675-7313
■ "Artists" took over this "funky" Fells Point "biker bar"
and the Eclectic "gourmet" fare is "truly creative"; a meal
here is something "like going to Mom's house" – if she
wore "Harley accessories."

Phillips Harborplace S 15 | 15 | 15 | $23 |
Harborplace, 301 Light St. Pavilion (bet. Calvert & Pratt Sts.),
410-685-6600
Phillips Seafood Grill S
White Marsh Mall, 8200 Perry Hall Blvd. (Honeygo Blvd.),
410-931-0077
See Washington, DC, Alphabetical Directory.

Piccolo's 🆂   17 20 17 $23
Brown's Wharf, 1629 Thames St. (foot of Broadway on Pier), 410-522-6600
◪ When approached by water taxi (or private yacht) with moderate expectations and not on weekends ("to avoid crowds"), this "upscale" Italian on a Fells Point pier does fine – especially if you nab an "awesome" waterside seat, watch the tugboats in the harbor and order pasta and one of its winning wines; in contrast, the "large dining room feels impersonal and touristy."

Pier 500 🆂   18 20 18 $27
HarborView Marina, 500 HarborView Dr. (Key Hwy.), 410-625-0500
◪ A "straight-up" martini and an "away from everything" Harbor view are the highlights of a visit to this marina restaurant; the "cramped, crowded" interior and comings and goings of too many chefs have left its identity in disarray, but perhaps the latest menu of regional Maryland seafood (a "mixed success") will stick.

PIERPOINT 🆂   26 18 21 $31
1822 Aliceanna St. (bet. Ann & Wolfe Sts.), 410-675-2080
◼ Nancy Longo's "national stature" derives from her "imaginative" interpretations of Maryland seafood classics, her ability to transform the freshest ingredients into "memorable" comfort food and her generosity as a teacher; the major complaint about her "cozy, stylish", "intelligent" Fells Point bistro is that it's "too small."

POLO GRILL 🆂   26 25 24 $38
Inn at the Colonnade, 4 W. University Pkwy. (bet. Canterbury & Charles Sts.), 410-235-8200
◼ Say what you will about its "who's who" "power scene" and "snooty" attitude – this Contemporary American's grill-room updates are "almost always impeccably prepared" and served "whether it's New Year's Eve or brunch"; and if you "know everyone" in the "clubby" room "it's fun" – if not, you can always eat the same "good food" at the bar; N.B. a new chef (summer 1996) should not rock this solid ship.

PRIME RIB 🌑🆂   28 25 27 $41
1101 N. Calvert St. (Chase St.), 410-539-1804
◼ The epitome of "swanky", "let's get dressed up dining", this "fancy" Downtowner brings a "touch of NY to town" and demonstrates the timeless appeal of "consistently excellent" beef, seafood and dry martinis and "solicitous service" by earning top ratings for food (No. 2 for popularity and service) in this year's *Survey*; N.B. be sure to park in the garage.

Puffin's [S] 23 | 18 | 21 | $22
1000 Reisterstown Rd. (Sherwood Ave.), Pikesville, 410-486-8811
■ "Upscale" (a bit "expensive for Formica tabletops") Pikesville crowd-pleaser offering a "very California (for Baltimore)" take on healthy eating; the focus here is on fresh vegetables, grains and grilled fish in an "artistic" environment; new owners (post-*Survey*) haven't fixed what ain't broke.

Purim Oak – | – | – | I
321 York Rd. (Chesapeake Ave.), Towson, 410-583-7770
This cavernous Korean with Pan-Asian aspirations draws Towson business types for lunch, students, families and moviegoers for dinner; penny-pinchers head straight for the all-you-can-eat buffet.

Purple Orchid [S] 24 | 20 | 21 | $27
(fka Orchid)
419 N. Charles St. (Franklin St.), 410-837-0080
■ A new name flags renewed emphasis on fusing Asian and French dining experiences (with "outstanding presentation" and service complementing "interesting" food) as well as a refurbishing of this "quietly elegant" Mt. Vernon townhouse; best of all, it's seldom crowded, making it a good "last-minute" bet.

Ralphie's Diner [S] 16 | 17 | 16 | $16
9690 Deereco Rd. (Padonia Rd.), Timonium, 410-252-3990
◪ A "run-of-the-mill place to eat during the week" with enough dineresque dishes and blue plate specials to occupy the kids; although many reviewers find this Timonium faux-diner useful for a good, "informal" meal, some say what was once fresh and "trendy" now seems like they're "faking it."

Ransome's Harbor Hill Cafe [S] 19 | 14 | 18 | $17
1032 Riverside Ave. (Cross St.), 410-576-9720
■ This "cute" neighborhood tavern "tucked away" near Federal Hill serves duck salad, "fresh-baked bread" and inventive pasta along with burgers and brews to a gentrified 'hood; there's a division between those who would "like to love it" (a minority) and those who do.

Red Hot & Blue [S] 20 | 15 | 17 | $17
11308 Reisterstown Rd. (High Falcon Rd.), Owings Mills, 410-356-6959
See Washington, DC, Alphabetical Directory.

Red Star [S] — 17 | 14 | 16 | $18

906 S. Wolfe St. (Thames St.), 410-327-2212

◪ Red stars point the way to this former Fells Point "brothel" that's now a gentrified place for lunch – that is, "when it's not too crowded" and you can take advantage of the "varied" menu of bar eats and "unusual" American choices; at night, you'll find raucous, "smoky", "crowded" goings-on that are often labeled "fun."

Redwood Grill [S] — ▽ 15 | 18 | 17 | $17

12 S. Calvert St. (bet. Baltimore & Redwood Sts.), 410-244-8550

◪ Updated bar and grill bidding for the Downtown lunch trade that makes dramatic use of a former car dealership's soaring space; but its shaky start in a "tough location" gives rise to comments like "tries hard, but doesn't quite make it"; N.B. it gets noisy and flashy at night.

Regi's — 18 | 18 | 16 | $17

1002 Light St. (Hamburg St.), 410-539-7344

◪ Diehards lament that this "nice Federal Hill bar with average food and good atmosphere" is "not the same since Regi sold it"; apparently, the new owners have "changed the American menu" and introduced "rotating art shows complete with curators" – which strikes some as a distinct "improvement"; service remains familiarly "slow."

River Watch [S] — 19 | 19 | 18 | $20

207 Nanticoke Rd. (Middleborough Rd.), Essex, 410-687-1422

◪ This "redneck riviera" on Hopkins Creek offers something for everyone – "crabs with a view", "savory seafood and sensational sunsets", a chance to "meet men with boats", a summertime singles scene, "great music", dancing, family dining and "good value"; sometimes you can even "catch a great meal" at this seafooder.

Ruby Lounge [S] — ▽ 24 | 24 | 21 | $25

(fka Donna's Restaurant)

800 N. Charles St. (Madison St.), 410-539-8051

■ Once again, Donna Crivello and company "score big" with this "dark, stylish", high-energy Mt. Vernon supper club where "martinis replace roasted vegetable salad" on a "superb" Eclectic menu designed for "regular eating"; the air of "NYC chic" is heightened by small tables and "waitresses with attitude"; N.B. park on Charles Street.

RUDYS' 2900 [S] — 27 | 23 | 25 | $37

2900 Baltimore Blvd. (Rte. 91), Finksburg, 410-833-5777

■ It's a "bit of a drive" to Finksburg, but that doesn't dampen admiration for this Continental-American's "dynamic, interesting food" (ranked No. 2 in Baltimore); here, a "pair of Rudys" display their "mastery" – one elevates service to an art form, while the other does "fabulous fish", game and dishes with "Austrian accents"; decor isn't bad, but not masterful.

Rusty Scupper 🅂   16 21 17 $22
402 Key Hwy. (Light St.), 410-727-3678

☑ Commanding Baltimore's "best" Inner Harbor view from virtually every seat and a spectacular deck for outdoor dining, this nautical tourist stop is "much better looking" since its post-*Survey* "overhaul"; but it remains to be seen if the seafood and service "are as good."

RUTH'S CHRIS STEAK HOUSE 🅂   24 21 22 $39
34 Market Pl., 600 Water St. (bet. Market Pl. & Gay St.), 410-783-0033
See Washington, DC, Alphabetical Directory.

Sabatino's ◑🅂   18 15 18 $22
901 Fawn St. (S. High St.), 410-727-9414

■ "A quintessential Baltimore restaurant – "average" food and decor "but appealing all the same" – this famous Little Italy "spaghetti house" is known for its "great" Bookmaker salad, massive red-sauced pastas and entrees and for staying open after the "bars close"; note that nonregulars are "sent to Siberia."

Saguaro's 🅂   17 16 15 $18
2 W. Pennsylvania Ave. (York Rd.), Towson, 410-339-7774

☑ This "attractive" SW range rider gets borderline reviews for its "colorful" Tex-Mex eats, grills and modern desert fare: "barely ok" vs. "very good even when the waiter brings the wrong dish"; but located where it is, in collegiate and suburban Towson, you can bet the bar is "full."

Saigon 🅂   ▽ 23 8 19 $13
3345 Belair Rd. (Erdman Ave.), 410-276-0055

■ The food's so reasonable at this "linoleum Vietnamese" on Belair Road "that if you get a bad dish", you can easily afford another; but chances are you'll love everything you try – "a Vietnam tour you'll want to repeat"; BYOB.

Samos ⇥   ▽ 24 7 19 $11
600 S. Oldham St. (Fleet St.), 410-675-5292

■ The highly edible outcomes of this archetypal Greek "hole-in-the-wall" include "excellent calamari", "wonderful stuffed grape leaves" and the "best chicken souvlaki", gyros and hamburgers in Highlandtown; prices couldn't be lower or customer satisfaction greater; if only it "were more than a carryout" with a few tables.

Sanders' Corner 🅂   15 17 15 $14
2260 Cromwell Bridge Rd. (Loch Raven Dr.), Glen Arm, 410-825-5187

☑ Whether you go to this "damn quaint" American "in the woods north of Towson" for a breakfast "like Mom's", an "extra-thick malted", a "romantic sandwich" or a drink with a "view on the porch", it can be "family-friendly" or "disorganized" depending on the hour; many prescribe "a chef transplant" before they'll go for dinner.

SAVANNAH S   25 23 23 $32
Admiral Fell Inn, 888 S. Broadway (Thames St.), 410-522-2195
■ Native and born-again Southerners salute Baltimore's "best new restaurant" – a "cheerful" Fells Point "nest" of Dixie living; besides "excellent", "refined" (but not fat-free), "new Southern food", it features a "creative selection" of martinis, cigars and wines; go for the "fabulous brunch" with "wonderful biscuits and corn bread."

Schultz's Crab House S   ▽ 21 13 19 $18
1732 Old Eastern Ave. (Walkern Rd.), Essex, 410-687-1020
■ "Call ahead to check if steamed crabs are in season" (and available) because that's the right time to visit this timeless, "real blue-collar" Essex seafooder; there's nothing fancy about the knotty pine dining rooms or the down-to-earth help, but, eat-in or carryout, its crabs are among the "best."

Sevilla's ◐S   ▽ 17 15 14 $22
(fka Rio Madrid)
4700 Eastern Ave. (Newkirk St.), 410-522-5092
☑ "Flamenco dancers", "great sangria" and a Spanish tapas bar and dancing (downstairs) reflect a shift from Lisbon to Madrid for this Brazilian hybrid in Highlandtown; the hokey "La Cucaracha" festivities are the drawing card, not the "hit-or-miss" food and service.

Sfuzzi S   18 19 17 $22
100 E. Pratt St. (Calvert St.), 410-576-8500
☑ Baltimore's link in this forged-in-Texas "Tuscan" chain is only a few minutes from Little Italy, but its California salads, "nouvelle" pasta and pizza and trendy "trappings" are decades apart in style; it's a "pass the focaccia, I can't hear you" kind of place.

Sidestreets S   ▽ 17 18 17 $21
8069 Tiber Alley (Main St.), Ellicott City, 410-461-5577
☑ "Adequate" for lunch or as an "end to a day in Ellicott City", this "middle-range" American's "musty" charms strike some as "quaint", others as "unpredictable and average"; still, it's hard to go wrong with Sunday brunch.

Silver Diner ◐S   14 16 16 $13
Towson Town Ctr., 825 Dulaney Valley Rd. (Fairmount Ave.), Towson, 410-823-5566
See Washington, DC, Alphabetical Directory.

Silver Spring Mining Co. S   ▽ 23 16 18 $15
(fka Silver Spring Inn)
8634 Belair Rd. (Link Ave.), Perry Hall, 410-256-6809
☑ This recently remodeled Belair Road standby still satisfies the basics – "sit, eat, pay, leave full and not feeling ripped off" – and has kept predecessor Marvin & George's sour beef and dumplings on its updated all-American bar food menu; note that the "upstairs dining room is better than the downstairs bar" for eaters.

Sisson's [S] — 19 | 18 | 18 | $21
36 E. Cross St. (bet. Light & Charles Sts.), 410-539-2093
■ "Order blackened anything" at Baltimore's original microbrewery, where the spicy Cajun eats (and newfangled American grills) "go great with the beer"; but most go to "enjoy the Baltimore-ness" of "Federal Hill's best" pub – "noisy", "crowded", and "hearty good fun."

Sotto Sopra [S] — – | – | – | M
405 N. Charles St. (Mulberry St.), 410-625-0534
Turning Baltimore's image of mod Italian dining topsy-turvy with its talented young chef from Milano cooking la vera cucina, and its "hip" gilded age decor, this "hot" new Italian on Charles Street has been having its moment; although sotto sopra means 'upside down', it seems like some knowledgeable folks are getting things right.

Speakeasy [S] — 19 | 20 | 18 | $23
2840 O'Donnell St. (Linwood Ave.), 410-276-2977
◪ For "plain and fancy", mostly Mediterranean food in a "very pretty", vaguely Edwardian room, this gussied-up Canton speakeasy has its takers – mainly those not "watching their cholesterol" and into desserts; those who "just have drinks" in the neat-looking bar tag upstairs as being "for people who eat with their wallets."

SPIKE & CHARLIE'S [S] — 24 | 20 | 20 | $29
1225 Cathedral St. (Preston St.), 410-752-8144
◪ Serving "adventurous, architectural" light fare and wine samplings in spare designer surroundings is no big deal in some cities, but across from the Meyerhoff & Lyric concert halls it is; despite some missteps ("slow" service), this "chichi but not imposing" New American "comes through" for everything from a "simple pizza at the bar" to "an elegant night out."

Stixx Cafe — 18 | 18 | 17 | $21
Club Ctr., 1500 Reisterstown Rd. (bet. McHenry Ave. & Old Court Rd.), Pikesville, 410-484-7787
◪ Pikesville's "in crowd" recommends this slick Cal-Asian for its "excellent sushi", "varied menu", "close to home" and shopping convenience and getting you "in and out without feeling rushed"; ratings are up a notch after an ownership change last year, although a few note it "needs to shape up."

Stone Mill Bakery [S] 🚫 — 23 | 15 | 19 | $22
1609 Sulgrave Ave. (Newbury St. & Kelly Ave.), 410-542-2233

Stone Mill Bakery (Cont.)
5127 Roland Ave. (Deepdene St.), 410-532-8669

Stone Mill Bakery & Ecole [S]
Greenspring Station, 10751 Falls Rd. (Greenspring Valley Rd.), Brooklandville, 410-821-1358
◪ "Billy Himmelrich deserves the credit" for bringing seriously excellent bread and croissants to Baltimore; his "heavenly" loaves and a few choice sandwiches and desserts make his bakery/cafes good "alternative" breakfast and lunch venues; prix fixe, BYO dinners at the Ecole on Friday and Saturday reflect a "passionate commitment" to "cutting edge" cuisine, but prompt some patrons to say "stick to the bread."

Strapazza [S] 16 | 13 | 16 | $15
300 Pratt St. (bet. Howard & Eutaw Sts.), 410-547-1160
1330 Reisterstown Rd. (Walker Ave.), Pikesville, 410-484-6906
Palace 9, 8775 Centre Park Dr. (Old Annapolis Rd.), Columbia, 410-997-6144
12 W. Allegheny Ave. (Washington Ave. & York Rd.), Towson, 410-296-5577
◪ Given the inevitable "crying baby" and the flavors of "Chef Boyardee", it may "feel like the relatives invited you over" when you take the kids to these "cheap Southern Italians" for "lots of pasta", pizza and "garlicky" entrees; of course, quality, appearance and service "vary" by location – the one near Camden Yards is the high-profile place.

Sunset [S] 20 | 19 | 17 | $20
625 Greenway Ave. (Aquahart Rd.), Glen Burnie, 410-768-1417
◪ If you thought that "country club–style decor" and "large, varied menus" of seafood, steak and American-Continental entrees went out with the '50s, think again; efforts to revive this Glen Burnie "suburban strip" eatery are welcomed in an "area that needs it"; it's "romantic" and "cozy around Christmas", but some find service "amateurish and familiar."

Surfin' Bull [S] – | – | – | M
2821 O'Donnell St. (Streeper St.), 410-675-9155
Dos hermanos "are striking out on their own" in an attractive room above a Canton bar with Latino seafood, flavorful beef, "homemade sangria" and their guitars; and, just like the American "immigrant dream" movies, it's a real family operation.

Sushi Cafe [S] ▽ 17 | 11 | 16 | $16
1640 Thames St. (Broadway), 410-732-3570
■ As trim and tidy as its well-made maki, this tiny Fells Point sushi bar does "great takeout" and slices a "quick", "cheap", "friendly" lunch; it's perfectly situated for a late-night "sushi fix" – but do remember that the "spicy" special rolls deliver a karate kick.

Sushi-Ya S 21 15 22 $18
Valley Ctr., 9616 Reisterstown Rd. (Greenspring Valley Rd.),
Owings Mills, 410-356-9996
■ A warm greeting puts diners at ease at this "clean",
personable Owings Mills Japanese; the "nicely rolled,
fresh-tasting maki, greaseless tempura", seaweed salad
and lots of cooked things to slurp and crunch please their
palates – and the BYO policy is kind to their pocketbooks.

Swallow at the Hollow S 11 7 14 $12
5921 York Rd. (Northern Pkwy.), 410-532-7542
◪ Looking "older than" most of its customers, this "smoky"
York Road "neighborhood pub would fit nicely in a pub
crawl" for "local color"; the equally "classic", "deep-fried
everything" bar fare is "cheap, filling, not very nutritious"
and tasty – and, of course, the place is filled with regulars
who "just drink."

Szechuan 22 11 20 $16
1125 S. Charles St. (Cross St.), 410-752-8409
◪ This "plain" South Baltimore BYO Chinese has many
years of cheap, "high-quality cooking" under its belt; dubbed
"Baltimore's Szechuan pioneer", it's the locale for fiery tofu
and eggplant dishes, "excellent fish" and whatever the
staff says is good.

Szechuan Best S 24 14 20 $16
8625 Liberty Rd. (Old Court Rd.), Randallstown, 410-521-0020
◪ Try to go to this Randallstown Taiwanese with someone
who can order from the Chinese menu, or "just ask and
they help"; that way you'll be able to sample the pick of
its "authentic" Cantonese seafood, dim sum and other
multiregional specialties; "when it's on" (usually), "it's
the best in the area."

Szechuan House S ▽ 22 18 23 $15
1427 York Rd. (Seminary Ave.), Lutherville, 410-825-8181
■ Although this Lutherville Chinese has a "nice room" and
"excellent personal service", a surprising number of its
customers have never seen the place; on the other hand,
ordering the "good, cheap" carryout and delivery as often
as they do, most have gotten "to know off-the-menu items"
intimately – "and they're great."

Tenosix S ▽ 18 16 18 $20
1006 Light St. (Hamburg St.), 410-528-2146
Noodles, pasta, spaghetti, soba, bean threads – call it what
you will; if it whirls, twirls, sops up sauce or serves as
ballast in a soup, you can get it fast, cheap and "beautifully
arranged" at this multicultural noodle shop south of the
Inner Harbor; the fast food, veggie-friendly concept (and
"exceptional" desserts) seem right in line with dining trends.

TERSIGUEL'S 🇸
25 | 24 | 24 | $35 |
8293 Main St. (Old Columbia Pike), Ellicott City, 410-465-4004
■ No one knows how to make Americans feel comfortable with Classic French cuisine better than Fernand Tersiguel; his "warm, welcoming" red townhouse in Ellicott City is "cheaper than going to Paris (but just as good)" and his customers feel they "can't go wrong" with his menu of "comforting favorites"; maybe the space is "cramped" and "best seen in a dim light", but so are plenty of lesser places in France.

T.G.I. Friday's ◐🇸
14 | 14 | 15 | $15 |
Towson Town Ctr., 668 Fairmount Ave. (Dulaney Valley Rd.), Towson, 410-828-4556
4921 Campbell Blvd. (Honeygo Blvd.), White Marsh, 410-931-3091
Restaurant Park, 5330 Benson Dr., Columbia, 410-312-2719
See Washington, DC, Alphabetical Directory.

Thai 🇸
23 | 14 | 19 | $17 |
3316-18 Greenmount Ave. (33rd St.), 410-889-7303
☑ Despite the influx of newer Thai restaurants in less "dubious" (safer) locales, this Waverly storefront is a "real survivor"; chalk it up to the "fabulous seafood in outstanding sauces, stunning use of herbs and spices" and doing "great things with squid"; even when you factor in occasional slips, it delivers a "mega-value" meal.

Thai Landing
23 | 14 | 21 | $18 |
1207 N. Charles St. (bet. Biddle & Preston Sts.), 410-727-1234
☑ In a city "blessed with good Thai food", this Charles Street offering provides a bit of "atmosphere", "even better" service and a chance to test your tolerance for heat; "even the nonstarred dishes are too spicy" for some and if you "ask for extra hot" – watch out; that advice also applies to the neighborhood.

Thai Orient 🇸
▽ 23 | 20 | 21 | $17 |
Valley Ctr., 9616-I Reisterstown Rd. (Greenspring Valley Rd.), Owings Mills, 410-363-3488
■ Shopping center Asian with the "right formula" for Owings Mills – "excellent Thai", "fantastic Chinese", crystal chandeliers, elaborate murals and "good advice" from polite help; too bad that "it's become so popular" it gets crowded at times.

Thames Street Tavern 🇸
▽ 15 | 15 | 15 | $13 |
1702 Thames St. (Broadway), 410-563-5423
☑ Before Hollywood film crews gave this Fells Point waterfront bar visibility beyond its upstairs harbor view, it was best known for major bedlam during "happy hour on Fridays", "classic" bar food and what passes for service in a twentysomething "hangout"; since then, it hired a chef (internationally inspired).

That's Amore 🅂   19 | 16 | 18 | $21
720 Kenilworth Dr. (West Rd.), Towson, 410-825-5255
See Washington, DC, Alphabetical Directory.

Timbuktu 🅂   – | – | – | M
1726 Dorsey Rd. (off I-295), Dorsey, 410-796-0733
Don't let the exotic "name fool you", this dark-paneled
dining room near BWI Airport is as Baltimore as can be;
indisputable proof are its "great crab cakes" and seafare-
oriented American menu.

TIO PEPE 🅂   26 | 23 | 23 | $35
10 E. Franklin St. (bet. St. Paul & Charles Sts.), 410-539-4675
🔳 A Baltimore perennial "favorite", this "Spanish wine
cellar" in the heart of Downtown has a compelling, sangria-
fueled "party" atmosphere with dungeonesque decor, dated
but good Continental dishes and courtly bows; despite
concerns about parking (across the street), there are few,
if any, slow nights.

Tomato Palace 🅂   19 | 17 | 18 | $16
10221 Wincopin Circle (Rte. 175), Columbia, 410-715-0211
▪ On the lakefront in Columbia is "Clyde's Italian cousin",
a lighthearted, child-friendly pasta and pizza place with
"calzone so good you'll weep" and a combo of fresh,
"interesting" food, wine, "value" and "fast" service that
mostly works; a "must" on a nice day.

Tomcat Alley   ▽ 22 | 19 | 22 | $21
1705 Aliceanna St. (Broadway), 410-327-7037
▪ There's always room for another atmospheric bar and
grill – especially one with a brick-walled courtyard, wines
by the miniglass, the "tastiest burger in Fells Point" and
contemporary dishes that are "clever" and "first-rate";
this start-up is a "little too full of itself", but don't let that
keep you away.

Tony Cheng's Szechuan 🅂   21 | 20 | 19 | $22
801 N. Charles St. (Madison St.), 410-539-6666
🔳 This "spacious, quiet" Mt. Vernon townhouse is an
unexpected (and relatively expensive) setting for "better
than most" Chinese food and service; regulars have
"liked it for years", others say "used to be good, but I still
go anyway", and many feel it would be "best if they could
build a parking lot."

Trattoria Alberto   ▽ 26 | 19 | 22 | $37
1660 Crain Hwy. (bet. Hospital Dr. & Rte. 100), Glen Burnie,
410-761-0922
▪ Italian expats don't judge a restaurant's pasta and veal
by its "strip mall" location and neither should you; they
consider this somewhat "pricey" Glen Burnie Northern
Italian a "real find", with a "commendable" chef and a
willingness to "remember your name"; "make arrangements
to sit back and eat a lot."

Tully's S   17 | 16 | 15 | $15
Putty Hill Plaza, 7934 Belair Rd. (I-695), Perry Hall,
410-665-9100
◪ "A model train runs around the ceiling perimeter, a
magician comes to the table" (weekend nights), there's
wing night and shrimp night and a Monday-night band –
were it not for these "positives", this Perry Hall bar would
have little to recommend it, except as a "place for greasy
bar food, many beers" and mating possibilities.

Turtle Bay Grille S   ▽ 12 | 14 | 15 | $16
Hunt Valley Mall, 118 Shawan Rd. (bet. I-83 & York Rd.),
Hunt Valley, 410-584-2625
◪ A desert-toned, "barn"-like eatery in Hunt Valley with
an open-ended menu that covers all the casual American
food bases from the Islands to the Southwest with "typical
mall" results; given the sprawling space, it's "good the
waiters are so full of energy."

Valley Inn S   15 | 17 | 17 | $24
10501 Falls Rd. (Hillside Rd.), Brooklandville, 410-828-8080
◪ "Some things never change" – notably, this "old
plantation" in Brooklandville whose "down at the heels,
romantic" appearance, "reliable" seafood and steak menu,
"experienced servers" and "gin and tonic" clientele have
been around forever; "if you know what Old Maryland
means", you can attend this "private club."

Velleggia's S   18 | 17 | 18 | $20
829 E. Pratt St. (Albemarle St.), 410-685-2620
◪ "An old name with an older cookbook" of "heavy"-
handed pastas and veal, the self-proclaimed 'oldest
restaurant in Little Italy' could use some updating; some go
to this "large, impersonal", ornate operation for its "old-
world charm" – most on a "two-for-one."

Victor's Cafe S   18 | 20 | 17 | $25
Pier 7, 801 Lancaster St. (President St.), 410-244-1722
◪ The wrap-around deck offers "fabulous" Downtown
skyline and harbor views "worth the price of admission",
which is just as well since this yearling's "strongly flavored",
around-the-world menu "needs fine tuning", the servers
could use more training and a "few things in the kitchen
need to be worked out"; N.B. don't skip dessert.

Vito's Cafe   – | – | – | I
10249 York Rd., (Warren Rd.), Cockeysville, 410-666-3100
"You don't have to go to Little Italy for good, reasonable
Italian food" say supporters of this strip-mall Italian in
Cockeysville; it's cheerful and bustling – not a place for
intimate dining – but the food tastes "homemade and
delicious" and the price is right; P.S. bring your own vino

Waterfront Hotel **S**   ▽ 17 | 19 | 18 | $20
1710 Thames St. (bet. Broadway & Ann St.), 410-327-4886

◪ A familiar scene to TV viewers ("*Homicide* films here") as well as to Fells Point pub crawlers, this "quaint" ("gloomy") old bar has become a "great people-watching place"; since it has "decent" American food and ok help, it's surprising that it's not that hard "to get a table on a Saturday night" in the upstairs dining room.

Weber's on Boston **S**   20 | 19 | 19 | $21
845 S. Montford Ave. (Boston St.), 410-276-0800

▪ It's "easy to get comfortable" at this handsome Canton restoration – with a "midweek hamburger" in the "cheery" bar and lots of Contemporary American bistro choices ("all done well") in the restaurant upstairs; "elegant yet unpretentious", it accommodates "young nongourmets" and serious wine buffs alike (the owner's brother makes wine in France).

Wharf Rat **S**   15 | 18 | 15 | $15
206 W. Pratt St. (Sharp St.), 410-244-8900

◪ Close enough to Camden Yards that many virtually "go through on the way to the ball game", this brewpub inevitably hosts a major 'before and after' scene; although most go to sample the "unbelievable variety" of microbrews, we hear that the British pub fare and pizza "isn't bad."

Wild Mushroom   23 | 20 | 20 | $20
641 S. Montford Ave. (Foster Ave.), 410-675-4225

▪ Mushrooms and Belgian beer would seem to be an odd coupling, yet those specialties have made this newish Canton bar in a vintage building "wildly popular"; it offers plenty of portobellos (some meat and fish as well), "youthful energy", a few tables and creatively mismatched chairs, long waits and "innovation with a smile" – all of which make its upstairs expansion good news.

WINDOWS **S**   21 | 24 | 21 | $24
Renaissance Harborplace Hotel, 202 E. Pratt St., 410-685-8439

▪ "The view is stunning", the space "attractive" (if a bit hotelish) and the Contemporary American food and service can be a notch or two above what's needed for a "nice business lunch"; this Downtown dining room is a "good choice" for meetings, with a "great lunch buffet" and a view-and-then-some Sunday brunch.

Windows on the Bay **S**   22 | 21 | 19 | $23
White Rock Marina, 1402 Colony Rd. (Ft. Smallwood Rd.), Pasadena, 410-255-1413

▪ At "sunset in warm weather", this "lovely" marina setting near Severna Park glows best; it's a "fine" place to soak up "local color" and eat "terrific fish" (or unsurprising American food); call ahead – it's "not easy to find "

203

Wing Wah S   ▽ 18 13 21 $13
509 Reisterstown Rd. (Slade Ave.), 410-653-0606
▨ A "throwback" to the "egg roll" and "fried rice" dynasty
of suburban Chinese food, this offering's carry-out business
was so popular that it set up a dining room; but takeout is
still the recommended option for a "tasty", "predictable"
fast-food fix in Pikesville.

Woman's Industrial Exchange   18 16 23 $10
333 N. Charles St. (Pleasant St.), 410-685-4388
▨ "Wonderful" "turn-of-the-century tearoom" that evokes a
"kind and gentle" era with every bite; it's presided over by
the "original staff" ("where else can you be waited on
by a 90-year-old?") serving "homemade", white-bread
food for what seems like the original prices; check out
the handicrafts before you leave; N.B. breakfast and
lunch, weekdays only.

Ze Mean Bean Cafe S   ▽ 20 22 19 $11
1739 Fleet St. (bet. Broadway & S. Ann St.), 410-675-5999
▨ This "mellow" coffeehouse in Fells Point has the "added
bonus" of some interesting Eastern European food; if you're
not "in a hurry", sink into the red damask couch, taste
some brewed beans and find out what "pierogi" means.

Zorba's S   ▽ 18 15 17 $18
4710 Eastern Ave. (bet. Oldham & Newkirk Sts.), 410-276-4484
▨ "Lots of regulars" at the bar of this Greektown nook
lend it "old-time atmosphere"; while the kitchen does an
"excellent" job with steak and grilled fish, "the chops and
octopus" are also recommended (on a "hit-or-miss" basis);
expect the help to be "low key."

F	D	S	C

Adam's Rib S
| 19 | 13 | 18 | $16 |

East Port Shopping Ctr., 321-C Chesapeake Ave. (Bay Ridge Ave.), 410-267-0064
589 Baltimore-Annapolis Blvd. (MacKenzie Rd.), Severna Park, 410-647-5757
219 N. Fruitland Blvd./Rte. 13, Salisbury, 410-749-6961
2200 Solomon's Island Rd./Rte. 4, Prince Frederick, 410-586-0001
169 Mayo Rd. (Old Solomon Rd.), Edgewater, 410-956-2995
■ "Absolutely the best ribs in the USA (including Texas)" and the "best value" too — once such a secret leaks, this "plain" suburban Annapolis BBQ could be mobbed by Baltimore and DC BBQ freaks; right now, it's a family-oriented, neighborhood place near the movies, where waiters "enjoy their work."

Angler S
| ▽ 18 | 15 | 18 | $17 |

3015 Kent Narrows Way S. (Rte. 18), Grasonville, 410-827-6717
■ A "convenient" stop "after sailing" or for a home-cooked "dinner on the way to the beach"; local "hunters and fishermen" eat steak and fried chicken, while tourists find a "Chesapeake seafood experience" and kind folks — no one goes to this "unpretentious" restaurant "for the decor."

Armadillo's ● S
| ▽ 15 | 15 | 16 | $18 |

City Dock, 132 Dock St. (Main St.), 410-268-6680
☑ "Great margaritas and the band upstairs" parlay an Annapolis City Dock location into big-time party time; think of it as "a friendly bar" with a "great waterfront location" and treat the Tex-Mex food as "pricey" fuel.

Bertucci's S
| 17 | 16 | 16 | $15 |

2207 Forest Dr. (bet. Rte. 2 & Riva Rd.), 410-266-5800
See Washington, DC, Alphabetical Directory.

Buddy's Crabs & Ribs S
| 14 | 13 | 15 | $17 |

100 Main St. (Market St.), 410-269-1800
■ "Other places have better" steamed crabs, BBQ, bar food, housekeeping and help (not to mention smaller crowds and shorter waits), but they don't have a "down by City Dock" location, which is why it's easy to "spot Navy cadets" and virtually everyone else at this hurly-burly "tourist trap"

Cafe du Vin S   – | – | – | M
Clocktower Plaza, 1410 Forest Dr. (Gemini Dr.), 410-268-6677
Blessed for bringing house-baked breads and well-selected wines to the Annapolis area, plus "creative sandwiches", pastries and "imaginative" Continental-American entrees, this take-out market/bakery/cafe offers multiple solutions to the 'what do we do about dinner' dilemma; for added inspiration, you can sample "over 40 wines by the glass."

Cafe Normandie S   23 | 21 | 20 | $26
185 Main St. (bet. Church Circle & Conduit St.), 410-263-3382
☑ A "charming" French bistro in historic Annapolis is bound to attract tourists, especially when its fireplace looks so "inviting on cold winter nights"; this one is also a "local favorite", highly praised by most, but not all ("nice but uninspired"), for its provincial fare and early-bird deals.

Cafe Sophie S⋻   – | – | – | M
401 Lovepoint Rd. (Historic Stevensville), Stevensville, 410-643-8811
If more people knew about this "jewel", a "lovely, small, owner-run" French boîte in Stevensville, it might lose its "refreshing" appeal; here, Lyon-born Suzanne Peach cooks carefully chosen, market-based bistro fare to order – as she would in her home; N.B. lunch Wednesday–Sunday, dinner Friday and Saturday.

California Pizza Kitchen S   18 | 14 | 17 | $16
Annapolis Mall, 22 Annapolis Mall (Jennifer Rd.), 410-573-2060
See Washington, DC, Alphabetical Directory.

Calvert House S   ▽ 19 | 14 | 18 | $21
401 Solomon's Island Rd. (Parole Plaza), 410-266-9210
◼ Although there's "nothing exceptional" about its American food or clean-cut appearance, this Parole seafooder will come as a "real surprise"; seldom does one find the combination of simplicity, "good quality" and "good value" – traits much appreciated by its early-bird clientele.

Cantler's Riverside Inn S   21 | 15 | 18 | $21
458 Forest Beach Rd. (on Mills Creek), 410-757-1311
◼ There's "no better crab pickin'" than at this "true riverside crab joint" near Annapolis; the crabs arrive "fresh off the boat daily", along with other local seafood, and the atmosphere is "great"; the "challenge is finding it" (call for directions) and being prepared to wait (even to park).

Carrol's Creek Cafe S   20 | 23 | 20 | $26
410 Severn Ave. (East Port Bridge), 410-263-8102, in Baltimore call 410-269-1406
☑ This contemporary seafood "vantage point" overlooking the harbor draws two kinds of trade – those who "go for a drink on the deck" and those who say the "imaginative" kitchen "doesn't rely" on the "scenic location"; P.S. if you lean toward the latter, ask for a "view table "

Chart House | 19 | 21 | 19 | $28 |
300 Second St. (Severn Ave.), 410-265-7166
See Washington, DC, Alphabetical Directory.

CHESTER RIVER INN S | 27 | 18 | 23 | $32 |
Castle Harbour Marina, 205 Tackle Circle (1 mi. off Rte. 50), Chester, 410-643-3886
■ Mark Henry (ex Milton Inn) gets rave reviews and near top marks in this *Survey* for "wonderful high-end and low-end", classically based Contemporary American fare at his Kent Island venue: "excellent food, great presentation", "pleasant people and place", "worth a detour, but don't dress up"; N.B. it's especially nice on the porch in summer.

Chick & Ruth's Delly ◐S⊄ | 18 | 14 | 18 | $11 |
165 Main St. (Conduit St.), 410-269-6737
■ From the "breakfast pledge of allegiance" (recited at 8:30 AM during the week, 9:30 AM on weekends) until after the bars close, Annapolis locals "meet their legislators" and everyone else at this Downtown "1930s-style" diner/ deli; go for "local color", magic tricks, milk shakes, chopped liver, a cheap feed, whatever – just go.

Corinthian S | 25 | 26 | 25 | $30 |
Loews Annapolis Hotel, 126 West St. (Lafayette St.), 410-263-1299
■ "Crisp tablecloths" and "elegant" appointments tag this Annapolis hotel dining room as *the* "fine dining" place; although "sometimes ordinary", it's capable of "five-star service", "steak cooked to perfection" and a "nice variety" of Contemporary American dishes.

Crab Claw S⊄ | 21 | 17 | 17 | $21 |
Navy Point, 156 Mill St. (Talbot St.), St. Michaels, 410-745-2900
☑ "One of St. Michaels' oldest, most bustling crab houses", beloved by boaters, lets you watch the river traffic from its pierside prospect, and the "seafood and crabs are great"; unfortunately, it's "now haunted by the tour bus crowd", which overwhelms the help.

Fergie's S | ▽ 17 | 19 | 21 | $24 |
Oak Grove Marina, 2840 Solomon's Island Rd. (off Rte. 2 next to South River Blvd.), Edgewater, 410-573-1371
■ The South River window view "at sunset" (and "value" deals) season the "good, not great" food at this "aim-to-please" American "suitable for a businessman's lunch."

Giolitti Deli S | ▽ 22 | 8 | 15 | $11 |
2068 Summerville Rd. (bet. Rte. 2 & West St.), 410-266-8600
■ This "authentic Italian cafe and grocery store outside Annapolis is not to be missed" for its breads, pastas and entrees – they often inspire "spur-of-the-moment" meals; it's also a treasure trove of "specialty ingredients" and good wine so you can "do it yourself" at home.

Griffin's at City Dock ◑ S   18 | 19 | 17 | $19
2224 Market Space (Main St.), 410-268-2576

Griffin's West St. Grill
2049 West St. (Rte. 2), 410-266-7662

■ "Good management", "good bar", "good atmosphere", "good American food in the heart of Annapolis", "good everything" — why can't those City Dock tourist traps learn from this well-designed, gargoyle-themed pub?; P.S. go for "oysters at the bar" paired with "wine by the glass."

Harris' Crab House S   21 | 15 | 19 | $20
433 N. Kent Narrows Way (off Rte. 50 under Kent Narrows Bridge), Grasonville, 410-827-9500

■ Cracking crabs at this "real Maryland crab house" just over the Bay Bridge will "extend your vacation" — the picnic tables on the upper deck, "water, water everywhere" and "great sunsets" are the "essence of the shore"; it's "family-owned", locally favored and hard to find.

Harry Browne's S   23 | 22 | 23 | $28
66 State Circle (bet. Maryland Ave. & East St.),
410-263-4332, in Baltimore call 410-269-5124

■ If it were possible to keep a "secret" near the State House, this classy Continental would be it; it brings a touch of *Casablanca* to the "Circle" with strong drinks, "well-served", "reliably good" food and a location "far enough from the tourists to provide a lovely, leisurely meal"; in summer, the patio is a "popular" retreat.

Holly's S   ▽ 15 | 10 | 18 | $18
108 Jackson Creek Rd. (Rte. 50), Grasonville, 410-827-8711

■ For travelers, this "old-fashioned diner" offers a chance to eat the "best chicken salad in the US", "great fried chicken" and "vanilla milk shakes" instead of "Route 50 fast food"; for locals, it's "of extreme importance" as a meeting place.

Imperial Hotel S   ▽ 27 | 27 | 27 | $37
Imperial Hotel, 208 High St. (Cross St.), Chestertown, 410-778-5000

■ Cap "a wonderful escape" to a colonial-era Chesapeake Bay port with a "most enjoyable" Contemporary American meal in this "charming" inn's dining room; Carla and Al Missoni, who were responsible for its "lovely" restoration, "know and care, especially about wine."

INN AT PERRY CABIN S   27 | 29 | 26 | $49
Inn at Perry Cabin, 308 Watkins Ln. (Talbot St.), St. Michaels, 410-745-2200

■ Maybe it's a "schlep and a bit too fussy", but very few would turn down a meal (or overnight stay) at this luxurious manor on the Eastern Shore; it's "definitely a special-occasion experience" with "beautifully served", modern Continental food matched by award-winning wines and a patio with a breathtaking water view.

Ironstone Cafe ▽ 27 | 23 | 24 | $28
236 Cannon St. (Cross St.), Chestertown, 410-778-0188
■ This "informal" eatery in historic Chestertown has "character" – a rough-edged, "creative simplicity" reflected in the short, eclectic, Regional American menu and "pleasant" atmosphere; if you'd stumbled upon it while exploring the town, you'd call it a "real find."

LA PICCOLA ROMA S 24 | 21 | 22 | $29
200 Main St. (bet. Church Circle & Conduit St.), 410-268-7898
■ In historic Annapolis, this "intimate", Victorian-feeling storefront's Northern Italian food and "gracious" hospitality reflect Mary and Gino Giolitti's Roman restaurant family roots; many consider it Annapolis' "best."

Lewnes' Steakhouse S ▽ 29 | 21 | 22 | $42
401 Fourth St. (Severn Ave.), 410-263-1617
■ Sometimes there's nothing like a big, juicy steak – "cholesterol be damned"; when so inclined in the Annapolis area, this "men's club" steakhouse with its "big portions, big prices" approach to "excellent steak and seafood" is "the only place to go."

Maria's Italian Ristorante ◗S ▽ 20 | 16 | 18 | $23
12 Market Space (Randall St.), 410-268-2112
☑ It's on Market Square, but it has the air of a side-street trattoria in Rome; this Southern Italian is a "local place" with a "home-like atmosphere" and "predictable" fare; surrounded by tourist meccas, it's a "good solid choice."

Marmaduke's Pub S 16 | 17 | 16 | $18
301 Severn Ave. (3rd St.), 410-268-1656, in Baltimore call 410-269-5420
■ At Eastport's semi-official "sailboat racing headquarters", a polished mahogany pub with "pretty good" burgers and "seasonal seafood", docksiders swap scuttlebutt "after Wednesday night races"; for those less nautically inclined, there's a weekend sing-along upstairs.

McGarvey's ◗S 19 | 18 | 18 | $19
8 Market Space (Pinkney St.), 410-263-5700
■ After the sails go down, "tourists and shoppers" make way for a "rowdy yachty crowd" at this popular seaporter where the "classic American saloon food" (chili, burgers, black bean soup) is "good" and the bar is "better" – "this is the place for oysters and a real taste of Annapolis."

Michael Rork's Town Dock S ▽ 22 | 17 | 20 | $28
125 Mulberry St. (waterfront), St. Michaels, 410-745-5577
☑ Boaters can dock at Michael Rork's (ex Hampton's) St. Michaels "crowd-pleaser" – a sprawling indoor-outdoor, casual-serious dining and entertainment complex with "seafood galore", a "great staff" and "sunset on the bay" views; those who "order from the daily specials" are most likely to get one of his "great" meals.

Mick's 16 16 16 $16
Annapolis Mall, 187 Annapolis Mall (off Parole Rd.), 410-224-4225
See Washington, DC, Alphabetical Directory.

Middleton Tavern 20 21 18 $23
2 Market Space (Randall St.), 410-263-3323
◪ "Cozy", colonial-era tavern with "lots of history", a "working fireplace", "great oyster shooters", "good pub grub" and seafood – no wonder it's swamped by tourists and "preppy sailors"; the bar is a hangout for an "older crowd" – with "food secondary" and service in third place.

Mike's Crab House [S] ▽ 16 15 14 $18
3030 Riva Rd. (White Point Rd.), Riva, 410-956-2784
◪ "Ok for crabs" and beer, with a "pretty setting by the river", an outdoor deck and its "own dock for boats", this Annapolis-area crab house is decidedly less appealing inside; at night, "casual slumming" in the bar is more of a draw than the "average" burgers and seafood, although local workers come here for lunch.

NARROWS [S] 23 23 21 $27
3023 Kent Narrows Way S. (Rte. 18), Grasonville, 410-827-9500
■ A contender for "best crab cakes" and crab soup in the area; this Kent Narrows viewspot mixes a "great Bloody Mary" and its "traditional and nontraditional shore menu is always good", too; though it seems "almost too fancy" to be fixing shore food, it's "very relaxing", "not overpriced" and will cook your catch, at the lowest entree price, as long as it's gutted and scaled.

NORTHWOODS [S] 27 22 25 $35
609 Melvin Ave. (Ridgely Ave.), 410-268-2609, in Baltimore call 410-269-6775
■ The "lovely prix fixe meal" ($25.95 Sunday–Friday) is Continental ("not cutting edge"), the candlelit residential setting "pleasant" (if "slightly cramped") and the service "unsurpassed"; this "special-occasion place" rates a spot on almost everyone's 'Tops in Annapolis' list because it's "consistent", "quietly festive" and "a good deal."

O'Brien's ◐ [S] ▽ 16 17 16 $21
113 Main St. (Green St.), 410-268-6288, in Baltimore call 410-269-0099, in DC call 301-261-2100
■ Don't take a politico to this clubby Annapolis tavern "when the assembly is in session" – there will be "too many handshake interruptions" to your spiel (later in the evening, the distractions are youthful meetings of a different kind), the raw bar, steak and seafood won't overwhelm, and, though we're told "the place has improved dramatically", it still "could use some decor."

O'Leary's Seafood [S] 23 20 21 $32
310 Third St. (Severn Ave.), 410-263-0884
■ Recommended by Annapolis 'finatics' for "swimmingly" fresh fish "prepared to your request"; the cottagelike premises are as simple as the "casual" concept (which translates service-wise as "expect to wait"), and though prices may seem high for the setting, they're reasonable for high-quality seafare.

Outback Steakhouse 20 16 19 $21
Hechinger Plaza, 2207 Forest Dr. (Riva Rd.), 410-266-7229
See Washington, DC, Alphabetical Directory.

Paul's on the South River [S] ▽ 22 23 22 $34
3027 Riva Rd. (Old Riva Rd.), Riva, 410-798-5272
◪ "Walking out on the pier" is a pleasant coda to a business lunch at this "nice"-looking "water place" near Annapolis, or you can sail in for a "romantic" meal; the "varied" American menu "emphasizes seafood" – understandably, as it has three seafood market sibs; some find it "ho-hum."

Rams Head Tavern 🌙[S] 18 19 17 $20
33 West St. (bet. Church Circle & Calvert St.), 410-268-4545
■ "Annapolis' best bet" for "good microbrews to wash down innovative pub fare"; this handsome brewpub with a "historic atmosphere" has one of the "best beer selections in Maryland" – over 130 bottled brews and 24 on draft along with a trellised brick patio for summertime quaffs; service is not on "par."

Red Hot & Blue 20 15 17 $17
201 Revell Hwy. (Rte. 50 at Old Mill Bottom Rd.), 410-626-7427
See Washington, DC, Alphabetical Directory.

Reynolds Tavern [S] ▽ 20 24 20 $26
7 Church Circle (Franklin St.), 410-626-0380
◪ "Filled with history and good food", this "Williamsburg-like", colonial-era re-creation is a "wonderful location for a reception"; the "Chesapeake Bay dishes", rack of lamb and plain American food can be very "good if you hit it right" – the same goes for the service.

Riordan's 🌙[S] 19 17 18 $20
26 Market Space (Main St.), 410-263-5449
◪ One of several "middle of the road" Market Space taverns where "what you see is what you get" – "friendly" fun, a "good steak" or "some of the best bar food" and a "perfect place for Sunday brunch"; what you don't get is innovation or much service or, unless you go upstairs, "quiet" conversation.

Saigon Palace S ▽ 23 | 13 | 19 | $20
West Annapolis Shopping Ctr., 609-B Taylor Ave. (Rowe Blvd.),
410-268-4463
■ A welcome "change of pace" for Annapolis dwellers,
their local Vietnamese offers lots of "vegetarian choices"
and "good specials" in a "try-hard" storefront setting;
occasional "French twists" are a reminder of colonial
Indochina – it's all very "not terrifying."

Scirocco Mediterranean Grill S ▽ 24 | 23 | 22 | $30
2552 Riva Rd. (Rte. 665), Riva, 410-573-0970
◪ There aren't many Annapolis-area restaurants suitable
for business and dress-up dining, and fewer still with the
ambition to offer a menu spanning Africa, Spain, Italy
and Greece; while this Mediterranean villa is sometimes
"uneven" and "amateurish", its emphasis on seafood and
open-hearth and grill catch the prevailing breeze.

T.G.I. Friday's 14 | 14 | 15 | $15
Annapolis Harbour Ctr., 2582 Solomon's Island Rd.
(Patuxent Blvd.), 410-224-4870
See Washington, DC, Alphabetical Directory.

TREATY OF PARIS S 24 | 25 | 23 | $34
Maryland Inn, 16 Church Circle (bet. Main & Duke of
Gloucester Sts.), 410-216-6340, in Baltimore call 410-269-0990
◪ "Colonial atmosphere" and "all that jazz" sums up historic
Annapolis' "finest", a "Revolutionary War"–era relic with a
blend of Chesapeake seafood and contemporary classics,
"erratic" charm and a "food orgy" brunch; weekend sounds
in the tavern feature the likes of Charlie Byrd.

208 Talbot S ▽ 28 | 23 | 26 | $37
208 N. Talbot St. (bet. North St. & Dodson Ave.), St. Michaels,
410-745-3838
■ This enchanting St. Michaels Contemporary American
townhouse earns accolades from nearly all quarters:
"professional, serious, very pleasant", "most imaginative",
"reasonable prices for quality", "as near perfect as you can
get"; it's "best when the chef-owner is behind the range",
which he mostly is; N.B. Saturday night is prix fixe only.

Indexes to Baltimore Restaurants

Special Features and Appeals

TYPES OF CUISINE

Baltimore Indexes

Baltimore Indexes

Candle Light Inn
Elkridge Furnace
GlasZ Cafe
Hampton's of Towson
Harry Browne's
Henninger's Tavern
Hersh's Orchard Inn
Inn at Perry Cabin
Josef's Country Inn
King's Contrivance
Manor Tavern
Marconi's
Metropol Cafe
Northwoods
Peerce's Plantation
Rudys' 2900
Sunset
Tio Pepe
Treaty of Paris

Crab Houses
Backfin
Bo Brooks
Buddy's
Cantler's Riverside
CJ's
Crab Claw
Fishery
Gabler's
Gunning's (Dorsey)
Gunning's (Bklyn.)
Harris' Crab House
Jimmy's Famous Sea.
Kaufmann's Tavern
Kelly's
Mike's Crab House
Obrycki's
Schultz's Crab Hse.

Delis
Attman's Deli
Chick & Ruth's
Giolitti Deli
Miller's Deli
Nates & Leons

Eclectic
Bandaloops
Cafe Tattoo
Chester River Inn
Foster's
GlasZ Cafe
Gr. Amer. Melt. Pot
Joy America
Louie's Bookstore
Margaret's Cafe
Martick's
Metropol Cafe
Morning Edition
One World Cafe
Peter's Inn
Puffin's

Regi's
Ruby Lounge
Stixx Cafe
Tenosix
Victor's Cafe

French
Cafe Bretton
Cafe du Vin
Cafe Manet
Cafe Normandie
Cafe Sophie
Jeannier's
Martick's
M. Gettier
Stone Mill Bakery
Tersiguel's

French (New)
Purple Orchid

German
Haussner's
Josef's Country Inn

Greek
Acropolis
Ikaros
OPA
Samos
Zorba's

Hamburgers
Alonso's
Charred Rib
Claddagh Pub
Crease
Duda's Tavern
Gr. Amer. Melt. Pot
Harryman House
Jenning's Cafe
Kelly's
Kelsey's
Manor Tavern
Marmaduke's Pub
McCabe's
McCafferty's
McGarvey's
Mick's
Middleton Tavern
Mt. Washington
Perring Place
Rams Head Tavern
Ransome's
Redwood Grill
Samos
Sidestreets
Sisson's
Swallow at Hollow
T.G.I. Friday's
Thames St. Tavern
Tomcat Alley
Weber's

NEIGHBORHOOD LOCATIONS

BALTIMORE

NEARBY MARYLAND

ANNAPOLIS/EASTERN SHORE

SPECIAL FEATURES AND APPEALS

Breakfast
(All major hotels and the following best bets)
Baugher's
Bel-Loc Diner
Cafe du Vin
Cafe Hon
Cafe Normandie
Chick & Ruth's
Donna's Coffee Bar
Double T Diner
Holly's
Jimmy's
Morning Edition
Nates & Leons
New Towne Diner
One World Cafe
Stone Mill Bakery
Woman's Ind. Exchange
Ze Mean Bean

Brunch
(Best of many)
Anastasia
Bertha's
Cafe Hon
Carrol's Creek Cafe
Champagne Tony's
Chart House
Clyde's
Corinthian
Donna's at BMA
Hampton's
Harry Browne's
Harryman House
Hersh's Orchard Inn
Hull St. Blues
Imperial Hotel
Josef's Country Inn
Kelsey's
Lista's
Louie's Bookstore
Manor Tavern
Margaret's Cafe
Marmaduke's Pub
Metropol Cafe
Michael Rork's
Morgan Millard
Morning Edition
Paolo's
Pavilion at Walters
Peerce's Plantation
Phillips Harborplace
Pier 500
Pierpoint
Polo Grill
Rams Head Tavern
Ransome's

Red Star
Savannah
Sidestreets
Spike & Charlie's
Thames St. Tavern
Treaty of Paris
208 Talbot
Victor's Cafe
Waterfront Hotel
Weber's
Windows
Windows on the Bay
Ze Mean Bean

Buffet Served
(B = brunch; L = lunch; D = dinner)
Akbar (B,L)
Anastasia (B)
Banjara (L)
Bombay Grill (L)
Bombay Peacock (L)
Cafe Bombay (L)
Carrol's Creek Cafe (B)
Corinthian (B)
Fergie's (L)
Harry Browne's (B)
Harvey's (B)
Hull St. Blues (B)
Manor Tavern (B)
Metropol Cafe (B)
Michael Rork's (B,D)
Mughal Garden (L)
New No Da Ji (L,D)
Orchard Market (B)
Peerce's Gourmet (B)
Phillips Seafood (B)
Polo Grill (B)
Purim Oak
Saigon Palace (L)
Scirocco (B)
Treaty of Paris (B)
Weber's (B)
Windows (B)

Business Dining
Bamboo House
Berry & Elliot's
Boccaccio
Bombay Grill
Brass Elephant
Cafe Bombay
Corinthian
Due
Hampton's
Helmand
Hersh's Orchard Inn
King's Contrivance
Liberatore's

Linwood's
Milton Inn
O'Brien's
Pierpoint
Polo Grill
Prime Rib
Rudys' 2900
Ruth's Chris
Sabatino's
Sfuzzi
Thai Landing
Windows

BYO

Adrian's
Al Pacino Cafe
Cafe Zen
Desert Cafe
Di Pasquale's
Ethel & Ramone's
Fazzini's
Hampton Tea Room
Orchard Market
Peerce's Gourmet
Saigon
Samos
Stone Mill Bakery
Strapazza
Sushi Cafe
Sushi-Ya
Szechuan House
Vito's Cafe
Ze Mean Bean

Caters

(Some good bets,
in addition to
hotel restaurants)
Attman's Deli
Bare Bones
Brass Elephant
Cafe Hon
Cafe Manet
Di Pasquale's
Due
Fisherman's Wharf
Giolitti Deli
Josef's Country Inn
Joy America
Kawasaki
King's Contrivance
La Tesso Tana
Liberatore's
Linwood's
Lista's
Matsuri
Metropol Cafe
Mo's Seafood Factory
New No Da Ji
OPA
Orchard Market

Peerce's Gourmet
Pierpoint
Red Hot & Blue
Rudys' 2900
Saigon Palace
Samos
Sfuzzi
Spike & Charlie's
Sushi Cafe
Velleggia's

Dancing/Entertainment

(Check days, times and
performers for entertainment;
D = dancing)
Angelina's (guitar)
Antrim 1844 (piano)
A-1 Crab Haven (piano)
Armadillo's (bands)
Bare Bones (bands)
Bay Cafe (varies)
Berry & Elliot's (D/DJ)
Bertha's (jazz)
Bombay Grill (sitar)
Bombay Peacock (sitar)
Bowman (comedy)
Burke's (comedy)
Cacao Lane (varies)
Cafe Tattoo (bands)
Champagne Tony's (harp/piano)
Chester River Inn (bands)
Da Mimmo (soft rock)
Fergie's (piano)
Gunning's (Dorsey) (karaoke)
Hampton's (jazz/piano)
Hampton's of Towson (piano)
Harry Browne's (varies)
Harvey's (varies)
Hersh's Orchard Inn (piano)
Hunt Ridge (keyboard)
Imperial Hotel (jazz)
J. Patrick's (varies)
Kaufmann's Tavern (karaoke)
Kelly's (karaoke)
Linwood's (jazz)
Louie's Bookstore (classical)
Luigi Petti (piano)
Marmaduke's Pub (sing-along)
McCafferty's (bands)
Metropol Cafe (poetry/varies)
Michael Rork's (D/varies)
Middleton Tavern (bands)
Morning Edition (varies)
New Orleans Cafe (varies)
O'Brien's (D/varies)
One World Cafe (folk/jazz)
Phillips Harborplace (piano)
Piccolo's (bands)
Prime Rib (bass/piano)
Rams Head Tavern (varies)
Red Star (tarot cards)

Delivers*/Takeout

Dessert & Ice Cream

Dining Alone
(Other than hotels)
Cafe Hon
Café Pangea
Donna's
John Steven, Ltd.
Linwood's
Louie's Bookstore
Margaret's Cafe
Matsuri
Pavilion at Walters
Samos
Sushi Cafe
Windows

Family Style
Friendly Farms
That's Amore

Fireplaces
Anastasia
Antrim 1844
A-1 Crab Haven
Bandaloops
Bombay Grill
Bowman
Cacao Lane
Cafe Normandie
Chart House
Da Mimmo
daniel's
Elkridge Furnace
Foster's
Harryman House
Hull St. Blues
Imperial Hotel
Inn at Perry Cabin
La Piccola Roma
Luigi Petti
Manor Tavern
Middleton Tavern
Milton Inn
O'Brien's
Ocean Pride
Peerce's Plantation
Regi's
Reynolds Tavern
River Watch
Sanders' Corner
Thames St. Tavern
Tony Cheng's
Treaty of Paris
Turtle Bay
Valley Inn
Velleggia's
Weber's
Ze Mean Bean

Game in Season
Birds of a Feather
Brass Elephant
Cafe Sophie

daniel's
Hampton's
Imperial Hotel
Inn at Perry Cabin
Joy America
La Tesso Tana
Metropol Cafe
M. Gettier
Polo Grill
Rudys' 2900
Sotto Sopra
Tersiguel's
Trattoria Alberto

Health/Spa Menus
(Most places cook to order to meet any dietary request; call in advance to check; almost all health-food spots, Chinese, Indian and other ethnics have health-conscious meals, as do the following)
Akbar
Dalesio's
Harvey's
Hoang's
Kelly's
Margaret's Cafe
One World Cafe
Puffin's
Thai
Wild Mushroom

Historic Interest
(Year Opened)
1740 Milton Inn*
1740 Rams Head Tavern*
1744 Elkridge Furnace*
1747 Reynolds Tavern*
1750 Middleton Tavern*
1762 Savannah*
1772 Treaty of Paris*
1774 O'Brien's
1790 Harryman House*
1797 Hampton Tea Room*
1808 daniel's*
1820 Bertha's*
1820 La Piccola Roma*
1830 Valley Inn*
1844 Antrim 1844*
1850 Brass Elephant*
1850 Martick's*
1850 Wild Mushroom*
1860 Cacao Lane*
1860 Weber's*
1860 Woman's Ind. Exchange*
1871 McGarvey's*
1871 208 Talbot*
1880 Henninger's Tavern*
1880 Manor Tavern*
1886 Sanders' Corner*

Offbeat

Outdoor Dining

Regi's (S)
Reynolds Tavern (G)
River Watch (P,W)
Ruby Lounge (P)
Rusty Scupper (P,W)
Saguaro's (S)
Sanders' Corner (P)
Sfuzzi (P)
Spike & Charlie's (P)
Stixx Cafe (P)
Stone Mill Bakery (S)
Strapazza (S)
T.G.I. Friday's (P)
That's Amore (P,S)
Tomato Palace (P,W)
Tomcat Alley (G)
Victor's Cafe (P,W)
Weber's (S)
Wharf Rat (S)
Windows on the Bay (P,W)
Ze Mean Bean (S)

Outstanding Views
Bamboo House
Bay Cafe
Berry & Elliot's
Carrol's Creek Cafe
Chart House
Cheesecake Factory
Donna's at BMA
Hampton's
Inn at Perry Cabin
Joy America
Lista's
Michael Rork's
Paul's
Peerce's Plantation
Phillips Harborplace
Piccolo's
Pier 500
River Watch
Sanders' Corner
Victor's Cafe
Windows
Windows on the Bay

Parking
Most Outer Baltimore
locations have accessible
parking, plus the following
Inner Baltimore and
Annapolis-area locations
(L = parking lot;
V = valet parking;
$ = discounted parking;
* = validated parking)
Angler (L)
Armadillo's (L)
Berry & Elliot's (L)*
Boccaccio (V)
Caesar's Den (V)

Cafe Normandie ($)
Cantler's Riverside (L)
Carrol's Creek Cafe (L)
Champagne Tony's (L)
Chart House (L)*
Chester River Inn (L)
Chiapparelli's (V)
Ciao Bella (V)
Corinthian (L,V)*
Dalesio's (V)
Da Mimmo (V)
Di Vivo's (L)
Faidley's (L)
Germano's (V)
Hampton's (V)
Hampton's of Towson (L)
Louie's Bookstore (L)
Marconi's (V)
Polo Grill (L,V)
Prime Rib (L)
Ruth's Chris (V)
Sabatino's (V)
Savannah (V)
Scirocco's (V)
Sisson's (V)
Sotto Sopra (V)
Treaty of Paris (V)
Windows (L)
Windows on the Bay (L)

Parties & Private Rooms
(Any nightclub or restaurant
charges less at off hours;
* indicates private rooms
available; best of many)
Anastasia*
Antrim 1844*
Bamboo House
Baugher's*
Bertha's*
Boccaccio*
Brass Elephant
Cacao Lane*
Candle Light Inn*
Captain Harvey's*
Carrol's Creek Cafe*
Chester River Inn*
Chiapparelli's*
Corinthian*
Dalesio's*
Da Mimmo*
daniel's*
Donna's at BMA*
Friendly Farms*
Hampton's of Towson*
Hampton Tea Room*
Harry Browne's*
Harryman House
Haussner's*
Hersh's Orchard Inn*
Imperial Hotel*

Inn at Perry Cabin*
Joey Chiu's*
King's Contrivance*
La Tesso Tana*
Liberatore's*
Lista's*
Manor Tavern*
M. Gettier*
Michael Rork's*
Middleton Tavern*
Milton Inn*
Paul's*
Peerce's Plantation*
Phillips Seafood*
Pier 500*
Polo Grill*
Reynolds Tavern*
Rudys' 2900*
Savannah*
Spike & Charlie's*
Stone Mill Bak./Ecole*
Tersiguel's*
Tio Pepe*
Treaty of Paris*
208 Talbot*
Wild Mushroom*

People-Watching
Cafe Hon
Donna's Coffee Bar
Due
John Steven, Ltd.
Linwood's
Louie's Bookstore
O'Brien's
Paolo's
Polo Grill
Ruby Lounge
Sabatino's
Sotto Sopra

Power Scenes
Corinthian
Due
Hampton's
Harry Browne's
King's Contrivance
Lewnes' Steakhouse
Liberatore's
Linwood's
O'Brien's
Pierpoint
Polo Grill
Prime Rib
Tio Pepe
Windows

Pre-Theater Menus
(Best of many; call to check
prices, days and times)
Brass Elephant
Cafe Normandie

Candle Light Inn
Fergie's
Jeannier's
King's Contrivance
Michael Rork's
Owl Bar
Purple Orchid
Ruby Lounge
Scirocco
Sotto Sopra
208 Talbot

Prix Fixe Menus
(Call to check prices,
days and times)
Akbar
Angelina's
Antrim 1844
Bombay Grill
Bowman
Brass Elephant
Cafe Normandie
Champagne Tony's
Corinthian
Fergie's
Germano's
Gunning's (Dorsey)
Hampton's
Hampton's of Towson
Harryman House
Inn at Perry Cabin
Jeannier's
Joy America
King's Contrivance
Northwoods
Orchard Market
Palermo's Grill
Purple Orchid
Reynolds Tavern
Rudys' 2900
Scirocco
Sotto Sopra
Stone Mill Bak./Ecole
Tersiguel's
Treaty of Paris
208 Talbot

Pubs
Alonso's
Bertha's
Harryman House
Jerry D's Saloon
John Steven, Ltd.
Manor Tavern
McGarvey's
Ransome's
Reynolds Tavern
Tomcat Alley
Weber's

Baltimore Indexes

T.G.I. Friday's
Thai Landing
That's Amore
Wild Mushroom

Romantic Spots
Akbar
Antrim 1844
Cacao Lane
Desert Cafe
Henninger's Tavern
La Tesso Tana
Milton Inn
Northwoods
Prime Rib
Sotto Sopra
Treaty of Paris
208 Talbot

Saturday Dining
(B=brunch; L=lunch;
best of many)
Angler (L)
Baugher's (L)
Cacao Lane (L)
Cafe Hon (B,L)
Cafe Normandie (L)
Cafe Sophie (L)
Cantler's Riverside (L)
Charred Rib (L)
Chester River Inn (L)
Donna's at BMA (L)
Gabler's (L)
Grand Palace (L)
Haussner's (L)
Inn at Perry Cabin (L)
John Steven, Ltd. (L)
Josef's Country Inn (L)
La Tesso Tana (L)
Liberatore's (L)
Linwood's (L)
Louie's Bookstore (L)
Marconi's (L)
Michael Rork's (L)
Middleton Tavern (L)
Narrows (L)
One World Cafe (L)
Pavilion at Walters (B,L)
Piccolo's (L)
Polo Grill (L)
Sabatino's (L)
Sanders' Corner (L)
Treaty of Paris (L)
Wild Mushroom (L)
Windows on the Bay (L)

Sunday Dining
(B=brunch; L=lunch,
D=dinner; best of many)
Amicci's (L,D)
Baugher's (L,D)
Cacao Lane (L,D)

Cafe Normandie (L,D)
Cafe Sophie (L)
Cafe Zen (L,D)
Carrol's Creek Cafe (B,D)
Cheesecake Factory (L,D)
Dalesio's (D)
daniel's (D)
Donna's at BMA (B,D)
Double T Diner (L,D)
Due (D)
Friendly Farms (L,D)
Grand Palace (L,D)
Harry Browne's (B,D)
Harryman House (B,D)
Hull St. Blues (B,D)
Imperial Hotel (B)
Inn at Perry Cabin (L,D)
Jimmy's Famous Sea. (L,D)
Joy America (L,D)
La Piccola Roma (D)
La Tesso Tana (L,D)
Linwood's (D)
Louie's Bookstore (B,L,D)
Margaret's Cafe (B,L,D)
Michael Rork's (B,L,D)
Morning Edition (B,L)
Narrows (L,D)
Northwoods (D)
O'Leary's (D)
Paolo's (B,L,D)
Pavilion at Walters (B,L)
Piccolo's (L,D)
Pierpoint (B,D)
Polo Grill (B,D)
Prime Rib (D)
Ruby Lounge (D)
Rudys' 2900 (D)
Saigon (L,D)
Sanders' Corner (B,L,D)
Savannah (B,D)
Sotto Sopra (D)
Trattoria Alberto (D)
Treaty of Paris (B,L,D)
208 Talbot (B,D)
Weber's (B,D)
Ze Mean Bean (B,D)

Singles Scenes
Bay Cafe
Bill Bateman's
Hersh's Orchard Inn
Jilly's
Marmaduke's Pub
McGarvey's
Michael's
Middleton Tavern
Mt. Washington
Nacho Mama's
Nick's
Obrien's
Rams Head Tavern

Baltimore Indexes

Red Star
River Watch
Rusty Scupper

Sleepers
(Good to excellent food, but little known)
Antrim 1844
Cafe Bretton
Cafe Sophie
Cafe Zen
Chester River Inn
Ciao Bella
Claddagh Pub
Elkridge Furnace
Fazzini's
Giolitti Deli
Grand Palace
Gunning's (Dorsey)
Hampton's of Towson
Harris' Crab House
Imperial Hotel
Ironstone Cafe
Lewnes' Steakhouse
Matsuri
Perring Place
Peter's Inn
Reynolds Tavern
Saigon
Saigon Palace
Samos
Thai Orient
Tomcat Alley
208 Talbot
Windows on the Bay

Teflons
(Gets lots of business, despite so-so food, i.e. they have other attractions that prevent criticism from sticking)
Bay Cafe
Bel-Loc Diner
Double T Diner
Mt. Washington
Phillips Harborplace
Silver Diner
T.G.I. Friday's

Teas
(See also *Coffeehouses* & *Dessert* Indexes)
Bertha's
Hampton Tea Room
Harbor Court Hotel
Inn at Perry Cabin
Ze Mean Bean

Visitors on Expense Accounts
Corinthian
Da Mimmo

Due
Hampton's
Harry Browne's
Inn at Perry Cabin
Joy America
King's Contrivance
Lewnes' Steakhouse
Liberatore's
Linwood's
Marconi's
Michael Rork's
Milton Inn
Northwoods
Pierpoint
Polo Grill
Prime Rib
Rudys' 2900
Ruth's Chris
Savannah
Scirocco
Sotto Sopra
Tersiguel's
Tio Pepe
Treaty of Paris
208 Talbot

Wheelchair Access
(Check for bathroom access, almost all hotels plus the following)
Adam's Rib
Akbar
Al Pacino Cafe
Amicci's
Anastasia
Angelina's
Angler
Bamboo House
Ban Thai
Bare Bones
Baugher's
Bay Cafe
Berry & Elliot's
Bertucci's
Bill Bateman's
Bo Brooks
Boccaccio
Bombay Peacock
Bowman
Brasserie
Burke's
Cafe Bretton
Cafe Hon
Cafe Normandie
Cafe Tattoo
Cafe Troia
Cafe Zen
Cal. Pizza Kit.
Candle Light Inn
Captain Harvey's
Carrol's Creek Cafe

Baltimore Indexes

Baltimore Indexes

That's Amore
Tomato Palace
Trattoria Alberto
Tully's
Turtle Bay
Victor's Cafe
Wharf Rat
Windows on the Bay
Wing Wah

Wine & Beer Only
Amicci's
Attman's Deli
Cafe Manet
Cal. Pizza Kit.
Chick & Ruth's
Faidley's
Field's Pharmacy
Gabler's
Giolitti Deli
Hampton Tea Room
Hoang's
Holly's
Jimmy's
Ledo Pizza
Margaret's Cafe
Matsuri
Miller's Deli
PaperMoon Diner
Silver Diner
Strapazza
Szechuan
Tenosix

Winning Wine Lists
Dalesio's
Hampton's
Linwood's
Milton Inn
Prime Rib
Rudys' 2900
Savannah
Tersiguel's
Tio Pepe
Tomcat Alley

Worth a Trip
Kent Narrows
    Chester River Inn

Chestertown
    Imperial Hotel
Ellicott City
    Tersiguel's
Fallston
    Josef's Country Inn
St. Michaels
    Inn at Perry Cabin
    Michael Rork's
Taneytown
    Antrim 1844
Westminster
    Baugher's

Young Children
(Besides the normal fast-food
places; * indicates children's
menu available; best of many)
Armadillo's*
Bare Bones*
Baugher's*
Bertucci's*
Bill Bateman's*
Buddy's*
Cal. Pizza Kit.*
Canopy
Cantler's Riverside*
Chart House*
Chiapparelli's*
Double T Diner*
Fazzini's*
Friendly Farms*
Holly's*
Ledo Pizza*
Mama Lucia*
Mick's*
Outback Steakhouse*
Paolo's*
Phillips Harborplace*
Phillips Seafood*
Red Hot & Blue*
Silver Diner*
Strapazza*
Tomato Palace*
Windows on the Bay*

Wine Vintage Chart 1983-1995

This chart is designed to help you select wine to go with your meal. It is based on the same 0 to 30 scale used throughout this *Survey*. The ratings (prepared by our friend Howard Stravitz, a law professor at the University of South Carolina) reflect both the quality of the vintage and the wine's readiness for present consumption. Thus, if a wine is not fully mature or is over the hill, its rating has been reduced. We do not include 1984 and 1987 because, with the exception of '87 cabernets, those vintages are not recommended.

WHITES	'83	'85	'86	'88	'89	'90	'91	'92	'93	'94	'95
French:											
Burgundy	20	28	29	21	29	24	19	28	20	25	24
Loire Valley	–	–	–	–	24	23	15	19	22	23	24
Champagne	22	28	25	24	26	28	–	–	–	–	23
Sauternes	25	22	28	29	25	26	–	–	–	19	22
California:											
Chardonnay	–	–	–	–	–	24	22	27	26	23	22
REDS											
French:											
Bordeaux	25	27	26	25	28	27	16	19	23	24	25
Burgundy	23	26	13	26	27	29	21	23	25	22	23
Rhône	25	26	20	26	28	27	26*	16	23*	22	24
Beaujolais	–	–	–	–	–	–	22	15	22	23	24
California:											
Cab./Merlot	18	27	25	16	22	27	26	25	24	23	24
Zinfandel	–	–	–	–	–	22	20	20	20	21	20
Italian:											
Tuscany	–	27	16	25	–	25	17	–	19	–	20
Piedmont	–	26	–	24	27	27	–	–	19	20	25

*Rating and recommendation is only for Northern Rhône wine in 1991 and Southern Rhône wine in 1993.

Bargain sippers take note: Some wines are reliable year in, year out, and are reasonably priced as well. These wines are best bought in the most recent vintages. They include: Alsatian Pinot Blancs, Côtes du Rhône, Muscadet, Bardolino, Valpolicella and inexpensive Spanish Rioja and California Zinfandel.